Of Monarchs
and Black Barons

Of Monarchs and Black Barons

Essays on Baseball's Negro Leagues

JAMES A. RILEY

Foreword by Monte Irvin

McFarland & Company, Inc., Publishers
Jefferson, North Carolina, and London

LIBRARY OF CONGRESS CATALOGUING-IN-PUBLICATION DATA

Riley, James A.
   Of Monarchs and Black Barons : essays on baseball's Negro Leagues / James A. Riley ; foreword by Monte Irvin.
       p.   cm.
   Includes index.

   ISBN 978-0-7864-6542-2
   softcover : acid free paper ∞

   1. Negro leagues — History. 2. Baseball — United States — History. 3. African American baseball players. I. Title.
   GV875.N35R56 2012
   796.357'64 — dc23   2012010819

BRITISH LIBRARY CATALOGUING DATA ARE AVAILABLE

© 2012 James A. Riley. All rights reserved

No part of this book may be reproduced or transmitted in any form or by any means, electronic or mechanical, including photocopying or recording, or by any information storage and retrieval system, without permission in writing from the publisher.

Front cover image *detail* Jerry Veney of the 1913 Champion Homestead Grays

Cover design by David K. Landis (Shake It Loose Graphics)

Manufactured in the United States of America

McFarland & Company, Inc., Publishers
   Box 611, Jefferson, North Carolina 28640
       www.mcfarlandpub.com

For
Andy and Mark
Graham and Delaney

Grandchildren are the dessert
in the feast of life.

Table of Contents

Foreword: Reviving Memories (by Monte Irvin)   1
About Monte Irvin   5
Introduction   7

- For the Love of the Game: Negro Leagues Baseball Had a History of Its Own   11
- Fleetwood Walker: The Real First   19
- John McGraw and Chief Tokohama: Baltimore's Brush with Breaking the Barrier   25
- When Rube Foster Faced the Chicago Cubs   28
- The 1910 Leland Giants   33
- Pete Hill: The Greatest Black Outfielder of the Deadball Era   37
- John Henry (Pop) Lloyd: The Black Honus Wagner   43
- The Texas Cyclone: Smokey Joe Williams   48
- The Early Leagues: 1920–1932   57
- Mysterious Dave Brown: One Shot Short of Stardom   71
- The First Dark October: A Look at the Inaugural Negro World Series   76
- Duel of Two Dark Aces: The Showdown Between Willie Foster and Bullet Rogan   82
- The 1933 East-West All-Star Game: The First East-West Classic   87
- The Baltimore Baseball Nobody Knows   94
- Boojum: The Most Ferocious Hitter and Fiercest Competitor Ever to Play the Game   100
- Biz Mackey: The Man Who Made Campy a Catcher   111
- Slim Jones: A Season in the Sun and a Winter in the Cold   116
- Jimmie Crutchfield: Small and Proud   120

- Not the Only Game in Town: Pittsburgh's Other Teams — 125
- Buck Leonard: He Could Do It All — 129
- Don't Forget About Josh — 133
- The Thunder Twins: Black Baseball's Power Tandem, Josh Gibson and Buck Leonard — 137
- Ray Dandridge: Dandy — 142
- Ray Dandridge and the Newark Eagles' Million Dollar Infield — 145
- Willie Wells: El Diablo — 150
- Leon Day: A Living Legend of the Negro Leagues — 153
- Buck O'Neil: The Dean of the Monarchs — 159
- Bill Byrd: Baseballer's Black Spitballer — 165
- Dave Barnhill: Impo — 170
- Edsall Walker: The Catskill Wildman — 175
- Gene Benson: Baseball Pioneer — 179
- Wild Bill Wright: A Mexican Legend Comes Home — 183
- Johnny Davis: Cherokee — 188
- Piper Davis: The Man Who Made Mays — 192
- Felix "Chin" Evans: The Winning Pitcher in the Last Black All-Star Game Before Robinson Broke the Color Line — 201
- Red Moore: He Could Pick It! — 206
- Buck Leonard on Jackie Robinson: The Negro Leagues Superstar Talks About Jackie's Signing and the Aftermath — 212
- Eddie Klep: The Reverse Jackie Robinson — 217
- Toni Stone: Lady at the Bat — 224
- Baseball with a Rumba Beat — 228
- When "The Babe" Came to Mobile — 231
- President Bush Hits a Homer: Negro League Players Honored at the White House — 235
- A Bit of Americana—1986 Ballpark Dedication Renews Memories — 239
- Buck O'Neil: A Remembrance — 257
- Remembering Ray: The Hot Corner Hall-of-Famer Will Not Be Forgotten — 260
- Buck Leonard: A Tribute — 265

Index — 269

Foreword: Reviving Memories
by Monte Irvin

Reading these stories brought back a flood of fond memories for me.

I was born in 1919, a year before Rube Foster founded the first Negro National League, and was fortunate enough to have started my professional baseball career in the new Negro National League before its demise in 1948. Soon afterward, I signed with the New York Giants and began the second part of my baseball career that led to two National League pennants and a World Series victory in 1954.

A few years earlier I had been privileged to experience the equivalent thrill in the Negro World Series when my team, the Newark Eagles, defeated Satchel Paige and the Kansas City Monarchs to win the 1946 Championship.

Those years in the Negro Leagues will always have a special place in my heart. I was young and everything was a new experience for me. Some of the happiest moments of my life were spent in the ballparks where we played and on the bus rides in between the games. Times were hard but the camaraderie we shared back then can never be duplicated.

Baseball was king at that time, and I played with and against some of the greatest players of all time. There was so much great talent in those days. Players like Josh Gibson, Buck Leonard, and Satchel Paige, just to name three of the very best. It's just a shame that people never had a chance to see these great players.

It was a double injustice. The first was that most of these outstanding players never had an opportunity to play in the major leagues, and the second — and perhaps the greater of the two — was that most baseball fans never had the opportunity to see them play.

During the years that I was in the Negro Leagues, the Homestead Grays were the top team. They won nine straight Negro National League pennants and their two superstars were Josh Gibson and Buck Leonard. They did for the Grays what Babe Ruth and Lou Gehrig did for the New York Yankees. In fact they were called the "Black Babe Ruth and Lou Gehrig."

Josh was the greatest hitter I ever saw, black or white. Nobody hit the ball farther than he did. Buck was a dead pull hitter, with a quick bat, and he feasted on fastballs. He hit a lot of home runs, too, but not as many — and definitely not as far — as Josh did.

Satchel was a natural. He didn't have a curve when I first saw him, but he didn't need it with his fastball and the great control that he had. By the time he finally got to the major leagues in 1948, he had already been pitching for more than 20 years in the Negro Leagues. He could have pitched for any major league team at any time during those years.

There were a couple of other top players, from an earlier time, that I want to mention. First is John Henry Lloyd, who was one of the all-time great shortstops. I was about nine years old when I saw him play in East Orange, and he was playing first base then.

The other player was Oscar Charleston, who was well past his prime when I came into the league, but is another all-time great that I saw play when I was a kid. He was with the Pittsburgh Crawfords then and had moved himself to first base, but he was still a formidable ballplayer. In his prime he was a center fielder and many people consider him the Willie Mays of his time. Some even say he was the better of the two, but I played with Willie on the Giants and I will say this: Nobody played center field better than Willie Mays.

Monte Irvin starred in the Negro Leagues for eight years with the Newark Eagles, but is pictured here when he was with the New York Giants after the elimination of baseball's color line.

Willie was my roomie with the Giants and the best teammate I ever had, but I also had some great teammates with the Newark Eagles before that. I was an 18-year-old youngster when I first joined the Eagles, and several of my old teammates are included in this anthology. Among them are Ray Dandridge, Leon Day, Willie Wells, Johnny Davis, Jimmie Crutchfield and Biz Mackey.

I got to know all the Newark Eagles players, and there were several that I really admired. I want to mention three at the top of the list. First of all was Leon Day. Leon was a great pitcher and had a real good fastball, a good curve and control of both pitches. He could also hit, run and play other positions when not pitching.

During that time, we had a million dollar infield. The two players that really made that infield famous were Ray Dandridge and Willie Wells. They were two of the finest infielders I've ever seen.

I've never seen any third baseman who could make the fielding plays any better than Ray Dandridge. You had to see his play to fully appreciate it. People would have paid just to see him play third base. He was something special, and fans loved him. He was definitely the best we ever had in the Negro Leagues.

Willie Wells was the best shortstop that I saw during my professional baseball career. He played a shallow shortstop, but had exceptional quickness and was expert at going back on line drives and pop flies. Wells also was one of the best curveball hitters I ever saw, and was a fast, aggressive baserunner. He was a clutch player who always came up with the big fielding play or a key hit when it was needed.

Many players that I played *against* are also featured in this anthology. It was almost like meeting old acquaintances again and revived more good memories from the past. Included from the Negro National League are Josh Gibson, Buck Leonard, Boojum Wilson and Edsall Walker from the Homestead Grays; Bill Wright and Bill Byrd from the Baltimore Elite Giants; Gene Benson and Slim Jones from the Philadelphia Stars; and Dave Barnhill from the New York Cubans. From the Negro American League are Buck O'Neil from the Kansas City Monarchs; Piper Davis from the Birmingham Black Barons; Chin Evans from the Memphis Red Sox; and Red Moore from the Atlanta Black Crackers.

I also played against Jackie Robinson, but not in the Negro Leagues. When he played his only season in 1945 I was guarding German POWs in Europe during World War II. But I *did* play against Jackie in the major leagues when he was with the Dodgers and I was with the Giants. Baseball fans remember the battles our teams had in that heated rivalry, and the contributions made by former Negro League players in those hard-fought games.

Think about how different it would have been without Jackie, Roy Campanella, Don Newcombe, Joe Black, Junior Gilliam, and Sandy Amoros for the Dodgers; and Willie Mays, Hank Thompson, and Ruben Gomez, along with myself, for the Giants.

Without the color line, that same difference could have been added to baseball history from the beginning. But that's just the way it was back then. They didn't want blacks to play in the big leagues at that time. That prevailing mindset resulted in the color line, but it also created the world of black baseball, where we developed a rich history of our own.

The author has preserved the distinctive qualities of that history and the spirit of the players who made it what it was. I have known Jim Riley for over 30 years. We first met in the summer of 1981 when I was still working in the Baseball Commissioner's office. Jim was a pioneer in the field of Negro Leagues baseball research and is the most knowledgeable person about the players and history of the Negro Leagues. In addition to the articles included in this anthology, he has written extensively on the subject, including the landmark volume *The Biographical Encyclopedia of the Negro Baseball Leagues* and my autobiography, *Monte Irvin: Nice Guys Finish First*.

I thought that us getting together for my book was a perfect match. We were always on the same page and the many days we sat around talking about those times was something I really enjoyed. I have visited in his home and he has visited in mine. The friendship of Jim and his wife Dottie has been invaluable to me.

Through the years we have spent a lot of time together at various functions and reunions at many locations, from Cooperstown to Mexico City. The accounts of two of these events are included in this anthology and are among my most memorable.

The first is when President George Herbert Walker Bush invited me, along with Leon Day, Jimmie Crutchfield and Josh Gibson, Jr., to the White House in 1992, for special recognition as representatives of the Negro League Players Association during Black History Month. The other is when the East Orange Oval Park in my hometown was renamed Monte Irvin Field in my honor on June 6, 1986.

On a closing note, I will repeat that reading these accounts rekindled the warm memories from those events. I commend the publisher for making all of these wonderful stories available in a single volume.

About Monte Irvin

Monte Irvin's life experience has placed him in position to provide a unique perspective on the effect of the color line on baseball history.

In one respect, he was one of the *fortunate* ones. When the major leagues were opened to black ballplayers, he was still young enough to make the transition from the Negro Leagues. Although he was 30 years old and his best years were behind him when he broke in with the New York Giants, he still played in eight major league seasons.

But at the same time, from a different perspective, Monte was also one of the *unfortunate* ones. He spent eight seasons in the Negro Leagues at the beginning of his baseball career and eight seasons in the major leagues at the end of his baseball career. In between was a super season in the Mexican League, followed by three years in the United States Army during World War II. Those three years in service of his country came during his baseball prime and were, in essence, the heart of his career. Coupled with the residual fallout from the three-year layer of athletic rust in the aftermath, his baseball career suffered adversely as a consequence.

Monte was an all-star performer in both the Negro Leagues and in the major leagues. His greatest thrill in baseball came when he stole home in the 1951 World Series against the New York Yankees. In that Series, Monte also tied the record at that time for most hits in a World Series with 11. Still, as great as his career was, it would have been even more impressive had he not lost those three prime seasons.

Following his outstanding achievements on the diamond, Monte embarked on another successful venture in baseball when he served as a Special Assistant to Baseball Commissioner Bowie Kuhn. In that pioneering role, he paved the way for other African American executives in baseball's front offices, but the best was yet to come.

The capstone of Monte Irvin's baseball endeavors came on August 6, 1973, a day that he will always remember, when he was inducted into the National Baseball Hall of Fame at Cooperstown, New York. Monte's Hall of Fame plaque reads:

"Regarded as one of Negro leagues' best hitters, star slugger of Newark Eagles won 1946 Negro League batting title. Led N.L. in runs batted in and paced 'miracle' Giants in hitting in 1951 drive to pennant. Batted .458 and stole home in 1951 World Series."

Introduction

Each essay herein is designed to stand on its own merit and is complete; yet when considered as a whole, this anthology presents a mosaic of the entire spectrum of black baseball during an era when America's game was separated by a color line. Based on 40 years of research and hundreds of interviews with surviving participants and observers, this volume preserves a backdrop for this crucial and unique time in our country's history, and captures the special essence and flavor of the Negro Leagues.

The first player of African ancestry to play in baseball's recognized major leagues was William Edward White, who appeared in two games in 1879. He was followed by the Walker brothers, Fleetwood and Welday, in 1884. The fourth African-American, Jackie Robinson, did not make his major league debut until 1947. This 63-year gap has become known as the era of "black baseball"—a time when two generations of players of African ancestry were excluded from the existing major leagues.

This anthology provides meaningful insights into the world of black baseball, from the nineteenth century through Jackie Robinson's entry into the major leagues and even beyond the eradication of baseball's color line. The focus, however, is squarely on the first half of the twentieth century when baseball *was* separated by a color line. The reader will journey back in time to experience baseball as it existed on the darker side of that line.

In that world, we learn about Rube Foster, Smokey Joe Williams and other black hurlers of the deadball era who pitched against white teams that featured major leaguers, and can view summaries and examine boxscores of outstanding black-vs.-white contests against Hall of Fame pitchers such as Grover Cleveland Alexander, Walter Johnson and Rube Marquard. We also meet superstar John Henry Lloyd—called the "black Honus Wagner"—and Pete Hill, the first great black outfielder, who was rumored to be sought by major league teams in 1910.

After our look at the deadball era, we turn to the establishment of the early black leagues and then to their halcyon years, where readers will learn about the formation of various leagues, franchises and dynastic teams; and

The first three players from the Negro Leagues voted into the National Baseball Hall of Fame were Satchel Paige (1971), Josh Gibson (1972) and Buck Leonard (1972).

enjoy historic highlights such as the first Negro World Series (1924), the first Negro Leagues All-Star game (1933), and the exciting pitching duel between future Hall of Famers Bullet Rogan and Willie Foster to determine the 1926 Negro National League Championship.

Perhaps most pleasing to readers will be getting introduced to many of the greatest, most colorful and otherwise intriguing players who populated the world of black baseball. Some are famous and others are lesser known, but all have stories that will command attention.

Included among this disparate group are many members of the National Baseball Hall of Fame. Foremost among this celestial aggregation is the Homestead Grays' great power tandem of Josh Gibson and Buck Leonard, called the "Thunder Twins," who were approached by Washington Senators owner Clark Griffith about playing in the major leagues years before Branch Rickey signed Jackie Robinson.

Monte Irvin, who might well have been the player to break the color line had it not been for World War II, is also featured, along with three of his teammates from the Newark Eagles, the celebrated triad of Ray Dandridge, Leon Day and Willie Wells.

Rounding out the Cooperstown entries are Jud "Boojum" Wilson, considered by Satchel Paige to be one of the two best hitters he ever faced, and Biz Mackey, Roy Campanella's mentor, who was voted to the first East-West All-Star game ahead of Josh Gibson.

Buck O'Neil captured the hearts of America with his appearance in Ken Burns' superlative *Baseball* documentary, and is among the other outstanding players showcased. Joining O'Neil in this group is a roster that includes Wild Bill Wright, who starred in the outfield for the Baltimore Elite Giants and is a member of the Mexican Hall of Fame; Bill Byrd, one of the last legal spitball pitchers; Slim Jones, regarded as faster than Lefty Grove by Buck Leonard, who faced both pitchers; Piper Davis, a star player and manager of the Birmingham Black Barons, who discovered and developed Willie Mays; Gene Benson, an outfielder who perfected the "basket catch" long before Willie popularized it in the major leagues; James "Red" Moore, a flashy fielding first sacker who often entertained fans by taking throws behind his back; Jimmie Crutchfield, an outfielder who pleased fans in the same fashion with flyballs; Johnny Davis, a slugging outfielder called "Cherokee" by his teammates; Dave Barnhill, a diminutive fastball pitcher given the name "Impo" because he looked like a little imp out on the mound; Felix "Chin" Evans, whose curveball was labeled a "mountain drop"; and Homestead Grays lefthander Edsall Walker, who would stick a fastball in a batter's ribs just to get his attention.

Other players of special interest are Toni Stone, the first female player in the Negro Leagues, and Eddie Klep, a white pitcher signed by Cleveland Buckeyes owner Ernie Wright in 1946 to be the "reverse Jackie Robinson."

Also, of course, there is Jackie Robinson himself, who carried the essence and flavor of the Negro Leagues into the major leagues. Jackie owes a debt of gratitude to all the players in black baseball, who kept the flame burning. Without their sacrifices, there would have been no proving ground for Robinson to use as a stepping stone for his historic entry into the mainstream of major league baseball.

These Negro League veterans endured the injustices they faced, but remained un-embittered and eventually overcame the circumstances and existing conditions of their times, so that future generations would only read about these conditions and not have to experience them.

After once being ignored to the point of invisibility, former Negro Leaguers have been celebrated in rediscovery with a variety of awards, honors and recognitions coming their way. With the belated acknowledgement of their rightful place in baseball history, the long bus rides, low pay and exclusion from the major leagues were all put in the rear view mirror.

For the Love of the Game: Negro Leagues Baseball Had a History of Its Own

Baseball is our National Pastime. Its history holds a special fascination, which eradicates class distinctions and makes it America's game. Its continuity possesses a unique timelessness, which supersedes age differences and bonds generations together. The baseball diamond is a common ground, serving as a "field of dreams" for every American.

But there was a time when such dreams could never become a reality for a youngster with dark skin. For over half a century, black baseball players were excluded from the recognized major leagues, necessitating the formation of their own teams and leagues. That segment of baseball history remains nebulous to most observers, but the game they played was imbued with a style and flavor all its own, and has become known as "Black Baseball."

Had it not been for this parallel baseball world, there would have been no Jackie Robinson and, without Jackie Robinson, the current crop of black baseball stars would not have their multi-million-dollar contracts. Instead they would be taking a long bus ride for a short paycheck, scuffling around the country playing baseball wherever they could, against whomever they could.

Willie Mays, who began his professional baseball career with the Birmingham Black Barons, understood those conditions that existed before the color line was eradicated, and was reminded of them every time he looked in his wallet. But today's modern athlete has little knowledge of Black Baseball, and even less appreciation for the sacrifices made by players from that generation.

Once the floodgates were opened, the reservoir of black talent supersaturated organized baseball, making expansion a direct and inevitable result of baseball integration. Beginning with Jackie Robinson in 1947, six of the first seven National League Rookie of the Year Awards went to former Negro Leaguers. The resultant effect on major league baseball has been inestimable.

Imagine baseball in the post–World War II era without the excitement that black players have added to the game.

The baseball memories that have been created by black stars have provided increased enjoyment for millions of fans and have become a part of baseball lore. Images of Jackie Robinson dancing off third base and stealing home in the 1955 World Series; Willie Mays running down Vic Wertz' long drive and making "*the catch*" in the 1954 World Series; Bob Gibson's record-breaking 17 strikeouts in the 1968 World Series; or last season's climactic last-pitch World Series finish with Joe Carter's dramatic home run giving the Toronto Blue Jays another World Championship, are indelibly etched into fervent memories.

Without the legacy of black baseball, we would have missed Ty Cobb's stolen base marks being eclipsed by Maury Wills (season) and Lou Brock (career), and would have lost the thrill of watching all-time home run king Hank Aaron in pursuit of Babe Ruth's lifetime home run record.

The same excitement generated by black stars in the major leagues was being generated by their counterparts in black baseball. They never played in the recognized major leagues, never earned big salaries, and were rarely mentioned by the leading sports papers. But they formed a big league of their own and made a reluctant sporting world take notice of the brand of baseball they played. With few exceptions, they remain enigmatic specters still hidden in the sundown shadows of baseball history.

These players were drawn from every remote realm of the Americas, possessing only two common characteristics — their complexions were dark, and they could *play* the game of baseball. Eleven of these great players have been inducted into the National Baseball Hall of Fame in Cooperstown. The legendary Satchel Paige, arguably the greatest pitcher of his generation, heads the list. Paige was followed by the Homestead Grays' power tandem, Josh Gibson and Buck Leonard, who earned the appellation "The black Babe Ruth and Lou Gehrig."

Other enshrinees include Oscar Charleston, the Negro Leagues' equal of Willie Mays; John Henry Lloyd, called the "black Honus Wagner"; Martin Dihigo, the most versatile man to ever play baseball, who starred as a pitcher, outfielder and infielder and is a member of the Hall of Fame in three countries; Cool Papa Bell, whose incredible speed and consistent hitting made him an invaluable part of any ballclub; Ray Dandridge, often called the "black Brooks Robinson"; Judy Johnson, another solid hitter and superlative fielder at the hot corner; Rube Foster, who excelled as a pitcher, manager, owner and league official; and Monte Irvin, who was a superstar in the Negro Leagues before entering the Army during World War II and subsequently joining the New York Giants.

Satchel Paige is the nearest thing to a legend ever to come out of the Negro Leagues. His nimble wit, colorful personality, pea-sized fastball and amazing control made him a household name. His unique aura is representative of the special qualities that permeated black baseball.

Even by conservative standards, there is another score of these forgotten heroes who also merit a plaque at Cooperstown. The last living star of this magnitude is Leon Day, an ace fastball pitcher with the Newark Eagles, who missed election by a single vote in the Veterans Committee balloting last year.

Other leading candidates who have impeccable credentials include Smokey Joe Williams, considered as Satchel Paige's equal, if not his superior;

Biz Mackey, a superior receiver and handler of pitchers, who was Roy Campanella's mentor; and superstar shortstops Willie Wells and Dick Lundy, who were virtually equal to Lloyd as all-around ballplayers. In their respective primes, each was a member of a "million dollar infield" but on today's market, they would command five million apiece.

Deserving pitchers include Willie Foster, considered the best black left-hander of all-time; Bullet Joe Rogan, who played in the outfield when not toeing the rubber; and Cannonball Dick Redding, a deadball era pitcher with outstanding velocity.

Other qualifiers are Pete Hill, the top outfielder from the deadball era, whose all-around play was comparable to Ty Cobb, Tris Speaker and Shoeless Joe Jackson; Cristobal Torriente and Turkey Stearnes, slugging outfielders from baseball's golden era, who could also field and run the bases; Louis Santop, a catcher with a strong arm and stronger bat, who was the leading slugger during the deadball era; and fiercely competitive Jud "Boojum" Wilson, a pure hitter who ranks among the best in the game. This list is not all-inclusive, and many other sundown stars from black baseball should also be considered.

Black baseball covers the first 80 years of professional baseball but, for the first quarter century, black players were permitted (albeit on a limited basis) to play with white teams and in white leagues. The first black professional baseball player was Bud Fowler, who began his pro career in 1872, and the first black major leaguer was Fleetwood Walker, who appeared with the Toledo ballclub of the American Association in 1884.

The first black professional team, the Cuban Giants, was formed in 1885 and gained immediate popularity. In 1887, efforts were made to organize a black league, but it folded after only a week. Teams continued to play as independent ballclubs and a viable league was not established until 1920 when Rube Foster, the father of black baseball, organized the first Negro National League. Foster's team, the Chicago American Giants, had dominated black baseball during the deadball era, and continued their winning ways, capturing the first three league pennants.

The charter members of Foster's league represented cities in the midwest, and in 1923 a second league, the Eastern Colored League, was formed. After a year of co-existence, the two leagues played the first Negro World Series, with the Negro National League Champion Kansas City Monarchs besting the Eastern Colored League Champion Hilldale Daisies in a hard-fought ten-game series that included one tie. The Series continued for four years until the Eastern League broke up early in the 1928 season. The American Negro League, a replacement eastern league, operated during 1929 but folded after a single season, and no World Series was played.

The Negro National League, already faltering after Foster's death, fell victim to the Depression after struggling through the 1931 season. The following year was chaotic, as teams disbanded, throwing multitudes of players into free agency. Homestead Grays owner Cum Posey made a valiant effort to provide a stable league, organizing the East-West League, but it did not even survive the season. The Negro Southern League, formerly a minor league, was a beneficiary from the infusion of quality players from the folding franchises, and was accorded major league status for a single season.

Into this organizational void stepped Gus Greenlee, who rallied his business associates, most of whom were numbers bankers, and together they formed the second Negro National League. This was the only black major league operating from 1933 to 1936, and in the absence of a World Series, the league played a split schedule and had a championship play-off between the winners of the first and second halves. The dominant team during this time was Greenlee's Pittsburgh Crawfords, an aggregation that is most often designated as black baseball's greatest team. At one time they fielded five future Hall of Famers: Satchel Paige, Josh Gibson, Oscar Charleston, Cool Papa Bell and Judy Johnson.

While the new league returned a measure of stability to black baseball, that same year Greenlee pulled a financial rabbit out of his hat when he conceived the idea for a black all-star game, patterned after the Major League All-Star Game. Billed as the "Game of Games," the first East-West All-Star Game was played Sunday, September 10, 1933, at Comiskey Park. Promptly at 2:30, on a dark and dreary day and amid a drizzle that threatened to escalate into a storm, the umpires emerged from the home dugout "like groundhogs searching for that proverbial shadow" and set the historic game in motion with a stentorian call of "Play Ball!"

The decision was greeted by 20,000 howling fans, who braved the weather to watch as Chicago American Giants ace left-hander Willie Foster took the mound for the West and delivered the game's first pitch to Cool Papa Bell, the East's leadoff batter. In an exciting contest, the lead changed hands five times before the outcome was finally determined. Mule Suttles smashed a scorching home run into the upper deck of the left-center field stands for the first All-Star Game round-tripper, and added a game-winning double and three RBI. But the choice for the game's MVP would have to be Willie Foster who, with no rule against pitching more than three innings, pitched the entire game in the 11–7 West victory.

The success of the first game led to a renewal the following season, and the annual classic became the single most important event in the world of black baseball, being attended by crowds of up to 60,000. Dramatic climaxes to highly competitive, closely contested games the following two years firmly ensconced the East-West game in a permanent place in black baseball. The

1934 contest was a 1–0 pitchers' duel, with the East's Satchel Paige, Slim Jones and Harry Kincannon combining for the shutout to even the All-Star series at one game apiece. Slugger Mule Suttles enhanced his claim to All-Star notoriety when he won the 1935 game with a three-run homer off Martin Dihigo in the bottom half of the 11th inning to win the game as he had in the inaugural classic.

Homers were often the All-Star highlight, and the 1939 game was won with one swing of the bat, when the St. Louis Stars' Dan Wilson lifted the West to a comeback victory with a dramatic two-run homer in the bottom of the eighth inning.

But sometimes the pitcher stole the spotlight, as Leon Day did with his superlative performance in the 1942 game. With the East nursing a one-run lead over Satchel Paige, Day entered the game in the seventh inning, with two outs and the tying and go-ahead runs on base, and promptly retired the first batter on a ground ball to shortstop Willie Wells. Over the remaining two innings, the right-handed fastball artist's stint on the mound was similar to Carl Hubbell's famous feat in the 1934 Major League All-Star Game. Day struck out five of the six batters he faced, the last four in succession. Only cleanup slugger Willard Brown even touched the ball, fouling out to catcher Josh Gibson.

The popularity of the East-West game helped black baseball survive during the darkest years of the Depression. The concept proved to be as profitable as it was popular, and in some years there were two games played. The second game was usually held late in the season in an Eastern City, but the game played in Comiskey Park was *the* game. The East-West games also served to showcase the talent which was being excluded from the recognized major leagues. Among the large crowds at the annual extravaganza were many white sports reporters and baseball scouts who helped promote recognition for these great black players.

In 1937 the Negro American League organized in the west and the Negro National League was restructured as an eastern league. This alignment conformed to the East-West game constraints, and continued until the demise of the Negro National League after the 1948 season, when the young black players began to be taken into organized baseball in large numbers. These dozen seasons provided a period of stability and prosperity, especially during World War II.

The Kansas City Monarchs became charter members of the Negro American League and captured five flags in the league's first half-dozen seasons. During these years, their dominance in the west was more than matched by the powerful Homestead Grays in the east, who won nine consecutive pennants (1937–1945), and added a tenth flag in 1948.

For most seasons during this period, both leagues followed the split season format, with a League Championship Series to determine the league champions. In 1942 the Negro World Series was renewed, with the Negro American League Champion Kansas City Monarchs playing the Negro National League Champion Homestead Grays. The Series continued until the dissolution of the Negro National League in 1948.

For all practical purposes, the demise of the Negro Leagues came with the stroke of a pen. When Jackie Robinson affixed his signature to a Brooklyn Dodger contract, he signed the death warrant of the Negro Leagues. Unlike the phoenix, it failed to be reborn in its own likeness, but instead was resurrected in a new form — fused with the white leagues to make baseball whole again. This fusion created a unique renaissance, returning the lost soul to our National Pastime and preserving the essence of black baseball to be passed on to future generations.

The foregoing overview of black baseball spotlights the Negro Leagues' effect on major league baseball, and first appeared in the 1994 Athlon Baseball Annual.

In the intervening years, additional baseball memories have been created by ballplayers who once would have been absent from the major league scene. Three of the most heralded of these more recent memories are Sammy Sosa pushing Mark McGwire to a new single season home run record in 1998; Barry Bonds breaking that mark a scant three years later and then surpassing Hank Aaron's lifetime total in 2007 to become the first player since Babe Ruth to consolidate these two cherished records.

Other events and changing conditions have introduced additional variance from the information provided in the text, generally strengthening and giving greater credibility to the content of the original article.

For instance, the "conservative" estimate that "another score of these forgotten heroes" merited Hall of Fame election has been proven accurate as the 11 Negro leagues members of the Hall of Fame at that time have now been increased to 30 (plus five executives), beginning with Leon Day's election in 1995, the year after this article appeared in print. Listed by name among this "score" were Smokey Joe Williams, Biz Mackey, Willie Wells, Willie Foster, Bullet Rogan, Pete Hill, Cristobal Torriente, Turkey Stearnes, Louis Santop and Jud Wilson — all of whom are now Hall of Famers. Inexplicably, two identified by name in this list — Dick Lundy and Dick Redding — were overlooked. The list was not all-inclusive and others not named who have been inducted are Hilton Smith, Ben Taylor, Mule Suttles, Ray Brown, Willard Brown, Jose Mendez, Andy Cooper and Frank Grant.

The election of Willie Foster and Jud Wilson enhances the Pittsburgh Crawfords' claim as black baseball's greatest team. Both players were with the Crawfords for a season (albeit not the same one), so instead of once fielding "five future Hall of Famers" the roster number now becomes six.

Another conservative statement by today's standards is the "five million" dollar assessment of the salaries that would be commanded by Willie Wells and Dick Lundy. Today their value would be measured in double-digit millions.

At the time the article was published, Fleet Walker was the first known black player in the major leagues. Recently, William Edward White has been identified as being of mixed parentage, thus now having that distinction with his debut in 1879.

Fleetwood Walker: The Real First

The visiting Cleveland team took the field for their pre-game practice. As the tall, slender catcher whipped the ball around the infield, the hometown Louisville fans watched with more than casual interest. The Louisville manager was also watching the player closely, but for a different reason. As the infield workout continued, he approached the umpire and insisted that the catcher not be allowed to play. Cleveland's manager vigorously protested playing the game without his starting catcher, but the umpire ruled in favor of the home team, and Cleveland's star catcher was not allowed to take the field for the beginning of the game.

Disgusted with the decision, he sat silently on the sidelines and watched as the replacement receiver encountered one difficulty after another while trying to handle the unfamiliar position. At the end of the inning the substitute returned to the bench complaining about his battered and bruised hands. At the beginning of the second frame, he reluctantly took his place behind the plate but, after only a few pitches, refused to continue and the game was halted. On the sidelines, the star catcher sat quietly, watching the developments on the field.

Aware of the situation, the crowd grew restless and called out to let him play. Sensing the mood of the crowd and concerned with the possibility of a lost gate, the Louisville ballclub's Vice-President left the stands and made his way to the field to try to resolve the dilemma by making a personal appeal to the shunned catcher to accede to the cries of the crowd. The player listened attentively to the official's persuasion but, still simmering from the slight at the beginning of the game, he was hesitant to take the field. Reluctantly, he consented and, as he walked past the grandstands, the fans cheered and called his name in support. Standing behind the plate for a minute, he hesitated again, but peeled off his warm-up jacket and began warming up. Taking some throws and rifling the ball to the infielders, he demonstrated the same brilliance that had won the fans' approval during the pre-game drills.

While the Cleveland catcher was dazzling the fans, Louisville's two best players walked off the field in protest. Supported by the exit of his players to the clubhouse and ignoring the will of the crowd, Louisville's manager renewed his demands that the Cleveland player not be allowed to play. With the nearly 3,000 fans in the crowd and the Louisville team's executive in favor of letting him play, the umpire was "between a rock and a hard place" and had to make a decision that would be unpopular with someone. The home team remained adamant against the catcher's entry into the game and, ultimately, their refusal to play prevailed. With the team facing the prospect of forfeiture, the young catcher was again removed from the field.

In response, the 3,000 patrons booed, hissed and jeered the Louisville players for the remainder of the game, switching partisanship to the visitors. As the banished player watched from the sidelines, the crowd cheered the home team's every mistake, and openly rooted for the visiting Clevelanders. With the third baseman assuming the emergency catching chores, the team strove valiantly for victory but suffered a 6–3 defeat. Cleveland's pitcher was handicapped with poor support, as his regular battery mate sat on the bench, forbidden to play because his skin was too dark.

It is highly doubtful that anyone present, including the young catching star himself, thought that there was even a remote possibility that less than three years later, he would become the first black ever to play in the major leagues — and he would be beginning his major league career in this very same town.

Who was the player? Not Jackie Robinson. Robinson would not play in the major leagues until 1947. The year of this player's major league debut was 1884, and his name was Moses Fleetwood Walker. Even a casual observer of baseball knows about Jackie Robinson's role in breaking baseball's color barrier. Yet it was Walker who was the first black to play in the major leagues, preceding Robinson by 63 years. In contrast to Robinson, Fleetwood Walker and his place in baseball history is virtually forgotten, and his presence on a major league ballclub has become an almost forgotten footnote in baseball history. But now he is being rediscovered.

Fleetwood Walker played with the Toledo Blue Stockings in the American Association in 1884 and, until recently, was thought to be the first black player in the major leagues.

Born October 7, 1857, at Mount Pleasant, Ohio, a small village in eastern Ohio with a substantial Quaker populace that served as a way station on the underground railway for fugitive slaves on their way to Canada, the family soon moved to Steubenville, Ohio. At the age of 20 Walker entered Oberlin College, and in the spring of 1881 joined the college's first varsity baseball team. After leaving Oberlin, he also played two seasons (1882–1883) while attending law school at the University of Michigan. As a college man who attended predominantly white schools and played both with and against white players on the baseball diamonds, Walker's background was similar to that of Robinson.

However, Walker's pioneering entrance failed to open the floodgate permitting the flow of black talent into the major leagues, as did Robinson's appearance. At the time of Walker's debut, the Civil War was as recent as the Vietnam War is today, and both baseball and civil rights were still in their infancy. Although not commonplace, during the tenuous times as baseball evolved into a professional sport, some black Americans played alongside their white counterparts on integrated ballclubs. One of these was Fleet Walker. Entering the professional ranks in 1883 with the Toledo Blue Stockings of the Northwest League, he batted .251 and earned a reputation as a durable catcher.

The next season, the Toledo ballclub joined the American Association, a major league of the era, and Walker batted .263 as the team's starting catcher. After joining the team, Walker was generally well received at home by players and spectators, but on the road he was subjected to harassment, much as Jackie Robinson was to endure two generations later. Fans were especially active in the league's two southern cities, Baltimore and Louisville, and he was frequently subjected to verbal abuse and threats of bodily harm from anonymous sources.

Ironically, Walker played his first major league game May 1, 1884, against the Louisville Eclipse, the same team that had denied him the right to play three years earlier when he was with a semi-pro team. The residual memories of the unpleasant experience from his previous trip to this southernmost league city evidently troubled Walker, and his performance in his major league debut was not impressive, as he went hitless in four at-bats and committed five errors in a 5–1 defeat.

Manager Charles Morton showed confidence in Walker by keeping him in the lineup despite a slow start, but in addition to threats and jeers that he faced from the fans on the road, Walker had an everyday racist presence in the form of Toledo's ace hurler, Tony Mullane. Mullane had a distaste for Negroes, and refused to take signs from Walker. In an interview with a *New York Age* reporter 35 years later, Mullane acknowledged Walker as a top catcher and admitted that he had deliberately crossed up Walker on pitches. According to the old-time pitcher's account, Walker walked out to the mound and politely, but firmly, informed the star hurler that the practice would not continue. "Mr. Mullane, I'll catch you without signals," he said, "but I won't catch you if you are going to cross me when I give you a signal." He then turned and walked back behind the plate. For the rest of the season, he caught Mullane without knowing what pitch was coming.

Although known primarily for his defensive skills, Walker was hard-pressed to survive under this tacit agreement. In 1884, the American Association permitted pitchers to throw overhand, which coupled with the primitive mitts in use, caused considerable bruising to catchers' hands. The Mullane arrangement increased the already precarious situation, and nagging injuries plagued Walker throughout the season. In mid–July he suffered a more serious injury when a foul tip resulted in a cracked rib. Thereafter, he played sparingly and ineffectively until he was released in early September. At the time of his departure, the press called him a conscientious and popular player. Among the regulars on the team, only Mullane and second baseman Sam Barkley hit for a higher average than Walker.

During the season, Fleet was joined on the team by his brother Welday, who served as a replacement outfielder for an injured player. But neither of the brothers was ever to play in the major leagues again, and there was not to be another black player in the majors until 1947 when Jackie Robinson joined the Dodgers.

However, Walker played minor league ball for the remainder of the decade, appearing with four different teams. In 1887, three years after becoming the first black major leaguer, Walker registered another first while with Newark, when he paired with George Stovey to form the first black battery in organized baseball. It was Stovey who prompted Chicago White Stockings superstar Cap Anson to refuse to play in a scheduled exhibition game against Newark, setting the stage for future exclusion of blacks from the established leagues.

With Newark, Walker led the league in putouts, stole 36 bases and hit .263 for the year. When the team folded in the fall, he was signed by Syracuse and paired with Bob Higgins in 1888 to form another black battery, while helping the team capture the International League championship. Late in the season, in an exhibition game against Chicago, Cap Anson reiterated his position against black players and insisted that Walker be withheld from the starting lineup. Without Walker behind the plate, Syracuse lost the game, 3–0, to Anson's White Stockings. By 1889, Walker's last season in organized baseball, he was the only black player in the league.

Ending his professional career with a .228 batting average, he secured employment as a railroad clerk and continued living in Syracuse. Walker was a popular personage in Syracuse, but he also nurtured a drinking problem. In April 1891, while walking through a rough section of the city in an inebriated condition, he was accosted by a group of men that included a petty criminal named Patrick Murray. An argument ensued and after being struck by Murray, Walker pulled a knife, stabbed his attacker in the groin and fled the scene. Walker was arrested and charged with first degree murder, but when his case came before the court on June 3, 1891, the jury acquitted him on the grounds of self-defense, and the verdict was greeted by applause from the spectators.

Afterward, Walker moved back to his childhood home in Steubenville, but his personal setbacks continued. His wife died in 1893 and he was left with two sons and a daughter to rear alone. Demonstrating a personal resilience, Walker remarried five years later, and by 1903, he owned the Union Hotel and was publishing a newspaper, *The Equator*. In 1904, he relocated his family in nearby Cadiz, Ohio, where he worked as the manager of a local opera house for a year before leasing the opera house and showing motion pictures.

Intelligent, well-educated and a successful businessman, Walker lived a quiet and financially comfortable life. Although he had killed a white man and had been exonerated by a white jury, he became disillusioned later in his life, and was convinced that blacks could not receive justice from whites. In 1908 he wrote a treatise, *Our Home Colony,* advocating racial separation and a "back to Africa" policy for black Americans. However, Walker chose not to follow that policy himself, and enjoyed a prosperous decade. Saddened by the death of his second wife in 1920 and suffering infirmities that accompany advancing age, he sold his theatre business in the spring of 1922 and moved back to Steubenville briefly, before settling into retirement in Cleveland. Forgotten by baseball, embittered by discrimination and in failing health, Walker had less than two more years to live.

On May 11, 1924, he died of lobar pneumonia six hours after being admitted to Cleveland's City Hospital, and was returned to Steubenville for burial. Twenty-three years after Fleetwood Walker was interred and became a forgotten baseball pioneer, Jackie Robinson gained a lasting niche in baseball history by walking in Fleetwood Walker's footsteps.

This article was first published in the January-February 1994 issue of The Diamond: The Official Chronicle of Major League Baseball *under the title "63 Years Before Jackie Robinson: Fleetwood Walker Fought His Own Battle to Play in the Major Leagues."*

At the time, Fleetwood Walker was the first known black player in the major leagues. Recently, William Edward White gained that distinction when he was identified as being of mixed parentage, with a white father and black mother.

White was a student at Brown University when he filled in for an injured player at first base for two games with the Providence Grays, then a member of the National League, in 1879.

White's brief major league career did not ameliorate the discrimination that he faced, nor does it diminish Fleet Walker's pioneering role in the eventual elimination of baseball's color line.

John McGraw and Chief Tokohama: Baltimore's Brush with Breaking the Barrier

In 1954 Jehosie Heard became the first black ballplayer in Baltimore Orioles history. The little left-hander's stay with the club was brief, consisting of only two relief appearances for a total of three-and-one-third innings. If the legendary John McGraw had been successful in his plans, the first black Oriole would have played 53 years earlier.

In 1901, McGraw was an aspiring manager with the Baltimore Orioles in the newly organized American League. While quartered at the Eastland Hotel in Hot Springs, Arkansas, during spring training, he observed some black bellhops playing baseball on the hotel grounds and was especially impressed with the way one member of the group handled himself. The player under scrutiny was Charlie Grant, an excellent second baseman with five years' playing experience for top black ballclubs.

In need of quality ballplayers, McGraw devised a scheme to pass off the light-skinned Grant as an Indian in order to sign him for the Orioles. He changed Grant's name to Charlie Tokohama and informed the press that his new discovery was a full-blooded Cherokee. Grant practiced with the Orioles throughout the spring and accompanied the team north to Chicago, where he was exuberantly greeted by the city's black populace. When White Sox owner Charlie Comiskey heard about McGraw's deception, he exposed the ruse and Grant was dropped from the Orioles roster before opening day and never appeared in a regular season game.

Without Tokohama, McGraw managed the Orioles to a fifth place finish in 1901 before jumping to the New York Giants, where he became a managerial legend. If fate had been kinder, he would have also made Charlie Tokohama a legend, but baseball had to wait 46 years for Branch Rickey and Jackie Robinson to accomplish what John McGraw and Charlie Grant had attempted at the turn of the century.

This truncated version of John McGraw's subterfuge in making an abortive attempt to sign a black player to circumvent the color barrier in major league baseball first appeared as a sidebar titled "When a Barrier Almost Was Broken" in the 1993 All-Star Game Yearbook. A fuller account of this historic event would include additional information about the principal participants which should be of interest to the reader.

Grant had played in Chicago with the Columbia Giants in 1900 and was recognized by the black populace when he arrived with McGraw's aggregation. The reaction of the black fans alerted Charles Comiskey to McGraw's true intentions. Comiskey said that if McGraw was allowed to play Tokohama, he might sign a certain "Chinaman" of his acquaintance for the White Sox. McGraw did not fail to recognize the implication in the statement. The prompt release of Grant showed that the Orioles skipper had received the intended message.

After his failed ploy McGraw began 1902 in Baltimore but switched to New York during the season, where he managed the Giants for 31 years and won ten National League pennants and three World Series. He finished his career in 1932 with 2,763 victories, the second highest total behind Connie Mack (3,731). In 1933 he came out of retirement to manage the National League in the inaugural All-Star Game against Connie Mack's American League squad. John McGraw was elected to the Hall of Fame in 1937.

In contrast, Charlie Grant was almost forgotten.

Prior to McGraw's gambit Grant had played with two well-known black teams — the Page Fence Giants and Columbia Giants — and after being dropped by McGraw, he returned to the Columbia Giants for the 1901 season. Subsequently, he played on four championship black teams, with the Cuban X-Giants (1903) and Philadelphia Giants (1904–06). He is probably most identified with the Philadelphia Giants where he was teammates with Rube Foster, John Henry Lloyd, Pete Hill and Sol White,

In 1901 John McGraw attempted to pass off Charlie Grant as an Indian named Chief Tokohama and play him in the major leagues. Grant is pictured here five years later, sitting behind his Philadelphia Giants teammate Bill Monroe.

all of whom have been inducted into the Baseball Hall of Fame. Although Grant continued his baseball career through 1916, he never again played for top level teams.

After retiring from baseball Grant returned to his hometown, Cincinnati, Ohio, where he was born in 1879, and worked as a janitor in an apartment building. One hot July day in 1932, he was sitting outside the building when a passing car blew a tire, jumped the curb and hit him. The injuries suffered in the accident proved fatal for the former infielder who — briefly known as Chief Tokohama — once stood on the threshold of fame.

When Rube Foster Faced the Chicago Cubs

In 1909 the Chicago Cubs lost the National League pennant to Honus Wagner and the Pittsburgh Pirates, and found themselves without a World Series for the first time in four years. Rube Foster issued a challenge that would provide the Cubs with a fall series and possibly a fat paycheck. Foster's proposal would pit the best white team in Chicago against the best black team in Chicago in a Chicago series. Both teams, as defending champions, had suffered the loss of their titles. The Cubs lost to the Pirates, and Foster's team, the Leland Giants, had earlier lost a challenge match to the St. Paul Gophers for the Colored Championship of the west. However, in that series Foster had been out of action with a broken leg and unable to pitch for his team. Experts concede his presence would have made a difference in the outcome of the hotly contested playoff.

The Cubs-Leland Giants series was to be a three-game set played on the Cubs' home field. The first game was played on October 18 and featured the Lelands' veteran hurler, George Ball, against Cubs ace Mordecai "Three Finger" Brown. The Lelands lost the opener, largely due to a trio of errors by first baseman Bobby Marshall, a former football star at the University of Minnesota. Another controversial play occurred in this game when Joe Green was thrown out at home in an effort to score on a broken leg. Green had singled in the third inning and promptly stole both second and third base. However, in sliding at the hot corner he broke his leg. When the ball got away from third baseman Del Howard, Green was sent home by the third base coach and was thrown out a few steps from the plate while hobbling towards home as fast as he was able. After catcher Pat Moran put the tag on him, Green had to be carried off the field.

The final game was probably the best contest of the series. Featuring Pat Dougherty — at that time considered the best black left-hander ever — for the Lelands, and Orval Overall — sporting a season record of 20–11 with a 1.42 ERA — for the Cubs. The two hurlers locked in a pitchers' duel, with Overall and the Cubs emerging a 1–0 victor.

But it was the second game, with the well-known and colorful Rube

Foster taking the slab against the Cubs, that attracted the most attention. The game was played Thursday, October 21, 1909, and the Cubs' Big Ed Reulbach was given the nod to oppose Foster. With the big black Texan on the mound, the fans knew that anything could happen and they were not disappointed — something *did* happen.

In Ring Lardner's account of the game for the *Chicago Tribune*, he described the action leading up to the final scene.

> It happened that the Giants had pounded Mr. Reulbach for a whole host of runs — namely five in the third inning. Edward retired in the sixth in favor of Orval Overall, who wouldn't let the enemy score at all. By dint of scraping and saving, the Cubs collected two tallies off the tricky Foster before the ninth was arrived at. It was Rube's first appearance since July 12th, when he busted his leg. He was going along well enough to win easily until he had disposed of Joe Tinker in the final round. Bugs [the contemporary term used for "fans" — ed.] were hastening for the exits when their steps were arrested by singles of Moran and Overall. Heinie Zimmerman had been hitting the ball on the nose most of the afternoon, and he didn't disappoint this time. His safe wallop filled the bases and the spectators began to realize that the Cubs weren't whipped after all. James Sheckard refused to offer at any bad ones and was passed. This forced Pat across the plate with a tally. Frank Schulte, afterwards the hero of the play, sent a sharp grounder to Wallace whose throw got Overall at the plate.
>
> Now there were two out, the bases full and two runs needed to tie the score. Up strode brave Captain Howard and smote one he liked against the right field boards for a clean single, clean enough to allow both Zimmerman and Sheckard to count and Schulte to reach third.

At this point Hollywood could take over the plot. The score was tied and the winning run was on third base with two outs. Foster's reputation as a tactical and psychological genius was well earned. The baseball minds and bettors alike were running the possibilities around in their minds. What would the great Rube Foster do? Would he intentionally walk the next batter to load the bases and give his infield a force out at

Rube Foster was the foremost pitcher in black baseball during the first decade of the twentieth century. He was also the manager in the 1909 series against the Chicago Cubs, and would later become the team owner as well. Foster (standing) is pictured two years earlier with Lelands teammate Nate Harris.

any base? Would he try to tantalize the batter into swinging at a bad pitch? Or would he pretend to intentionally walk the batter and try to sneak a strike over on him while he wasn't expecting it? Maybe he was tiring and would bring in a fresh pitcher to relieve him. Since the game had appeared to be all over but the shouting, no one was warming up. If he was looking for relief, he would need to stall for time so the relief pitcher could get warmed up before coming into the game. The possibilities for a Hollywood ending were innumerable. But even the most imaginative Hollywood scriptwriter would never have come up with the improbable way the game actually ended.

Fay Young, sportswriter for the *Chicago Defender*, wrote an account of the game almost 40 years later. In his article he described the closing events of the game.

> Rube had gone along in major league style until the ninth inning, at which time he was enjoying a 5–2 lead.
>
> In the ninth he was touched for four hits and three runs which tied the knot five all.
>
> Rube walked over to the Giants bench to talk to Pat Dougherty. He wanted Pat to relieve him. The Cubs players converged around umpire Meyer over near first base. They were on the playing field. Several fans got into the argument. Some fans edged over the third base line.
>
> Frank Schulte was on third at the time. Foster claimed he called "time." He stood with his back to the plate with the ball in his hand. He was explaining to Meyer that he was "not stalling" as the Cubs players had claimed. During the discussion, Schulte sneaked home.
>
> Foster demanded that Schulte be sent back to third as both the Cubs players and spectators were on the field of play. Meyer said the run counted.

Meyer was a white semi-pro umpire who had called the game from behind the pitcher's mound. He maintained that during the argument with Foster, he did not hear Rube call time and that Schulte going home unmolested with the winning run was within the confines of the rules. The contemporary media indicated that even the rabid Cubs fans agreed that Schulte's stolen base was a "dirty steal" but insisted that nothing could be done about it.

Lardner agreed with that assessment and addressed the issue in his account of the game, wrapping up with a description of the other related activities on the diamond.

> The chances are that the game would have been protested if there had been anyone with whom a protest could have been lodged. Captain Foster asserted that he was not stalling at all, but merely asking Dougherty to take his pitching job away from him. Furthermore, he wanted to know how one Cub could be allowed to steal home when three or four others were standing on the diamond in conversation. There was no answer to this query since Meyer had made his ruling and the athletes had left the field.
>
> The Giants' fun was centered in the third. Ball was walked by Reulbach, and a

successful hit and run play with Strothers sent him to third, the hitsman stopping at first. Big Ed allowed Wallace's little roller to go through him and Ball scored. Wright sacrificed, and Payne drove in two more tallies with a single to right. Payne's steal of second, and Hill's single sent the former to third. A passed ball permitted Hill to scoot to second, and the fourth and fifth runs counted on Booker's safe drive.

Howard's smash off Strothers' chest enabled him to get to first base in the fourth. He advanced on Stanley's out. Archer, who was playing centerfield in the dear departed Hoffman's [sic] place, popped a fly to Strothers, but Tinker lined one to the right field barrier and Del trotted home. The next Cubs score was in the eighth off three hits. Pete Hill's nice throw to the plate prevented another run.

Fay Young's account of the game provided some additional insight into what happened *after* the game.

According to Young, "the umpire had to be escorted off the field to save him from bodily harm." There had been heavy betting on the game and the crowd turned ugly. The gamblers milled around the clubhouse for a long time, getting uglier by the minute. Billy Nielsen, a man respected by everyone, was selected to address the crowd with a general agreement to abide by his decision. Nielsen climbed on a chair so he could be seen above the milling melee and, in a demonstration of common sense and diplomacy, shouted to the angry throng, "All bets are off!"

That pronouncement soothed the mood of the crowd, but the bottom line was that Foster, a trickster himself, had been outfoxed. Without a doubt Rube, who had often victimized others in the same fashion, wanted revenge.

The next season he separated from owner Frank Leland and, by adding John Henry Lloyd, Bruce Petway, Home Run Johnson and other new players, built a much better ballclub. Then, after having the defeat fester for a year, he challenged the Cubs again. Although they had just won their fourth pennant in five years, the Cubs declined the invitation. Whether it was because they knew Foster had greatly improved his club and were afraid of losing, or whether it was due to the row from the previous encounter was never made clear. It would have been a great series. History is the loser.

This article was written as part of a series From the Negro League Archives *for* Oldtyme Baseball News. *Unfortunately, due to pecuniary considerations this excellent publication was unable to continue production. Thus, this account of the historic series of games has not appeared in print until now.*

Comments on this series of games:

The Cubs used their three top pitchers: Mordecai "Three Fingers" Brown (27–9), Orval Overall (20–11) and Ed Reulbach (19–10), but some of their regulars were absent from this series. Shortstop Joe Tinker was the only member of the vaunted double-play combination to play. Manager-first baseman Frank

Chance, who had missed much of the season with a broken bone in his shoulder, and second baseman Johnny Evers were both absent from the lineup. Starting center fielder Solly Hofman, third baseman Harry Steinfeld and catcher Johnny Kling, who had held out for the entire season, were also missing.

Del Howard, who had replaced Chance at first base after his injury, continued in his stead both at the position and at the helm. Young 22-year-old Heinie Zimmerman filled in for Evers at second base — and he would become the regular at this position in 1911. Ironically, in view of the heavy gambling on the series, ten years later Zimmerman would be declared ineligible to ever play baseball again for the remainder of his life, due to his association with known gamblers. Jimmy Archer, who had started behind the plate all year during Kling's holdout, moved to center field to replace Hofman, while backup catcher Pat Moran handled the chores behind the plate. Joe Stanley, a seldom used outfielder playing in his last major league season, filled in at third base.

For the Lelands, future Hall of Famer Pete Hill batted in the cleanup slot and Rube Foster batted himself 7th, while fellow moundsman Walter Ball played right field and batted 8th. This lineup was much inferior to Foster's 1910 Leland aggregation, a team that reigned supreme in black baseball. That season, Foster issued a challenge to the Cubs for a rematch but he was rebuffed. Unlike the previous year, the Cubs were in the World Series in 1910, which might have contributed to their decision not to accept the challenge.

Following is the box score of this historic game.

Box Score

LELAND GIANTS	AB	R	H	O	A	E	CHICAGO CUBS	AB	R	H	O	A	E
Wallace 3b	4	1	1	0	3	1	Zimmerman 2b	5	1	3	2	4	0
Wright ss	3	0	0	2	2	1	Sheckard lf	4	1	1	0	0	0
Payne lf	4	1	1	2	0	0	Schulte rf	5	1	0	1	0	0
Hill cf	4	1	1	2	1	0	Howard 1b	5	2	2	14	2	0
Moore 2b	4	0	1	1	2	0	Stanley 3b	4	0	2	0	1	0
Booker c	4	0	1	6	0	0	Archer c	4	0	2	2	0	0
Foster p	4	0	1	0	4	0	Tinker ss	4	0	1	3	4	0
Ball rf	3	1	0	1	0	0	Moran c	3	1	1	4	1	0
Strothers 1b	4	1	1	12	0	1	Reulbach p	2	0	0	1	3	1
							Overall p	2	0	1	0	0	0
Totals	34	5	7	*26	12	3	Totals	38	6	13	27	15	1

*Two outs when winning run scored.

Leland Giants	0	0	5	0	0	0	0	0	=	5	
Chicago Cubs	0	0	0	1	0	0	0	1	4	=	6

Two base hits — Moore, Sheckard, Wallace, Howard 2, Stanley. Stolen bases — Schulte, Payne. Hit by Pitcher — Moran. Passed Ball — Moran. Bases on balls — off Foster 1; off Reulbach 1. Struck out — by Foster 3; by Reulbach 1; by Overall 3. Umpire — Meyer. Time of game — 2 hours. Attendance — 2,000.

The 1910 Leland Giants

The 1910 Leland Giants were black baseball's first great team. Manager Rube Foster considered them the greatest baseball talent ever assembled, white or black. Featuring stars John Henry Lloyd, Pete Hill, Bruce Petway, Home Run Johnson, Frank Wickware and Pat Dougherty, the team fashioned a fabulous 128–6–1 record.

Founded in 1905 by Frank C. Leland, the Giants had quickly established themselves as a top team in the midwest. When Leland and Foster went their separate ways in 1910, Foster assumed complete control of the franchise, which legally retained the Leland Giants team name.

Foster aligned himself with John M. Schorling, Charles Comiskey's brother-in-law, and leased the old White Sox Park on 39th and Shields for their home games. He then formed a nucleus for the revamped club with top players from the old Leland Giants and the Philadelphia Giants.

The team assembled was virtually a black all-star team, but more than any other individual, Rube Foster is identified with the 1910 Leland Giants. A man almost bigger than life itself, he is considered black baseball's greatest manager, with the team becoming an extension of his philosophy and bearing his distinct imprint.

Foster molded players to fit his "racehorse" style of play. Good pitching, sound defense and an offense geared to the running game became the trademarks of his teams. All of his players were required to master the bunt and hit-and-run, so they could always push across some runs and avoid prolonged team slumps.

Essential to the Lelands' success during the 1910 campaign was the presence of John Henry Lloyd, the greatest black baseball player during the first two decades of the century. He was a complete ballplayer who could hit, run, field, throw, and hit with power. With the exception of Hans Wagner, the tall, rangy shortstop had no peer at his position.

Lloyd was a smart player who easily fit into the Foster style of play, as did center fielder Pete Hill, Foster's choice as team captain. This pair of superstars vied for designation as the most valuable player on the team. Also a five-tool player, Hill hit both for average and with power, was a nervy basestealer, fielded flawlessly and had a deadly arm.

Throughout the season, rumors persisted that Hill, under the guise of being an Indian or Cuban, was slated to play with a major league team the following year. Chicago White Sox ace (and future Hall of Famer) Ed Walsh, who faced the best in the American League for years, watched Hill play and declared him the equal of Ty Cobb. If an all-star team had been picked in 1910, Cobb and Hill would have flanked Tris Speaker to form the outfield constellation.

Two other established stars were Grant "Home Run" Johnson and Bruce Petway. Johnson, a right-handed slugger in the deadball era, was an established veteran shortstop in 1910 but shifted to second base in deference to Lloyd's outstanding ability. Petway was the premier catcher of the day and the first great receiver in black baseball history. His strong and accurate arm, regarded as one of the best ever, intimidated baserunners and kept him in demand by the best teams.

Pete Booker had been the starting catcher for the Leland Giants for the previous three seasons but when Bruce Petway joined the team, he moved to first base in deference to Petway's skills and developed into a solid first baseman.

Frank Wickware gained his most notoriety when he outdueled Walter Johnson two out of three games in 1913 and 1914, when both hurlers were in their prime, but when he arrived on the Chicago baseball scene in 1910 at age 22, the big right-hander was already noted for his blazing fastball, mound presence, coolness under pressure, and smooth delivery. Experienced diamond observers called him "the most sensational pitcher seen for some time" and, although only a rookie, he quickly developed into the ace of the staff, supplanting Rube Foster and Pat Dougherty.

Dougherty, described by the press as a "big side-wheeler," was the top left-hander in the game and had won both of the Leland Giants' victories in the five-game playoff against the St. Paul Gophers in 1909.

Grant "Home Run" Johnson was one of four players from the 1910 Leland Giants who were recruited to play against the Detroit Tigers and Philadelphia A's in a Cuban winter exhibition series.

Flanking Pete Hill in the outfield were two class outfielders, Frank Duncan and Jap Payne. Duncan, a popular and reliable player with all-around ability, was a successful leadoff man and proved to be an effective table-setter with his consistent hitting and basestealing. Payne was already an established veteran who could help a team in many ways. A complete ballplayer, he was a good hitter with above average power, an excellent basestealer, and a proven fielder with a good arm.

Wes Pryor and Fred Hutchinson were signed by Foster from the Chicago Unions and were predicted to be future stars. Pryor was the starting third baseman and Hutchinson, a utility infielder, was a good glove man with a great arm. Sam Strothers was in his third season with the Lelands as a back-up catcher. He also served as a utility player, filling in at first base or in the outfield.

Bill Lindsay began the 1910 season with a team in Kansas City, earning the nickname "the Kansas Cyclone," but after pitching against Foster's Leland Giants late in the year, the big, hard-throwing right-hander found favor in the manager's appraising eye and Rube signed him to pitch with the Lelands for the remainder of the season. Tragically, after developing into a star hurler, he died only four short years later.

Another short-time member of the mound corps was a pitcher named Harper, who pitched for the Leland Giants in the Florida Winter League and came north with them in the spring.

After winning the Florida Hotel Winter League title, Foster's squad played exhibitions on their way back to Chicago for the opening of their regular season, May 14. There was no Negro league at that time so the Lelands joined the Chicago League, comprised of white semi-pro teams, and supplemented their schedule by playing some independent black teams.

Rube penciled himself into the opening day lineup and hurled a 5–2 victory on their hosts' home field. The Lelands home opener was the next day and one of the largest crowds of the season turned out for speeches, bands, and other festivities. The Leland Giants' bats provided the fireworks for the occasion as they raked the opposing Gunthers pitcher for a 5–1 victory in their league opener to send the fans home happy.

The Lelands' diamond success continued unabated and they recorded 35 consecutive victories before their first defeat on June 12, when playing three games in a single day proved to be more than they could handle.

As their notoriety increased, large crowds from the white populace began attending the Leland Giants games. Rube bragged that he had the best team in the country and issued a challenge to the world, making a standing offer of $500 to any team that could beat his ballclub.

The nearest rival to his claim for the top spot in black baseball was Jose

Mendez' Stars of Cuba, but during the season, the Leland Giants defeated the Cuban squad soundly, losing only a single contest in head-to-head competition. That defeat came the day before the heralded heavyweight title fight between Jack Johnson and James Jeffries, and was only their second loss of the season.

The most exciting of these hotly contested games was played at White Sox Park, as the two greatest black pitchers of the century's first decade hooked up in a pitching duel. Rube Foster and Cuban Jose Mendez battled for 11 innings before darkness ended the classic encounter in a 4–4 deadlock.

Another formidable opponent who challenged the Lelands' claim of baseball superiority was the West Baden Sprudels, a team managed by C. I. Taylor that would evolve into the Indianapolis ABCs, who brought their 29-game winning streak to Chicago. Undaunted, Foster took the mound and snapped the streak with a 4–2 victory. Two days later, Wickware won by the same score in 13 innings over Ben Taylor, who would later win fame as a great first baseman.

As the month of August got under way Lloyd, Hill, Johnson, Duncan, and Booker were all hitting over .350. Pete Hill, a deadball era slugger, was also credited with 14 home runs, 16 triples, and 12 doubles for the first ten weeks of the season.

In the Lelands' last home appearance, Bill Lindsay — a recent signee — hurled a 4–1 victory. As the Lelands continued their dominant play, Foster sought a post-season series with the Chicago Cubs and the Chicago White Sox, but both teams declined the challenge.

In the absence of an autumn series with the city's major league clubs, the team embarked September 11 on an eastern tour, where they defeated the best black teams in the East and also the professional white teams from the Tri-State League. After 18 straight victories, including a 9–1 triumph over Mike Donlin's All-Stars, the Leland Giants embarked October 5 for Cuba on their scheduled World Tour.

After arriving at Havana, with 8,000 fans in attendance for the opening game of a 16-game series, Lindsay pitched Foster's team to a 5–4 victory over the hometown Havana ballclub. Following the end of the Cuban winter league and a brief respite, Rube renamed the team the Chicago American Giants and a dynasty was born, with the club becoming a dominant force until Foster's departure from baseball.

This concise history of Rube Foster's superlative 1910 ballclub first appeared in the 1994 Negro Leagues Baseball Museum Yearbook.

The 1910 aggregation was the beginning of Rube Foster's dynasty and for the next 12 years the Chicago American Giants won every recorded championship except one.

Pete Hill: The Greatest Black Outfielder of the Deadball Era

Pick an all-star outfield from the deadball era and it would be Ty Cobb, Tris Speaker and Pete Hill. Pete who? Don't confuse him with Charlie Hustle, although Hill's hustle was one of the baseball attributes the two great players shared on the diamond. Little known now, but widely heralded and respected during his own era, Hill was generally conceded by old-timers to be second only to Oscar Charleston as the greatest black outfielder in the first half of the twentieth century. Of the current crop of players, Rickey Henderson (.325 BA, 28 HR, and 65 SB last season) best demonstrates the blend of power, speed and batting consistency that Hill exemplified. But even Henderson comes up short in comparison. Hill was a superior bunter, an expert hit-and-run batter, and a much better defensive player than Henderson.

A definite Hall of Fame caliber player, he was the best black outfielder of the deadball era, and was often compared to Ty Cobb — rightfully so. Like Cobb, Hill was a big man for his era, standing a shade over six feet and weighing around 200 pounds. Also like Cobb, he threw right-handed but batted left-handed and was a great hitter both for average and power. An amazingly consistent line drive hitter who used the entire field and excelled at bunting for base hits, he was a superior contact hitter and seldom struck out. In 1911 he was credited with hitting safely in 115 out of 116 games.

A complete ballplayer, Hill could field and run the bases as well as hit. The star center fielder was one of the fastest outfielders in the game, fielded flawlessly, and had a deadly arm. On the bases he was a very fast, graceful runner and a good basestealer. But more than that, he was a nervy baserunner who upset pitchers and infielders, as Jackie Robinson was to do a generation later. He was described by the media as a "restless type, always in motion ... trying to draw a throw from the pitcher."

Hill displayed more power, possessed a better throwing arm, and was generally a much better fielder than the legendary Cobb. But an objective evaluation would place him slightly behind Cobb in batting average and stolen bases. Tris Speaker would serve as a better model for comparison as an all-around player. At bat Hill hit for a comparable average, but had more home run power than Speaker. His fielding and baserunning skills were also very close to the performance level demonstrated by Speaker, but Hill was a little behind afield, while just a shade better on the bases.

Hill was a contemporary of John Henry Lloyd, who was called the black Honus Wagner, and the comparisons between the two black superstars were similar to the arguments in the white leagues about who was a better player — Cobb or Wagner? The diamond skills of the four greats of the era were so evenly matched that neither question was satisfactorily resolved. When the initial balloting for the Hall of Fame was conducted in 1936, both Cobb and Wagner were among the first group elected, along with Babe Ruth, Christy Mathewson and Walter Johnson. Cobb finished with the highest vote total, while Wagner tied Ruth for second place. Meanwhile, their black peers were totally ignored by the baseball world. In 1977 Lloyd was posthumously accorded his proper place at Cooperstown by the Special Committee on Negro Leagues, but Hill's accomplishments remain unrecognized by the Hall of Fame. Players who observed him in action never had any reservations about his greatness. Lloyd, his primary rival, was always high in his praise of Hill, and Homestead Grays owner Cum Posey, who was an observer of black baseball from 1910 through 1946, selected him on his all-time team.

In 1910 Pete Hill (front) and Bruce Petway (back) played against Ty Cobb and the Detroit Tigers in a winter exhibition series. Big Ed Walsh, Chicago White Sox future Hall of Famer, declared Hill to be the equal of Cobb.

Hill started his career with the Pittsburgh Keystones in 1899, leaving after two seasons to join the New York–based Cuban X-Giants, the dominant team of that time. In 1903, the outfield star moved to the newly organized Philadelphia Giants, where he first joined forces with Rube Foster. After helping the team win consecutive championships in 1905–1906, Hill accompanied Foster in a move to the Chicago Leland Giants. When Foster and owner Frank C. Leland split in 1910, Hill yielded to Foster's persuasion and signed with his club. The transition proved to be a good one, as Foster assembled a cast which comprised the greatest talent in black baseball at the time. The aggregation of stars finished the season with a record of 106–7, and manager Foster called it the greatest team, black or white, of all time.

Hill's smart, aggressive style of play epitomized the kind of ballplayer that Foster wanted for his racehorse baseball team, and his studied approach to the game made him Foster's choice as team captain. Hill responded to the role by smashing the ball for a .428 average to out-hit teammate John Henry Lloyd. If a MVP had been picked in black baseball that year, Hill would have been the choice.

That winter Foster took his troops to Cuba to compete against the island's best professional teams from the winter league. The Cubans featured Jose Mendez, who earned the sobriquet "the black Matty" because he pitched on even terms when matching arms with New York Giants great Christy Mathewson, splitting two decisions. Despite the presence of Mendez and an ample portion of "home cooking" from the umpires, Foster's men finished the series with eight wins against only five losses and a tie.

By coincidence, the Detroit Tigers and Philadelphia Athletics had also scheduled an exhibition tour against the island ballclubs. The Cubans, impressed by the success and diamond skills of the Leland Giants, signed their top players (Hill, John Henry Lloyd, catcher Bruce Petway, and infielder Grant "Home Run" Johnson) to play against the invading major league clubs. Fortified by the four black Americans, the Havana ballclub broke even against Detroit, winners of three consecutive pennants (1907–1909) before slipping to third place in 1910, and defeated the World Champion Athletics three games to two.

Facing pitchers Jack Coombs (30–9, 1.30 ERA), Chief Bender (23–5, 1.58 ERA), Eddie Plank (16–10, 2.01 ERA), George Mullin (21–12, 2.87 ERA), Ed Willett (16–11, 2.37 ERA) and Ed Summers (12–12, 2.53 ERA), Pete Hill batted a cool .333 in the 11 games. And that "ain't too shabby" against the American League's best, which included two future Hall of Famers (Bender and Plank) and the league leaders in wins (Coombs) and winning percentage (Bender).

The following season Foster's aggregation became known as the Chicago American Giants, and Hill remained with the team, providing solid hitting, outstanding fielding, superior baserunning, and responsible leadership to the ballclub for the next eight years. During this time, he was the best hitter on the team, hitting left-handers and right-handers equally well. Statistics extrapolated from existing boxscores show averages of .400, .357, and .302 for the seasons 1911, 1912, and 1914.

As captain of the American Giants, he continued to be a team leader and, being above draft age, remained a stabilizing presence when the team lost many younger players to military service during World War I. During his tenure with the organization, Foster often let Hill run the ballclub, and in 1919, the apprenticeship paid dividends when Hill assumed the reins of the

Detroit Stars as playing manager. In a showdown series against his old mentor, Hill led his team to victory over Foster's American Giants.

Although entering the last phase of his career, the transition to the rabbit-ball era presented no problem for Hill as he rapped out a .391 average in 1921, his last season with Detroit. Moving east from the Motor City, Hill managed the Baltimore Black Sox, and as the years passed, relegated himself to a role as part-time outfielder and pinch-hitter. But, even as he neared the end of his career, he remained a dangerous hitter. In 1924 Ben Taylor, Hill's successor as manager of the Black Sox, paid tribute to Hill. "The time was he was numbered among the greatest in the game and will probably never have an equal as a hitter. I think he is the most dangerous man in a pinch in baseball."

In addition to slapping black pitchers all over the ball park, he is credited with a .354 average against major league opposition in exhibition games and compiled a .307 average for six winter seasons in Cuba, including a league-leading .365 for the 1910–1911 campaign.

In 1951, 25 years after the popular, clutch-hitting "money player" closed out his brilliant 28-year career as one of black baseball's finest players, J. Preston "Pete" Hill passed away in Buffalo, New York.

John McGraw would have loved him.

This article was first published in 1991 in Oldtyme Baseball News *(Vol. 3, No. 5) as the feature* Forgotten Heroes, *which spotlighted the greatest black baseball players before 1947. In the article Pete Hill was described as "a definite Hall-of-Fame caliber player" and was also projected as the 1910 Most Valuable Player "if there had been a MVP Award in black baseball." In recent years the validity of these assertions has been affirmed, as Hill was elected to the Hall of Fame by a special committee in 2006 and was selected as the 1910 MVP in the ESPN Baseball Encyclopedia's ex post facto MVP Awards for black baseball in 2007.*

The following box scores and commentary appeared in the same issue of Oldtyme Baseball News *but on a separate page with a new heading.*

Pete Hill versus the Major Leaguers

In the 1910 Cuban winter series against the Detroit Tigers, the Havana club dropped the first game but in the second contest, Hill demonstrated his clutch hitting by knocking in all the runs (with two-out RBI) in a 3–2 victory. In the third inning he knocked in the first run of the game and in the seventh inning, after having fallen behind, 2–1, knocked in the tying and winning runs.

November 14, 1910
BOXSCORE

	DETROIT TIGERS							*HAVANA*					
	AB	R	H	PO	A	E		AB	R	H	PO	A	E
Schaeffer 2b	4	0	0	3	5	–	C. Morin rf	3	0	1	2	0	–
O'Leary ss	4	0	0	3	5	–	P. Hill lf	4	0	2	3	0	–
Crawford cf	4	1	2	1	0	–	G. Johnson 2b	3	0	1	2	3	–
Moriarty 3b	4	1	1	2	2	–	S. Lloyd ss	4	0	2	7	4	–
T. Jones 1b	3	0	0	10	0	–	H. Hernandez cf	4	0	2	0	0	–
McIntyre rf	3	0	1	0	0	–	A. Parpetti 1b	4	0	1	10	0	–
Stanage c	3	0	0	5	4	–	B. Petway c	4	1	1	2	1	–
Casey lf	2	0	0	0	0	–	Bustamente 3b	4	1	1	1	1	–
Summers p	3	0	1	0	0	–	L. Mederos p	3	1	1	0	5	–
Totals	30	2	5	24	16	–	Totals	33	3	12	27	14	–

Errors — O'Leary, Moriarty, McIntyre, Lloyd.
Doubles — Luis Bustamente.
Strikeouts — By Summers 4, Mederos 2.
Bases on balls — off Summers 2, Mederos 1.

	1	2	3	4	5	6	7	8	9		
DETROIT TIGERS	0	0	0	0	0	0	2	0	0	=	2
HAVANA	0	0	1	0	0	0	2	0	x	=	3

Ty Cobb was late leaving the U. S. for the exhibition series, and the teams had split four games before his arrival in Cuba. Chicago White Sox ace Big Ed Walsh had seen Hill play in the late summer and had praised him as being equal to Ty Cobb. Hill faced Cobb in the last two games of the series and, playing up to Walsh's declaration, matched his white counterpart's performance. In the first encounter both players went hitless, but in the second contest each one had a pair of hits, including one for extra bases, and their teams split the games. Although there were rumors that Hill was headed for the majors with an Indian or Cuban moniker, the greatest black outfielder and the greatest white outfielder of their generation were never to play on the same diamond again.

December 4, 1910
BOXSCORE

	DETROIT TIGERS							*HAVANA*					
	AB	R	H	PO	A	E		AB	R	H	PO	A	E
Schaeffer 2b	5	0	2	1	3	–	C. Morin 3b	5	1	2	0	2	
O'Leary ss	5	2	2	3	4	–	P. Hill lf	4	0	2	6	0	–
Cobb rf	5	3	2	1	0	–	G. Johnson 2b	2	0	1	2	5	–
Crawford cf	5	2	3	2	0	–	S. Lloyd ss	5	0	2	4	4	–
Moriarty 3b	5	1	3	1	2	–	H. Hernandez cf	4	0	0	1	1	–
T. Jones 1b	4	1	0	12	0	–	A. Parpetti 1b	4	1	1	10	0	–
McIntyre lf	3	1	1	3	0	–	B. Petway c	3	1	1	4	2	–
Stanage c	4	1	1	4	1	–	L. Padron rf	3	1	0	0	2	–
Mullin p	4	1	2	0	3	–	L. Mederos p	1	0	1	0	0	–

	DETROIT TIGERS							*HAVANA*					
	AB	R	H	PO	A	E		AB	R	H	PO	A	E
							L. Gonzalez p	0	0	0	0	1	-
							B. Pareda p	1	0	0	0	0	-
Totals	40	12	16	27	13	-	Totals	32	4	10	27	17	-

	1	2	3	4	5	6	7	8	9		
DETROIT TIGERS	3	2	0	0	6	1	0	0	0	=	12
HAVANA	1	1	0	0	0	0	1	0	1	=	4

Errors — Schaeffer, O'Leary, Jones, Morin, Lloyd, Parpetti, Mederos
Triples — Crawford, Mullin, Cobb. Doubles — McIntyre, Hill. Stolen bases — Padron.
Sacrifice hits — Petway, Johnson. Left on bases — Detroit 3, Havana 6.
Double plays — Morin, Johnson and Parpetti; O'Leary, Jones; Mullin, O'Leary, Jones.
Strikeouts — by Mullin 4, Gonzalez 1, Pareda 1.
Bases on balls — off Mullin 3, Pareda 1.
Hit by pitcher — by Gonzalez (Jones), by Mullin (Gonzalez).
Hits — off Mederos 5 in 2 innings, Gonzalez 8 in 3 innings, Pareda 3 in 4 innings.
Time 2:10. Umpires — Billy Evans, E. Gutierrez. Scorer — Conejo.

In the renowned Detroit series, Cobb (.368) and Crawford (.360) had been out-hit by Lloyd (.500), Johnson (.412) and Petway (.389). However, in the subsequent series against the Athletics, their collective batting average was halved and Hill compensated for this loss of productivity by his teammates by ripping the ball for a .412 average.

December 16, 1910

BOXSCORE

	PHILADELPHIA ATHLETICS							*HAVANA*					
	AB	R	H	PO	A	E		AB	R	H	PO	A	E
Hartzel lf	3	1	1	2	0	-	C. Morin 3b	4	1	1	0	4	-
Lord cf	6	1	1	4	0	-	P. Hill lf	4	1	3	5	0	-
McInnis 1b	4	0	0	1	3	-	G. Johnson 2b	3	1	1	0	1	-
Murphy rf	5	0	0	0	0	-	S. Lloyd ss	4	1	2	3	6	-
Davis 1b	5	0	1	13	1	-	B. Petway c	4	0	0	4	1	-
Barry 2b	4	1	2	2	3	-	A. Parpetti 1b	3	0	0	13	1	-
Derrick ss	4	1	1	2	5	-	H. Hernandez cf	4	0	1	1	0	-
Thomas c	3	1	1	3	2	-	L. Padron rf	4	0	0	1	0	-
Bender p	4	1	2	0	2	-	L. Mederos p	1	0	0	0	0	-
							P. Parada p	1	0	0	0	2	-
							a — V. Gonzalez	1	0	0	0	0	-
Totals	38	6	9	27	16	-	Totals	33	4	8	27	15	-

	1	2	3	4	5	6	7	8	9		
PHILADELPHIA	0	0	1	0	3	0	0	2	0	=	6
HAVANA	2	0	0	0	0	2	0	0	0	=	4

Errors — Lloyd 2, Parpetti, Hernandez
Home runs — Lord. Triples — Barry. Doubles — Morin, Lloyd. Stolen bases — Hernandez.
Double plays — Barry, Davis and McInnis; Thomas and Barry.
Left on bases — Philadelphia 8, Havana 5
Strikeouts — by Bender 1, Mederos 2. Pareda 1
Bases on balls — off Mederos 2, Pareda 2, Bender 3.
Hits — off Mederos 5 in 5 innings, Pareda 4 in 4 innings.
Time 1:50. Umpire — E. Gutierrez. Scorer — Conejo.

John Henry (Pop) Lloyd: The Black Honus Wagner

John Henry Lloyd was the greatest black baseball player of the first two decades of the twentieth century. A superlative shortstop and superior hitter, he was called the black Honus Wagner but some observers said that Wagner should be called the white John Henry Lloyd. The dark superstar was a complete ballplayer who could hit, run, field, throw, and hit with power — especially in the clutch — and was the greatest shortstop of his day, black or white. Wagner himself said, "I am honored to have John Henry Lloyd called the black Wagner. It is a privilege to have been compared to him."

Lloyd's presence on a team meant the difference between winning and losing, and his skills were always in great demand. Free agency was a part of black baseball and Lloyd availed himself of the advantages. "Where the money was," Lloyd said later in life, "that's where I was." And wherever he was, the championship usually followed. Before his career was over, he had played with a dozen different ballclubs.

Although black baseball's statistics are incomplete, Lloyd, a left-handed batter, consistently hit over .300 and sometimes topped .400. The eighth edition of *The Baseball Encyclopedia* published by Macmillan lists a lifetime .368 batting average in the Negro Leagues. Cuban baseball records show a lifetime .321 mark for the 12 winter seasons that he spent there. A highlight of Cuban baseball lore is the renowned 1910 series when Lloyd, playing for a Cuban team, hit .500 against Ty Cobb's Detroit Tigers to lead all hitters and outshine the immortal Cobb.

Cobb, along with Honus Wagner, was among the first five players elected to the National Baseball Hall of Fame in 1936. Had it not been for baseball's unwritten but firmly entrenched color line, John Henry Lloyd would have probably also been in that elite group. However, with the extant socio-political constraints, it was be over 40 years before the "black Wagner" finally received that honor. In 1977, in recognition of his phenomenal 27-year career with top black baseball clubs and his contributions to baseball, John Henry Lloyd was inducted into the National Baseball Hall of Fame at Cooperstown, New York.

Lloyd rose to that greatness from humble beginnings. He was born April 25, 1884, in Palatka, Florida. His father died when he was an infant and his mother later remarried, leaving the youngster to be reared by his grandmother. His formal education was restricted and, like most black youngsters of the era, he dropped out of school early. To help earn money for the family, he worked as a delivery boy and, as a teenager, as a porter with the Southern Express Company in Jacksonville.

The youngster's passion for baseball had started with a local team in Palatka and he joined a baseball club in Jacksonville called the Young Receivers. His play on the Jacksonville sandlots eventually led to semi-professional baseball with the Macon (Georgia) Acmes, where he was a catcher and second baseman. In 1906 he went north as part of a youth movement initiated by the Philadelphia-based Cuban X-Giants, one of the top black ballclubs in the country. After only one season with the X-Giants, Lloyd joined Sol White's defending champion Philadelphia Giants as a shortstop for three seasons before being lured to the midwest by Rube Foster. Foster's Chicago Leland Giants was the greatest aggregation of black talent up to that time and Lloyd finished the 1910 season with a .417 batting average.

In 1911 Lloyd returned east to join the newly formed New York Lincoln Giants. A smart ballplayer, Lloyd knew inside baseball and at mid-

John Henry Lloyd was the best black player of the Deadball Era, and was compared to Pittsburgh Pirates superstar Honus Wagner. Wagner, in turn, said, "I am honored to have John Henry Lloyd called the black Wagner."

season he was appointed manager. At the helm, Lloyd guided the Lincolns to three straight Eastern Championships, while batting .475, .376 and .363. In 1913 his team compiled a phenomenal 101–6 record and soundly defeated Rube Foster's Chicago American Giants in the Championship playoffs.

The following season Lloyd was enticed back to Foster's Chicago American Giants, where his stellar play led the team to three Western Championships. In both 1914 and 1917, Chicago defeated the Eastern Champions in playoffs. Lloyd's four-year tenure with Foster's team was temporarily interrupted in 1915, when he jumped back east to join the new Lincoln Stars ballclub for part of the season before returning to Chicago.

In January of 1918, with World War I raging in Europe, Lloyd took a job with the Army Quartermaster's Depot in Chicago. This displeased Rube Foster, who wanted him to play winter ball instead, and when the season started Lloyd accepted an offer to become playing manager for the Brooklyn Royal Giants. After his first season with the Royal Giants, he spent most of the 1919 campaign with the Bacharach Giants but returned to the Royal Giants for the 1920 season.

For the next three seasons, Lloyd was playing manager for a different team each year. In 1921 he was with the Negro National League Columbus Buckeyes, followed by a season at the helm of the Bacharach Giants. Then, in 1923, Lloyd hit .418 and guided Hilldale to the inaugural Eastern Colored League pennant. "He was a great man and a great teacher," said future Hall of Famer Judy Johnson, who played on that team. Despite winning the pennant, Lloyd was released because of alleged dissension on the team, and assumed the helm of the Bacharach Giants for two years. Having slowed a step in the field, he placed himself at second base, his first year at the position after 20 years at shortstop, and topped the league with a .444 batting average.

In 1926 he returned to the New York Lincoln Giants and remained at the helm until the franchise's demise following the 1930 season. In his first two seasons back with the Lincolns, he batted .349 and .375. In 1928, he made a further concession to his age and moved himself to first base and despite the early collapse of the league, he topped Eastern League hitters in both batting average (.564) and home runs (11). The next season Lloyd entered his hard-hitting Lincoln Giants in the American Negro League, where he hit .362 in the league's only season of existence.

In 1930 the Lincolns played as an independent ballclub and fielded their strongest team since Lloyd's 1913 powerhouse, but lost the playoff for the Eastern Championship. During the 1930 season, Lloyd's Lincolns were the host team for the first game ever played by black teams in Yankee Stadium.

The Lincoln Giants broke up after that season, but Lloyd was appointed manager of the Harlem Stars, a team that rose from the ashes of the Lincolns and evolved into the New York Black Yankees. His last year as an active professional player was spent with the Bacharach Giants in 1932. But Lloyd was considered the elder statesman of black baseball and in 1933, when the first East-West All-Star Game was played, Lloyd was selected to manage the East squad.

After his retirement from professional baseball, he settled in Atlantic City and continued as a player-manager for sandlot teams, including the Johnson Stars and the Farley Stars. The old warhorse played until he was 58 years old, while continuing to manage on into his sixties. A rugged competitor as a player, his aggressive play on the field contrasted with his easygoing nature off the field. He neither drank nor smoked and seldom used coarse language. In his managerial capacity Lloyd was a master at instilling confidence in younger players.

Lloyd worked as a custodian for the post office and the school system and, although he had no children of his own, during his latter years he served as a surrogate father to thousands of schoolchildren and became affectionately known as "Pop." In addition to his work, he served as Atlantic City's Little League Commissioner for many years. In recognition of his involvement with youngsters, Pop Lloyd Field was dedicated in his honor in 1949. That same year, Jackie Robinson, who had started his professional baseball career as a shortstop in the Negro Leagues, became the first black player to win the National League MVP Award.

Because baseball's color line kept Lloyd out of the major leagues, some observers say that he was born too soon. But at the dedication of his ballfield, Pop Lloyd dispelled this contention. "I do not consider that I was born at the wrong time. I felt it was the right time, for I had a chance to prove the ability of our race in this sport ... and ... we have given the Negro a greater opportunity now to be accepted into the major leagues with other Americans."

John Henry Lloyd died March 19, 1965, in Atlantic City, N.J., of arteriosclerosis after a two-year illness.

This article was written in 1998 when John Henry Lloyd was inducted into the Florida Sports Hall of Fame. The prestigious trophy awarded to each inductee now resides in John Henry Lloyd's locker at the Negro Leagues Baseball Museum in Kansas City, Missouri.

Since Lloyd had no children and no other family members could be located, the author was asked to accept on his behalf. In the acceptance speech, I contracted the information from the article to fit the time limitations, but inserted two anecdotes and concluded with Lloyd's own words from a speech he made in 1949 when

Atlantic City dedicated Pop Lloyd Field in his honor. These three supplementary excerpts from the speech as delivered follow:

> In 1938, when asked "who was the best player in baseball history?" a white St. Louis sportswriter replied, "If you mean in organized baseball, my answer would be Babe Ruth, but if you mean in all baseball, organized and unorganized, the answer would have to be a colored man named John Henry Lloyd."
>
> The story is told that when announcer Graham McNamee asked Babe Ruth the same question, the Babe gave the same answer: "John Henry Lloyd."
>
> On October 1, 1949, the city of Atlantic City dedicated Pop Lloyd Field in his honor. The words that he spoke at that time are appropriate for this occasion. And I will close with John Henry Lloyd's own words:
>
> "I gave my best when I was playing ball, and today I mean to give the best that I have in expressing appreciation of the honor that has been given me this day. I hope the young men, not only of Atlantic City but of the entire nation, will benefit from what I have tried to give the youth of America. And I promise that this day, more than anything else, inspires me to continue to live righteously, so that I may justify the confidence you kind folks have shown in me. Thank you one and all."

The Texas Cyclone: Smokey Joe Williams

The deadball era of black baseball paralleled that of the white leagues with pitching being dominant. Rube Foster, Jose Mendez, Frank Wickware, John Donaldson, and Cannonball Dick Redding all had their days of glory during this era. But the greatest pitcher of the first half of black baseball was a big, hard-throwing right-hander, who was given the name "Cyclone" because his fastball was described as moving like a pebble tossed by a cyclone. Years later he would move to the "smoky" steel city of Pittsburgh and become better known as "Smokey Joe" Williams.

However, the oral grapevine of black baseball history maintains that he received his nickname of Smokey Joe when Ross Youngs paid him the passing tribute, "Good game, Smokey" as he trotted past him after the National League champion New York Giants had just become the beneficiaries of an unearned run in the tenth inning to escape with a 1–0 victory against the legendary black hurler.

Whether this account is real or apocryphal, the fact is that competition against the white major leagues' best seemed to bring out the best in Joe Williams. A partial account of these games over a half-dozen seasons is indicative of the caliber of the pitcher who earned the nicknames "Cyclone" and "Smokey Joe."

When Smokey Joe Smoked Alex

In October of 1912, he hurled a 6–0 shutout of the New York Giants (who had just won the second of three consecutive National League flags) and struck out nine of John McGraw's finest and proudest. Making no distinction between the leagues, the following week Williams defeated Hal Chase's New York Yankees by the same score, 6–0.

An autumn later, on October 5, 1913, Williams faced the Philadelphia Phillies, who had finished second to McGraw's team, with the great Grover

Cleveland Alexander on the mound. Young Alex, a strong 26-year-old, had just completed his third consecutive 20-win season, winning a total of 69 games in his first three years in the National League. With a league-high seven shutouts and sporting a 22–8 record (which produced the third highest winning percentage in the league), Alex was backed by a major league squad and ready for the black semi-pro team.

Williams himself was also ready. His team, the New York Lincoln Giants, had completed their third consecutive season as the top black team in the east, winning 101 of 107 games played in 1913. Organized in 1911, the franchise's existence barely equaled Alexander's stay in the majors, but Williams' teammates included four other great players — John Henry Lloyd, Louis Santop, Grant "Home Run" Johnson and Spot Poles. Lloyd is in the Hall of Fame, Williams should have already joined him, and the other three are legitimate candidates for induction.

Pitching in exhibition games against major leaguers brought out the best in the Texas Cyclone. In a 1952 poll conducted by the *Pittsburgh Courier*, Smokey Joe Williams was voted the all-time top black pitcher, ahead of Satchel Paige.

The Phillies, on the other hand, were shorthanded with star slugger "Cactus Gavy" Cravath and Bill Killefer, Alexander's favorite receiver, absent from the lineup. Playing in Cravath's place was rookie Vern Duncan, who had appeared in only eight games with the Phillies during the season, while Killefer's replacement was Bill Reynolds, a youngster borrowed from the Yankees where he had caught only five games, one shy of his major league career total.

Examining the lineups with the luxury of an historical perspective, the objective conclusion is that the Lincoln Giants were the stronger team and should have been favored in the contest. But in the sociological climate of the times, the major leaguers were expected to win and the outcome was viewed as an upset.

The October 11, 1913 edition of the *New York Age* carried the following account of the game, paired with another significant contest:

Philadelphia Nationals Lose; Walter Johnson Defeated

Sunday two exhibition games were played in the state of New York which have set the fans to arguing as to the relative strength of some of our colored clubs as compared with the big league teams. At Schenectady the Mohawk Giants defeated a team composed of big leaguers with Walter Johnson, the sensation of the American League, doing the twirling. The Lincoln Giants defeated the Philadelphia Nationals with Alexander in the box.

Wickware of the Mohawks opposed Walter Johnson and the score ended 1–0. This fact was not reported in some of the daily papers.

Alexander looked like any other pitcher of [sic] the Lincoln Giants and was batted hard. On the other hand the professionals could do nothing with Williams. The score ended 9–2.

The Lincolns have played 107 games and won 101. The score of Sunday's game between the Lincolns and the Philadelphia Nationals:

LINCOLN GIANTS	R	H	O	A	E	PHILA NATIONALS	R	H	O	A	E
Poles cf	2	3	4	2	0	Devore cf	0	2	3	0	0
Gans lf	0	0	1	0	0	Reed ss	0	1	2	1	0
Lloyd ss	1	2	6	1	0	Becker 1b	0	0	11	0	1
Johnson 2b	0	1	1	2	0	Byrne 3b	1	0	1	1	0
Santop rf	0	0	0	0	0	Paskert lf	1	2	1	0	0
Grant 1b	0	1	6	1	0	Duncan rf	0	1	0	1	0
Wiley c	2	2	9	3	0	Doolan 2b	0	0	0	4	1
Williams p	2	1	0	2	0	Reynolds c	0	1	6	1	0
Francis 3b	2	2	0	0	0	Alexander p	0	1	0	2	0
Totals	9	12	27	11	0	Totals	2	8	24	10	2

	1	2	3	4	5	6	7	8	9		
LINCOLN GIANTS	0	0	3	3	0	3	0	0	x	=	9
PHILADELPHIA NATIONALS	0	2	0	0	0	0	0	0	0	=	2

First base on errors — Lincoln Giants 2. Two base hits — Poles, Grant, Wiley. Home run — Williams. Sacrifice hits — Gans 2. Stolen bases — Poles 2, Lloyd 4. Left on bases — Lincolns 2, Philadelphia 7. Double plays — Lloyd and Grant, Poles and Wiley. Bases on balls — off Williams 2; off Alexander 1. Struck out — by Williams 9; by Alexander 6. Hit by pitcher — By Williams 1 (Byrne). Umpire — Mr. Oldis. Time of game — 2 hours.

The game against the Phillies was just one of several superlative outings for Williams that fall. He also out-dueled Chief Bender (who registered a 21–10 ledger along with a league-high 12 saves and a 2.21 ERA for the World Champion Philadelphia Athletics), winning a 2–1 three-hitter from Connie Mack's ace hurler.

Although Williams' nine strikeouts in the Phillies game were impressive, in three other contests against major leaguers (Mike Donlin's All-Stars and Earle Mack's All-Stars) that fall, he whiffed 16, 13 and 14 respectively. In the second of these games, despite his strikeout total, Williams lost a 1–0 decision to the Phillies' nondescript hurler George "Dut" Chalmers. Williams gained a measure of revenge the following week when the two teams met again and he defeated Chalmers in a 7–3 contest. These two hurlers were to face off again two years later, when the Phillies were the reigning National League Champions.

Smokey Joe Defeats the National League Champions

In 1915, the Philadelphia Phillies won their first National League flag and battled the Boston Red Sox in a losing effort in the World Series that ended in Philadelphia on October 13 when Harry Hooper lifted a ninth-inning homer into the center field bleachers for a come-from-behind 5–4 victory. Two days later in New York, the Phillies played the New York Lincoln Giants and their ace hurler Smokey Joe Williams. The Phillies had lost to Williams each of the two previous autumns and now, as National League Champions, more than their individual pride was on the line.

Dut Chalmers, who lost the hard-fought fourth game of the Series, 2–1, was on the mound for the Phillies with only two days' rest — if rest could be the proper description for a man on his honeymoon. Chalmers had been married the night before. Ironically, his performance against the Lincoln Giants (8 IP, 7 H, 1 R, 6 K, 2 W) very closely approximated his World Series performance against the Red Sox (8 IP, 8 H, 2 R, 6 K, 3W), and in each case, Chalmers took a loss.

The Phillies boasted future Hall of Famer Dave Bancroft at shortstop, but were again handicapped by the absence of their star slugger, Cactus Gavvy Cravath, and receiver Bill Killefer, as well as first baseman Fred Luderus and outfielder George "Possum" Whitted. The missing Phillies regulars were replaced in the lineup by Bert Adams, a big, rangy Texan, who had hit .111 during his stint as the Phillies' third-string catcher that season; Joe Judge, a Washington Senators rookie first baseman who played in only a dozen games in 1915 but would go on to a distinguished 20-year major league career; Hack Eibel, a left-handed hitting minor league outfielder who had a cup of coffee with the Indians three years earlier; and a minor league outfielder named Sullivan.

However, the Lincoln Giants had undergone a change in personnel, resulting from a schism which developed in 1914 when the McMahon brothers, the original owners of the Lincoln Giants, organized a new team, the Lincoln Stars, and the players were split between the two franchises. The Lincoln Giants, although still one of the top teams in the east, had lost their top four players (John Henry Lloyd, Louis Santop, Grant "Home Run" Johnson and Spot Poles) and were no longer the powerhouse that they had been two years earlier.

The October 21, 1915 edition of the *New York Age* carried the following account of the game:

At Olympic Field six members of the National League champions, including five who saw service in the recent World's series, played against the Lincoln Giants before about 9,000 fans on last Sunday. So big was the crowd that ground rules had to be put into force. The Phillies with Joe Judge of Clark Griffith's Senators and Eibel of the Atlanta Club in the lineup, were defeated by a score of 1–0.

Chalmers opposed Cyclone Joe Williams on the mound, and was outpitched by the local hurler. Williams allowed the Quakers only five hits and fanned ten, while Chalmers was batted for seven bingles and whiffed only six. The only run of the game was scored in the eighth frame. Forbes was walked by Chalmers, Williams followed with a single and Earle sacrificed both. Bragg then crashed out a hit to center that sent Forbes home.

Chalmers was married last night in The Bronx, and the five members of the Philly team who played with him yesterday attended the wedding ceremony.

Next Sunday the Yankees will play the Lincoln Giants.

LINCOLN GIANTS

	AB	R	H	O	A	E
Earle cf	3	0	0	2	2	0
Bragg 3b	4	0	1	0	1	0
Wiley c	4	0	0	10	2	0
Hall lf	4	0	1	1	0	0
Grant 1b	3	0	2	7	1	0
Thomas rf	3	0	1	3	0	0
James 2b	3	0	0	1	3	0
Forbes ss	2	1	1	1	0	0
Williams p	3	0	1	2	1	0
Totals	29	1	7	27	10	0

PHILA NATIONALS

	AB	R	H	O	A	E
Stock 3b	3	0	0	1	0	0
Bancroft ss	4	0	0	1	0	0
Paskert lf	3	0	0	1	0	0
Niehoff 2b	3	0	1	3	2	0
Eibel rf	4	0	1	0	0	0
Sullivan cf	3	0	0	1	0	0
Adams c	3	0	0	6	2	0
Judge 1b	3	0	2	11	5	0
Chalmers p	3	0	1	0	3	0
*English	1	0	0	0	0	0
Totals	30	0	5	24	12	0

*Batted for Sullivan in the ninth inning.

	1	2	3	4	5	6	7	8	9		
Philadelphia Nationals	0	0	0	0	0	0	0	0	0	=	0
Lincoln Giants	0	0	0	0	0	0	0	1	x	=	1

Two base hits — Hall, Judge. Stolen bases — Eibel, Grant. Left on bases — Philadelphia 6, Lincoln Giants 6. Double plays — Chalmers and Judge. Bases on balls — off Williams 3 (Stock, Paskert, Niehoff); off Chalmers 2 (Earle, Forbes). Struck out — by Williams 10 (Bancroft, Sullivan 2, Adams 2 Chalmers 2, Eibel, Paskert, English'; by Chalmers 6 (Wiley, James 2, Bragg, Forbes, Williams). Umpire — Mr. Oldis. Time of game — 1 hour and 55 minutes.

The game was closely contested and using Chalmers' relative performances against the Red Sox and the Lincoln Giants as a measuring device, it seems that the Lincolns would have been competitive against the top major league clubs — at least when Smokey Joe was on the mound.

A week earlier, Williams had thrown a 3–0 shutout at a team of Federal League Stars (who thought they were major leaguers) but the game against the Phillies was his biggest one of the 1915 post-season. The previous season, the biggest game for the black Cyclone was when he faced the New York Giants' Rube Marquard.

Smokey Joe and Rube Battle to a Draw

After three consecutive National League pennants, John McGraw's New York Giants had finished second to George Stallings' "Miracle Braves," and Rube Marquard, after three consecutive 20-win seasons in which he totaled 73 victories, had slipped to a 22-game loser despite a respectable 3.06 ERA. Had he not encountered some hard luck, the ace lefthander could just as easily have reversed his 12–22 record since Mathewson, with no appreciable difference in his ERA (3.00), had won 24 games for the Giants. Disregarding the loss total, Marquard was still in his prime, only two weeks past his 25th birthday and six months away from his only career no-hitter, when he faced Smokey Joe Williams and the Lincoln Giants.

Both hurlers were in rare form and the game was ended by darkness with the score deadlocked at 1–1, with Marquard registering 14 strikeouts and Williams fanning an even dozen.

While both pitchers turned in impressive performances, Marquard's was the most impressive in this outing, since he was facing a better lineup of hitters. The Lincoln Giants fielded a solid lineup enhanced for this game by the addition of John Henry Lloyd, who had been with the Chicago American Giants during the regular season. The Giants, while composed primarily of major leaguers, were playing without a single regular in their lineup.

The October 29, 1914, edition of the *New York Age* carried the following account of the game:

Williams and Marquard Tie.

Harlemites were treated to a fast and interesting game of baseball last Sunday at Olympic Field when Cyclone Joe Williams, pitching for the New York Lincoln Giants, held Rube Marquard, pitching for the New York Giants of the National League, to a 1 to 1 tie, the (game) being called on account of darkness.

The game was a pitching duel between Marquard and Williams. Williams struck out twelve men and yielded only five scattered hits.

The Lincolns took the lead in the second inning. Lyons' double and James' single netted the Lincolns a run and the Giants tied the score in the seventh. With one down in the ninth and Devlin and Grant on second and third respectively, Williams fanned the next two batters.

LINCOLN GIANTS	R	H	O	A	E	NEW YORK (N.L.)	R	H	O	A	E
Earle cf	0	0	1	0	0	E. Grant ss	0	1	0	1	0
Wallace 3b	0	1	2	0	0	Beatty 2b	1	1	1	3	0
Wiley c	0	0	12	0	0	Devlin 1b	0	2	10	1	1
Lloyd ss	0	0	0	2	1	McCormick cf	0	1	0	0	0
L. Grant 1b	0	0	8	0	0	Piez lf	0	0	1	0	0
Lyons lf	1	1	2	0	0	Damarow 3b	0	0	0	1	1
James 2b	0	1	2	3	0	Tamm rf	0	0	0	0	0

LINCOLN GIANTS						NEW YORK (N.L.)				
	R	H	O	A	E		R	H	O	A	E
Gatewood rf	0	0	0	0	0	McLean c	0	0	14	2	1
Williams p	0	0	0	1	0	Marquard p	0	0	1	3	0
Totals	1	3	27	6	1	Totals	1	5	27	11	3

	1	2	3	4	5	6	7	8	9		
N. Y. NATIONALS	0	0	0	0	0	0	1	0	0	=	1
LINCOLN GIANTS	0	1	0	0	0	0	0	0	0	=	1

First base on errors — Lincoln Giants 3. Two base hits — Lyons, Devlin. Stolen bases — Tamm. Left on bases — New York 2, Lincoln Giants 1. Double plays — Lloyd, James and Grant. Struck out — by Williams 12 (Beatty, Damarow 2, McLean, Devlin, McCormick, Piez (3), Tamm, Grant, Marquard); by Marquard 14 (Earle 2, Wallace 2, Wiley 3, Williams 2, Lloyd, Grant 2, Lyons 2). Hit by pitcher — By Marquard (Gatewood). Wild Pitch — Marquard. Time of game — 1 hour 43 minutes. Umpire — Mr. Oldis.

Two weeks earlier Walter Johnson, pitching for a semi-pro team, had lost a 2–0 decision to the Lincoln Stars and, on the same day, Williams had hung a 10–4 loss on the Philadelphia Phillies with another Rube — Rube Marshall — on the mound. He would have to wait awhile to hang a loss on Rube Marquard, but the time *would* come.

Smokey Joe and Rube: The Showdown

After the 1915 season, when John McGraw's New York Giants had finished last after being favored to win the flag going into the season, the "Little Napoleon" began dismantling his pennant machine, divesting himself of old parts and replacing them with new ones. Two of the "old" parts that he discarded were Rube Marquard and Chief Meyers. Marquard was still in his prime but had a disagreement with the rotund dictatorial skipper and orchestrated his own trade to the Dodgers. Meyers had been an integral cog in the McGraw machine, but was nearing the end of his career as a productive player. Brooklyn manager Wilbert Robinson welcomed the pair with open arms and was rewarded with a pennant in 1916. But a year later McGraw was back on top with a revitalized team, while Uncle Robbie's Dodgers sank to seventh place.

Marquard, still a big winner, managed a 19-12 record for the seventh-place team. While Marquard continued to excel, the Chief, now 37 years old, had been traded away and had just completed his last major league season. The two veterans who had been teammates on four pennant-winning clubs over a six-year span, reunited to form the battery for a lackluster group of players assembled to challenge Joe Williams' Lincoln Giants.

The Lincoln Giants had fallen from their prominence and were now only one of several black teams that were playing baseball of the same general caliber. Oftentimes the Lincolns would split a doubleheader, winning the game that Williams pitched and losing the other game. The diminished batting strength of the team is indicated by Williams (although a good hitting pitcher) batting sixth in the order, but the Lincolns still fielded the better team.

However, the supporting cast was not important to the baseball aficionados who turned out en masse. The pitchers were the big attraction. Williams had pitched against other major league pitchers in the autumn of 1917, including Bullet Joe Bush and Chief Bender, and now the fans wanted to see the rematch between him and the Rube.

The October 18, 1917 edition of the *New York Age* carried the following account of the game:

Williams Bests Marquard

"Rube" Marquard, former Giant pitcher and now a member of the Brooklyn team of the National League, and Cyclone Joe Williams of the Lincoln Giants met in a pitcher's duel Sunday at Olympic Field in which the colored pitcher had the better of the argument. The Lincoln Giants defeated Marquard's All Leaguers by the score of 5 to 4.

The score does not give an idea of how freely Marquard was hit by the Lincoln Giants. They nicked him for fourteen hits, while Williams allowed but six.

Over 7,000 persons attended the game, which was a record-breaking attendance. Many stood in the field. The game lasted ten innings, the home team coming across with the necessary run. Chief Meyers, who played with the Boston Nationals most of the season, caught for the All Leaguers.

In the game's denouement, Dodgers owner Charlie Ebbets fined Marquard $100 for playing in the game against the black ballplayers. Thirty years later, Jackie Robinson would be playing a World Series game in the ballpark bearing Ebbets' name.

LINCOLN GIANTS	R	H	O	A	E	MEYERS & MARQ. LEAGUERS	R	H	O	A	E
Gans cf	0	1	2	0	0	Senck 3b	1	0	0	4	2
Wallace ss	0	1	3	4	1	Leonard 1b	2	1	14	0	0
Webster lf	1	3	1	0	0	Burnett ss	0	2	6	2	0
Hall rf	1	1	1	0	0	Meyers c	0	2	4	3	0
Pettus 1b	0	2	11	2	0	Walsh lf	0	0	0	0	0
Williams p	0	1	0	6	0	Flynn rf	1	1	0	2	0
Mongin 2b	2	2	1	1	0	Curry cf	0	0	2	0	0
Kennard c	1	2	11	0	0	Oertzen 2b	0	0	2	7	0
Miller 3b	0	1	0	1	1	Marquard p	0	0	0	2	0
Totals	5	14	30	14	2	Totals	4	6	28*	20	2

*One out when winning run scored.

	1	2	3	4	5	6	7	8	9	10		
M. and M. Leaguers	1	0	0	0	0	1	2	0	0	0	=	4
Lincoln Giants	0	0	2	0	0	0	2	0	0	1	=	5

First base on errors — Meyers and Marquard's Leaguers 2, Lincoln Giants 2. Two base hits — Meyers. Home Run — Flynn. Sacrifice hits — Miller 2. Stolen bases — Walsh. Left on bases —

Meyers and Marquard's Leaguers 6, Lincoln Giants 13. Base on balls — off Williams 4; off Marquard 1. Struck out — by Williams 10; by Marquard 3. Passed Ball — Meyers. Umpire — Mr. Oldis. Time of game — 2 hours.

―⚬⚬⚬―

"The Texas Cyclone" is actually an amalgamation of four connected stories about Smokey Joe Williams which were written as part of a series From the Negro League Archives *for* Oldtyme Baseball News. *Unfortunately, due to pecuniary considerations this excellent publication was unable to continue production and the articles never appeared in print until now.*

This glimpse into the Negro League Archives was designed to illustrate why Smokey Joe was selected as the all-time greatest pitcher over the legendary Satchel Paige by a special panel in a 1952 poll conducted by the Pittsburgh Courier. *In my 1983 book,* The All-Time All-Stars of Black Baseball, *I had stated, "Of all the players who ever played in the era of black baseball, Smokey Joe Williams is the greatest player not yet enshrined in the National Baseball Hall of Fame." In these articles I reiterated that position, declaring that Smokey Joe Williams should have already been inducted into the Hall of Fame.*

Sixteen years after I first set forth my original premise, on July 25, 1999 — my 60th birthday — I was present at Cooperstown when the Texas Cyclone was inducted into the Hall of Fame, along with another right-handed Texan with a smoking fastball — Nolan Ryan. Also inducted were George Brett, Robin Yount and Orlando Cepeda.

In 2006 Louis Santop, described in the article as one of three other "legitimate candidates," joined Smokey Joe Williams among the immortals at Cooperstown.

A final comment about the article: The sampling of box scores between black and white teams included here illuminates the hazards involved in making blanket statements about the percent of games won by black teams versus white "major league" teams.

The Early Leagues: 1920–1932

Part I: The Dark Knight

Rube Foster had a dream of black players and black teams playing in the major leagues. To make this dream become a reality, he recognized a more immediate goal — the establishment of a quality black league patterned after the white major leagues. Foster was certain that such a league would be the salvation of black baseball. He realized that for this league to be successful, each team must have access to its own ballpark. And of even greater importance, he knew there must be parity within the league.

As a new decade started, all pieces were waiting to be put into place for this innovative venture, but it required a man of Rube Foster's vision and abilities to take action. Foster drafted an article for the *Chicago Defender*, the midwest's most popular black newspaper, in which he described the existing conditions of black baseball and discussed the need for a league.

At the time, an atmosphere of mutual distrust between players and owners had developed from unethical practices involved in jumping teams and tampering with players. Foster insisted that an agreement was necessary between club owners, pledging to respect the rights of other owners and to not tamper with their players. Players, as they do today, preferred free agency and feared that an organization would restrict their income. He had to convince everyone that their salaries were based on the gate receipts, and that bigger parks meant bigger crowds and bigger paychecks.

Foster wrote, "We cannot get along without organization. Many colored men with money have begged to get into the game, but they want it patterned after the way leagues are conducted."

Part II: Rube's League

Foster's efforts paid off and on February 13, 1920, the National Association of Colored Professional Baseball Clubs (more commonly known as the

Negro National League) was organized during a meeting at the YMCA in Kansas City, Missouri. As the moving force in founding the first black league, Rube Foster was elected the league president and his old rival C. I. Taylor served as vice-president.

The league constitution was written by sportswriters Dave Wyatt (*Indianapolis Ledger*), Elwood C. Knox (*Indianapolis Freeman*) and Cary B. Lewis (*Chicago Defender*), along with attorney Elisha Scott from Topeka, Kansas. This august group worked all through the night and most of the next morning framing the black baseball "bill of rights."

The document was amended, approved and signed by the representatives of the teams present at the conference. Those signing were Rube Foster (Chicago American Giants), C. I. Taylor (Indianapolis ABCs), Tenny Blount (Detroit Stars), Joe Green (Chicago Giants), J. L. Wilkinson (Kansas City Monarchs), and Lorenzo S. Cobb (St, Louis Giants). John Matthews (Dayton Marcos) was ill and unable to attend the meeting but sent a special delivery letter supportive of the league. Each franchise was required to post a $500 fee to bind them to the league and the constitution.

Foster hoped that once the Negro National League became fully functional and was a successful operation in the midwest, he could extend the league membership to include every large baseball city in the east. Nat C. Strong, the white East Coast promoter and booking agent who virtually controlled black baseball in the east, sent a letter to the organizational meeting, expressing a cooperative spirit and a willingness to promote the best interests of black baseball all over the country. However, Foster had previously encountered some difficulties with Strong, remained distrustful of his motivation, and initially concentrated on building and nurturing a successful league in the midwest.

In an effort to achieve parity within the league, Foster dictated the relocation of some players to insure that each team would include top performers. He realized that star players and closely contested games would be the key to attracting large crowds to the ballparks.

Wisely, he set an example by distributing some of his own players to other teams. Foster sent superstar Oscar Charleston to Indianapolis and star pitcher Richard Whitworth to Detroit, while St. Louis owner Charlie Mills sent Jimmy Lyons to Detroit. In turn, Tenny Blount sent star players John Donaldson and Jose Mendez to Kansas City. In these transactions, Foster suffered the most damage by losing two star players.

The first Negro National League game was played on May 2, 1920, and Foster's Chicago American Giants dropped a 4–2 contest to C. I. Taylor's Indianapolis ABCs. But this was not an indication of what was ahead, as the American Giants soon began a winning streak and pulled far ahead in the standings.

Foster's team was an extension of his own personality and philosophy, and bore his distinct imprint. The players were molded to fit his "racehorse" style of play. Good pitching, sound defense, and an offense geared to the running game characterized his ballclub.

Foster's imaginative style of play and consistent application of "heady" inside baseball enabled the American Giants' dominance to continue, and they won the league's first three pennants. Starring for Foster's championship teams were center fielder Cristobal Torriente, second baseman Bingo DeMoss, third baseman David Malarcher and left-handed pitching ace Dave Brown. Jimmy Lyons, acquired after the inaugural season, helped the team capture the latter two pennants in their three-peat.

In 1923, Dave Brown jumped the team in the raiding wars by the Eastern League and then disappeared two years later after killing a man in a barroom fight. The loss of Brown weakened the team appreciably and the American Giants were dethroned by the hard-hitting Kansas City Monarchs.

Christobal Torriente, the slugging superstar for Rube Foster's Chicago American Giants, powered the team to consecutive championships in the first three years of the newly formed Negro National League (1920–1922).

The Monarchs were led by pitcher-outfielder Wilbur "Bullet" Rogan and several other former stars of the U.S. Army's black 25th Infantry Regiment's team. Rogan combined a great fastball and exceptional curve to become the top pitcher in the league. When he wasn't doing mound duty, he was the starting center fielder. Slugging shortstop Dobie Moore and slick fielding second sacker Newt Allen were other outstanding players for the new champions.

Following on the heels of the Chicago American Giants capturing the first three pennants (1920–1922), the Kansas City Monarchs won the next three Negro National League pennants (1923–1925). These three years encased the formation of the Eastern Colored League and the establishment of the first Negro World Series. Owned by J. L. Wilkinson, a highly respected white entrepreneur, the Monarchs became one of the best known and most successful black teams of all time.

Meanwhile, Foster ruled the league with an iron hand and worked tirelessly to keep the league together. Franchises entered, faltered and disbanded only to be replaced with another ballclub. During one league meeting, an owner went to sleep and woke up without a franchise.

In his capacity as league president and treasurer, Foster became an even more powerful influence on black baseball, but as his autocratic powers increased, some owners became alienated by his dictatorial manner.

Discord grew from his handling of monies generated by the league. Although he received no salary as president, Foster took five percent of the gate receipts of every league game and distributed them without answering to anyone.

In 1925, the opposition to his unrestricted powers had grown and he offered to resign. Although he received a unanimous vote of confidence from the other owners, the handwriting was on the wall. By then, the sharp mind that Foster had exhibited in his prime was showing the effects of the tremendous pressures and stress under which he had labored for many years. He claimed that his players had "laid down on him" and the mental deterioration that would soon lead to a nervous breakdown was beginning to manifest itself.

Sadly, Rube Foster, once larger than life, fell victim to psychological illness and was placed in a mental institution. After his incapacitation, his white business partner, John M. Schorling, handled the business affairs and Foster's protegé, Dave Malarcher, assumed the managerial duties for the American Giants.

Malarcher, who learned his baseball from the master, applied what he had learned from Foster to guide the American Giants to back-to-back pennants in 1926–1927, followed each time by victories in the Negro World Series over the Eastern Colored League's Bacharach Giants. Foster's influence was not limited to Malarcher's managing, as Rube's younger half-brother, Willie Foster, assumed the role of the "ace" of the American Giants' pitching staff and won many clutch games during each season.

However, the management side of the game did not transition as seamlessly, and Foster's absence left a void that could not be filled. In the spring of 1928, Schorling alleged that he was "squeezed out" by a conspiracy of the other owners to keep the best clubs out of Chicago, and sold the ballclub to William E. Trimble, a white florist.

While the Eastern Colored League had collapsed that same spring, the Negro National League staggered on for three more seasons before falling victim to the Great Depression. In the interim, the Monarchs added another flag in 1929 behind the superb hurling of Chet Brewer, while the St. Louis Stars won pennants in 1928 and 1930–1931.

These St. Louis teams featured the speedy James "Cool Papa" Bell, who Satchel Paige said could switch the lights off and get in bed before the room got dark. Also featured were Willie "Devil" Wells and George "Mule" Suttles.

This pair was called "Damon and Pythias" and would later play together on the Chicago American Giants and the Newark Eagles. Wells was one of the greatest shortstops of all time, black or white, and Suttles was a slugger who hit tape measure home runs as far as any player in the league.

At various times in the 12-year duration of Rube's League — the original Negro National League — 24 different franchises appeared, but three teams dominated the league, capturing all pennants during the league's existence. The Chicago American Giants won five titles, the Kansas City Monarchs won four, and the St. Louis Stars captured the remaining three. These three franchises, along with the Detroit Stars and the Cuban Stars, provided a solid foundation for the league's stability and continuity.

Part III: Eastern Colored League

After three years of a successful black league in the west, Hilldale owner Ed Bolden was the driving force in forming a black league in the east. In preparation for the 1923 season, the leading teams in the east met December 16, 1922, at the Philadelphia YMCA and formally organized the Mutual Association of Eastern Colored Baseball Clubs (more commonly known as the Eastern Colored League).

The owners served as the Board of Commissioners, which was the governing body of the league, and Ed Bolden was elected as the Chairman of the Board. New York Lincoln Giants owner James J. Keenan was appointed Secretary-Treasurer of the Association.

The impetus for establishing a new league in the east was accelerated by Rube Foster's increasingly obsessive and dictatorial behavior, which alienated many prospective baseball entrepreneurs. Previously, Bolden had been reasonably receptive to Rube's vision of expanding the NNL into the east, and in 1922 both his Hilldale club and John Connors' New York Bacharach Giants had been satellite clubs, with associate membership status, in Rube's league.

However, Foster's continued distaste for Nat Strong eventually caused a breach between himself and Bolden, who viewed black baseball in the east as having developed far beyond being simply an extension of the NNL — and under Foster's control.

Bolden valued the ballpark access and booking connections in metropolitan New York City that Nat Strong and his partner, Max Rosner, had cultivated over the years. Strong, in turn, envisioned an eastern league as a source of quality competition that could be booked into his newly acquired Dexter Park to play his Brooklyn Royal Giants and the Cuban Stars, another black team whose booking was under his control.

Other eastern owners and promoters also favored a new league comprised of the top eastern teams. Charles P. Spedden, business manager for the Baltimore Black Sox, thought baseball in the east had previously been lacking an efficient operating system and needed the structure of a well-organized league to overcome the deficiencies of the past.

Owner John Connors dissolved his Bacharachs team and most of the players were picked up by the Original Bacharach Giants of Atlantic City. Operating under the leadership of the original founders, Tom Jackson and Henry Tucker, the franchise sought membership in the newly created ECL.

Bolden wisely limited the initial season to six franchises. The teams and their owners were: Hilldale (Ed Bolden), Atlantic City Bacharach Giants (Thomas Jackson), New York Lincoln Giants (James J. Keenan), Brooklyn Royal Giants (Nat C. Strong), Baltimore Black Sox (George Rossiter), and Cuban Stars (Alejandro Pompez).

Bolden received some criticism for having so many white owners. Much of the denigration emanated from Foster, who railed against the league for having too much white involvement, including "white money," and labeling Bolden's actions as "race betrayal."

Only Bolden himself was an African-American owner. Pompez was Cuban and the other four were white Americans. Understandably sensitive to the racial innuendo contained in the criticism, Bolden took measures to ameliorate the expressed concerns, and, in the second year, the Eastern Colored League expanded, adding two new teams, both with black ownership. These new league members were the Harrisburg Giants (Colonel C. W. Strothers) and the Washington Potomacs (George W. Robinson), with long-time Indianapolis ABCs star Ben Taylor as manager.

Ed Bolden was employed in the Philadelphia Post Office and — in contrast to the huge, flamboyant Rube Foster — was a small, shy, quiet and modest man who preferred working in the background instead of in the spotlight. But like Foster, his own team dominated the league that he formed, with the Hilldale club winning the first three Eastern Colored League Championships in 1923–1925.

As the founder of the Eastern Colored League, he was also accountable for the player raids by eastern teams on the more established Negro National League. However, it was the New York Lincoln Giants, a charter member of the ECL, who actually started the "player war" in January of 1923 when the team signed the Chicago American Giants ace left-hander, Dave Brown.

Brown was the top pitcher in black baseball at the time and he was welcomed by the Lincoln Giants brain trust, comprised of owner James J. Keenan and manager Smokey Joe Williams. In contrast, Rube Foster, responding both as the NNL President and the aggrieved team owner, was livid. When Brown jumped, it ignited the incendiary situation and a player war broke out between the east and the west.

Ed Bolden and the other eastern owners openly defied Foster and enticed other NNL players to the east. Foster countered the piracy by once again redistributing players in an effort to restore a semblance of parity in his league, but two western teams were dissolved due to the east's raids.

Altogether 30 players from the NNL chose to play in the newly organized ECL. Bolden's Hilldale team benefited by the addition of four quality players: Raleigh "Biz" Mackey (from the Indianapolis ABCs), George "Tank" Carr (from the Kansas City Monarchs), Clint Thomas and Frank Warfield (from the Detroit Stars).

In 1923, under playing manager John Henry Lloyd, Hilldale won the first ECL pennant but because of the "player raids" on the NNL, there was no Negro World Series between the two league champions. Lloyd, often called the "black Honus Wagner," had some differences with Ed Bolden and, after the season, he was fired for alleged team dissension.

Second baseman Frank Warfield took the helm for Hilldale and lead the team to two more consecutive pennants (1924–1925). The top players from these teams were catcher Biz Mackey, third baseman Judy Johnson, catcher Louis Santop, center fielder Clint Thomas and ace hurler Nip Winters. Mackey, Johnson and Santop were future Hall of Famers.

After Hilldale's "three-peat" the next two pennants (1926–1927) were won by Atlantic City's Bacharach Giants, named after the city's mayor, Harry Bacharach. Shortstop Dick Lundy, who doubled as manager, and third baseman Oliver "Ghost" Marcelle formed an almost impregnable left side of the infield and were the mainstays of the team, along with clutch-hitting outfielder Chaney White and pitching ace Rats Henderson.

Each of the previous four seasons (1924–1927) was highlighted by a Negro World Series, and while those years were the high points of the early leagues, the nadir was in sight.

Ed Bolden suffered a nervous breakdown in September of 1927, only a year after Rube Foster's breakdown, and was quickly removed as Hilldale's president. The ECL also acted swiftly and Atlantic City attorney Isaac H. Nutter was selected to replace Bolden as the league president. Nutter was re-elected to that position in February of 1928, but unfortunately, his tenure was brief.

Bolden had regained control of the Hilldale franchise and chose to separate from the league and play as an independent team. Without his management, the Eastern Colored League folded early in the ensuing spring.

Although the ECL lasted only half as long as Rube Foster's NNL, there was much more stability due to fewer franchise changes. Ten different teams operated in the league, with only three being one-time franchises. In addition to the pennant winners, Hilldale (three flags) and the Bacharachs (two flags), the steadfast franchises were the Baltimore Black Sox, New York Lincoln Giants, Cuban Stars, Brooklyn Royal Giants, and Harrisburg Giants.

The one-time entries were the Washington Potomacs (1924), the Newark Stars (1926), who disbanded in mid-season with only a solitary win, and the Philadelphia Tigers (1928), who entered the league briefly during the ECL's last gasp before breaking up in the spring.

Part IV: Negro World Series

During the existence of the early leagues, there were four years (1924–1927) when each season was culminated by a Negro World Series between the two leagues.

The first Negro World Series was played in 1924 between the NNL Champion Kansas City Monarchs and Hilldale, the ECL Champion. Scheduled as a best-of-nine series, the two teams battled each other and ten games were required before the Monarchs edged Hilldale in a thrilling Series. One game ended in a tie and most of the games were closely contested.

Nip Winters, Hilldale's elongated lefty, won three games to take top honors among moundsmen. Monarchs ace Bullet Rogan won two games, as did aging manager Jose Mendez, who won a thrilling seventh game, 4–3 in 12-innings, before pitching a masterful three-hit, 5–0 victory in the final game to give the Monarchs the title in the first-ever Negro World Series.

The next season featured a rematch between the two evenly matched teams in the 1925 Negro World Series. However, Monarchs star pitcher Wilbur "Bullet" Rogan was injured shortly before the first game and missed the entire Series. His absence put the defending champions at a distinct disadvantage and Hilldale won the Series five games to only one win for the Monarchs. Future Hall of Famers Judy Johnson and Biz Mackey provided the offense, while left-handed pitching ace Nip Winters shared the spotlight with Rube Currie and spitballer Phil Cockrell.

There were only two more Negro World Series between these two leagues. In 1926 and 1927, with new manager David Malarcher at the reins, the Chicago American Giants won both the Negro National League flag and the Negro World Series, each time defeating the Eastern Colored League's Champion Bacharach Giants, under the leadership of playing manager Dick Lundy. Ten games were played the first year and nine the second year, before a winner was determined, with the American Giants, winning five games to three, excluding ties.

In this pair of World Series, future Hall of Fame pitcher Willie Foster, regarded as the greatest left-hander in the history of the Negro Leagues, won two games each year, including the clinching game each time. In 1926 Foster fashioned two one-run victories for the champion American Giants, including a 1–0 shutout in the final game. A year later, he won both the first and last game of the 1927 rematch.

An oddity of this pair of World Series is that each one featured a no-hit game, both times by the team that was on the losing end of the Series. In 1926 Bacharachs hurler Red Grier tossed a no-hitter to win the third game, 10–0. A year later, Luther Farrell tossed a no-hitter in the fifth game but barely edged the American Giants, 3–2, when the game was ended by darkness in the middle of the seventh inning.

These were the only Negro World Series played until 1942, when two later leagues launched a seven-year set of post-season series.

Part V: A Replacement League

After the collapse of the ECL, Ed Bolden spearheaded a replacement league called the American Negro League, which operated for a season before its inevitable demise. This was essentially the same league with a different name and restructured leadership.

The organizational meeting was held January 15, 1929, at the Citizens Republican Club in Philadelphia. The teams in the league were Hilldale, Baltimore Black Sox, New York Lincoln Giants, Atlantic City Bacharach Giants, Cuban Stars, and Homestead Grays.

Bolden was a unanimous choice for President of the ANL, with James Keenan elected Vice-President and George Rossiter voted Treasurer. In an unprecedented move, sportswriter Rollo Wilson was appointed Secretary. Conspicuously absent from a leadership position was Homestead Grays owner Cum Posey.

Until now, Posey had eschewed league membership for the scheduling flexibility of an independent ballclub, and he was accustomed to being in command and making decisions concerning his team. He was strong-willed and it was not in his nature to take a back seat to anyone. Nor was he inclined to be subservient to anyone else's authority. In the eyes of some observers, this presented a definite problem for Ed Bolden.

However, the office of league President empowered Bolden with more authority than he had possessed as Chairman of the Board of Commissioners with the ECL. Other conditions that were improved in the ANL were a better competitive balance among the teams and an enhanced adherence to schedules.

A downside for the new league was a relaxed enforcement of rules governing individual players, and Bolden's reluctance to confront the strong-willed Posey. Bolden viewed Posey as a valuable ally, and the Grays owner reciprocated by joining Rollo Wilson in defending Bolden from criticism. Among the critics was Syd Pollock, owner of the Havana Red Sox, who questioned the President's consistency in enforcing league policies. Despite the controversies that developed, the ANL completed the season and provided eastern fans with a good brand of baseball.

In what was to be the league's only year of existence, the Baltimore Black Sox won both halves of the split season to take the pennant. The Sox featured a million dollar infield of Oliver Marcelle, Dick Lundy, Frank Warfield, and Jud "Boojum" Wilson, going around the horn from third base to first base. Slugging outfielder Rap Dixon and ace pitcher Laymon Yokely also starred for the Black Sox.

Hilldale fielded a strong lineup that featured four future Hall of Fame players (Oscar Charleston, Biz Mackey, Martin Dihigo and Judy Johnson), and were runner-ups in the second half of the season.

Another impressive team in the league was manager John Henry Lloyd's hard-hitting New York Lincoln Giants. Although late in his career, Lloyd formed a formidable slugging triad with the powerful John Beckwith and outfielder Chino Smith, who was considered one of the two best hitters in black baseball by Satchel Paige. Chino captured individual honors in the league with a .464 batting average and 23 homers to lead the ANL in both categories.

With the end of the ANL season, the teams in the east returned to independent play, while their NNL counterparts continued for two more seasons without Rube Foster's leadership.

Part VI: Final Efforts in the East

The pressure of operating a league was tremendous and, ironically, the founders of both of the earliest leagues suffered nervous breakdowns due to the physical and psychological stress generated from their involvement in their respective leagues.

The celebrated Rube Foster was the first to fall victim to this condition. Bolden was felled little more than a year later. While Bolden was to recover and make a comeback in baseball with another franchise in a new league, Rube Foster's fate was more tragic. He was committed to the state asylum at Kankakee, Illinois, and was never to leave until his death barely more than two weeks before Christmas in 1930. Fans and admirers lined up for three days to view the casket.

In his lifetime, Rube Foster covered the entire spectrum of baseball participation, from the playing field to the front office, and he excelled at each level. In his prime he was the top pitcher in black baseball. Then he became the game's greatest manager and most innovative owner. Finally, as founder of the first black league, he was recognized as the father of the Negro Leagues.

Foster's career exemplifies the essence of black baseball. From the day he arrived on the baseball scene until his death, he stood astride the black sporting world like a Colossus — almost bigger than life itself.

Foster's funeral was sandwiched between the final two seasons of the league that he founded. While the St. Louis Stars were winning those last two NNL pennants, the teams in the east had returned to independent play.

In 1930, the New York Lincoln Giants fielded their strongest team since manager John Henry Lloyd's 1913 powerhouse. Consequently, the Lincolns faced the rugged Homestead Grays in a challenge playoff for the Eastern Championship. The Grays were strengthened that year by the late-season acquisition of a young catcher named Josh Gibson, who was destined to become the greatest slugger in the history of black baseball, and arguably the best player ever to play his position, bar none.

In the hard-fought, ten-game Eastern Championship Series, the Grays won four of the first six games, with the final four games being played at Yankee Stadium in a pair of twin bills on September 27–28.

The teams split the first doubleheader, with the Grays taking the second game after dropping the opener. Gibson homered in both games, but the feature of the day was his home run in the second game, a 460-foot, three-run circuit blast into the left field bleachers off left-hander Connie Rector that was the longest home run of the season in Yankee Stadium.

The next day, with the Lincoln Giants needing to win both ends of a doubleheader to salvage a tie in the series, their ace hurler Bill Holland attempted an iron man effort by pitching both ends of the twin bill. Holland won the opener, 6–2, but faltered in the second game and lost to the Homestead Grays, 5–2, giving the Grays the championship with six wins in the ten-game series.

Earlier in the season, the Grays' Smokey Joe Williams had made baseball history when he engaged in a famous pitchers' duel against Chet Brewer. Brewer struck out 19 batters and allowed only 4 hits, but Williams "smoked" 27 batters while tossing a one-hitter to shut out the Kansas City Monarchs, 1–0, in a 12-inning night game under the portable lighting system being pioneered by the Monarchs. Despite his success, Williams actually did not like pitching under the lights.

The following season, with Smokey Joe Williams and Willie Foster forming a sterling duo on the mound, and a slugging trio comprised of Josh Gibson,

Oscar Charleston, and Jud Wilson providing the power, the Grays fielded an even more dominant team. All five of these superstars were future Hall of Famers. Ted "Double Duty" Radcliffe, a member of that ballclub, called this 1931 aggregation the greatest team that he ever saw.

With the success of the back-to-back championships, his ballclub still in ascendancy, and the death of the NNL, Cum Posey was prepared for a greater challenge and was poised to initiate a more elaborate endeavor.

Part VII: Troubled Waters

When he founded the Negro National League, Rube Foster had said, "We are the ship, all else is the sea." Rube Foster passed away December 9, 1930, in a mental institution in Kankakee, Illinois. When Foster died, the ship had lost its rudder and its captain who had piloted the ship. With him went the heart and soul of the Negro National League. An early victim of the Great Depression, the league that Foster founded died within a year from a void in leadership during this economically troubled period.

Foster's league had struggled on for two years longer than the eastern leagues, which had folded after the 1929 season. With the collapse of the Negro National League, black baseball was thrown into a state of disorder.

The last two Negro National League pennants were won by the St. Louis Stars, who had a roster heavily punctuated by stars and superstars, including Willie Wells, Mule Suttles and Cool Papa Bell. But despite the wealth of playing talent, after their second flag, the team folded along with the league.

Those players and many other players from other teams that were disbanding threw a multitude of good players out of a job. Those teams that "scuffled" to continue during the chaotic conditions had their pick from among this glut of instant free agents.

The upcoming 1932 season had the appearance of a year of approaching chaos. Stepping into the breach was Cum Posey. After a year in the ANL and two years of independent play where his Homestead Grays were the top team in the east, if not in all black baseball, Posey was primed to take the leadership role in restoring a viable black league. To this end, he provided the impetus at a January 20–21 meeting of club owners in Cleveland for formation of the East-West League in an effort to salvage franchises from both early leagues.

Charter members of the ambitious project were the following teams, listed with their managers: Homestead Grays (Jud Wilson), Detroit Wolves (Dizzy Dismukes), Baltimore Black Sox (Dick Lundy), Hilldale (Judy Johnson), Washington Pilots (Frank Warfield), Newark Browns (John Beckwith), Cleveland Stars (Pimp Young), and Cuban House of David (Ramiro Ramirez).

Unfortunately, the geographical spread of league cities made travel too expensive for fiscal viability. Teams were highly motivated to play their home games, but were reluctant to travel long distances for away games to accommodate other ballclubs. The extant economic conditions were reflected on the business side of baseball and dictated the demise of the league in mid-season.

In what some considered a conflict of interest, Posey had maintained ownership in two separate franchises — his Homestead Grays and the thinly veiled ownership of the Detroit Wolves. Prior to finally scrubbing the season, Posey attempted to resuscitate the ailing league by consolidating the two franchises, with the Grays playing out the remainder of the schedules for both teams.

This required a mini-realignment of the surviving franchises. Detroit had stocked their lineup with former players of the St. Louis Stars, who had exited from the now defunct franchise. After winning the previous two pennants under the St. Louis banner, much of the team's nucleus was now wearing Detroit uniforms and had carried the team into first place prior to the merger. The reconfigured Grays absorbed some of these ex–Wolves, and fought to maintain that position by fighting off the surging Baltimore Black Sox.

After the league had finally folded, Commissioner Cum Posey announced On July 16, 1932, that his Homestead Grays had been awarded the first-half flag in the East-West League.

Some surviving franchises that continued to operate chose to remain independent ballclubs, rather than join the East-West League. Some of those were the Pittsburgh Crawfords, Chicago American Giants, New York Black Yankees, and Kansas City Monarchs.

The two strongest of these teams were the Pittsburgh Crawfords and Chicago American Giants. The Crawfords, playing their first full season under the competent leadership of owner Gus Greenlee and manager Oscar Charleston, quickly established themselves as a top team and were elevated to a position of prominence in black baseball.

The American Giants, playing under new owner Robert A. Cole, an undertaker with limited baseball acumen, later decided to affiliate with the Negro Southern League and played under the name of Cole's American Giants. With Dave Malarcher at the helm, the American Giants won the NSL pennant.

The New York Black Yankees, under manager George Scales, remained unaffiliated and played an independent schedule that included many semi-pro teams. Another historically top ballclub, the Kansas City Monarchs, did not return to play until mid-season, while the defending NNL champion St. Louis Stars disbanded completely.

With the East-West League's inability to overcome the financial difficulties that were encountered and complete the season, that left the field open for the Negro Southern League to become the only Negro League to finish the entire season.

The Negro Southern League had been another beneficiary of the free agent glut in the wake of the NNL's breakup. The NSL continued to operate and, with the influx of more skilled players fleeing the large city markets of the north where the disbanding teams were located, these southern teams advanced to a major league caliber and for the 1932 season, the Negro Southern League acquired major league status for the only time.

However, this situation was reversed after only one season, when Gus Greenlee and Tom Wilson organized a new Negro National League in 1933.

Part VIII: Transition to Stability

This bold move by Greenlee and Wilson ushered in the era of the latter leagues. After four years of operating as the only black major league, the second NNL was joined by the Negro American League in 1937 to introduce the halcyon years of the Negro Leagues.

When the NAL organized, their franchises were located in the midwest and south. The NNL then realigned as an eastern league. This dual league structure was patterned after the two white major leagues — the National League and the American League — and continued for 12 seasons (1937–1948). Structurally and financially, those years were the high-water mark for the Negro Leagues until the abolishment of the color line opened the flood gates of black ballplayers assimilating into organized baseball.

The decline of the Negro Leagues after this period was swift and irreversible. Still, the special essence and flavor of black baseball survived, and was carried into mainstream baseball with the infusion of talented black players into the major leagues.

This concise narrative is intended to provide a fertile background for understanding the circumstances and conditions which contributed to the establishment, growth and decline of black baseball's early leagues — and ultimately to the assimilation of black players into the mainstream of our National Pastime. This article has not previously been published.

Mysterious Dave Brown:
One Shot Short of Stardom

An aura of mystery followed Dave Brown wherever he went.

From his days pitching with the Dallas Black Giants, while the Great War was raging in Europe, until he killed a man in a barroom fight in New York City during the middle of the "Roaring Twenties" and virtually dropped off the face of the earth, bad news and controversy constantly dogged his footsteps.

During the winter following the 1917 baseball season in Dallas, the mysterious left-hander was involved in a highway robbery and was a fugitive from justice when Rube Foster, the owner-manager of the Chicago American Giants, signed him. Despite his fellow Texan's difficulty complying with the law, Foster liked what he saw when the gifted southpaw took the mound and, ignoring persistent rumors, put up a $20,000 bond to get Brown a parole from his highway robbery conviction.

The Chicago American Giants were the top black team in the country and the mysterious Texan mixed outstanding speed, a good curve, a hard drop and excellent control to quickly establish himself as the team's ace.

The heart of his meteoric eight-year presence in the black big leagues was the first three years of Foster's Negro National League, in which Brown's clutch pitching was a primary factor in the team's dominance. The American Giants' crafty and talented ace led the team to a triad of consecutive NNL pennants (1920, 1921, and 1922). Brown's ledger for those championship seasons shows marks of 10–2, 11–3 and 8–3 in league contests for a composite .784 winning percentage. In the middle season, 1921, he was also credited with three victories in a playoff against the Atlantic City Bacharach Giants, the top black club in the east.

When the Eastern Colored League was founded in 1923, Brown jumped to the east coast to join the New York Lincoln Giants, triggering a controversial "player war" between the two leagues that resulted in many established players joining the new league.

His first year in New York was personally disappointing, as he suffered

Dave Brown, the top lefthander in the Negro Leagues, jumped his contract and triggered a "player war" between rival leagues in 1923. He is pictured (top right) with the Santa Clara Leopards, considered the best team ever in the history of Cuba.

a losing season (4–7). However, his resilience manifested itself in 1924, when his superb control made him a consistent and effective pitcher, almost unbeatable when he was right—which was most of the time. That year he matched arms with the Brooklyn Royal Giants' reigning superstar, Cannonball Dick Redding, in a game for the New York City Championship and walked away with a 3–1 victory.

Following the 1924 season, veteran player-manager Ben Taylor—who had just completed a quarter century in black baseball—regarded Brown and the ECL Champion Hilldale ace Nip Winters as being "without doubt ... our greatest lefthanders." Taylor's recognition of Brown's exceptional pitching skills ameliorated the lingering fallout from his mysterious persona and reputation for not respecting the law.

Those alleged off-field criminal behavior patterns were not reflected between the lines or in the clubhouse. In those settings, Brown was not considered a troublemaker and was described by some teammates as being a "gentleman," a "timid, nice guy" and a "kind, wonderful fellow." Others described him as "jolly" and "joking all the time."

Whatever his true character, the popular pitcher was coveted by other teams in both black leagues and also in Cuba, where the best baseball outside of the U.S. was played. In three Cuban League winter seasons (1922–1925), he accumulated a 17–12 composite record. His most notable Cuban performance came in the winter of 1923–1924 when he posted an 11–5 record for the Santa Clara Leopards, an aggregation that is considered the greatest Cuban team of all time.

After he returned to the U.S. following his last Cuban winter season, he rejoined the New York Lincoln Giants in the spring, ready to begin a new year on the home diamond. On opening day of the Lincolns' 1925 Eastern Colored League season, Brown took the mound to the cheers of 7,000 partisan fans that turned out at the Catholic Protectory Oval to see their ace left-hander scatter seven hits while cruising to a 6–1 victory over the visiting Bacharach Giants. This was the last game he would ever pitch in the Negro Leagues.

Two days later, in the early hours of the morning, the mysterious Dave Brown shot and killed Benjamin Adair in a barroom on New York's West 135th Street after an apparent dispute over a cocaine transaction gone bad.

Brown's bent for criminal behavior formed bookends for his baseball career. He had begun his career in the black major leagues in 1918 after a brush with the law, and ended it abruptly in a like manner, when he again ran afoul of the law in 1925.

Teammates Oliver Marcelle and Frank Wickware were with him when the fight started and they were picked up by police officers the next day at the ballpark, but the elusive assailant was not there. Mysterious Dave Brown had disappeared to avoid a murder charge from the barroom incident.

While the FBI was searching for him, it was reported that he traveled throughout the Midwest, playing for semi-pro teams under the alias "Lefty Wilson." Sometimes he toured with Gilkerson's Union Giants, as he did in 1926, or played with a white team in Bertha, Minnesota, in 1927. He was also reported to have pitched with teams in Sioux City, Iowa, in 1929 and Little Falls, Minnesota, in 1930.

Future Hall of Fame shortstop Willie Wells, who ventured into postseason barnstorming with the Kansas City Monarchs, said that Brown played with the Monarchs down through the Midwest towards Mexico. "We all knew who he was," Wells recalled, "and we kept our bags packed so we could leave on a moment's notice if the law showed up." Wells further related that when the tour continued closer to the Mexican border, Brown left the team and did not go on into Mexico with the team because there would have been a passport problem.

Unverified rumors persisted for years of murky sightings of him appearing unexpectedly somewhere, almost like an apparition, and vanishing suddenly in the same manner. Even his death is clouded in mystery, with reports that he died in Denver, under mysterious circumstances.

Indeed, a fitting end for the mysterious Dave Brown.

Many athletes have squandered potential greatness for a variety of causes. This article presents an overview of one baseball player with great talent, who effectively forfeited his place in baseball history by his off-field exploits. To present a more complete picture of Dave Brown's career for baseball aficionados, some of the more memorable games of his relatively brief career are presented here.

In 1920 the Negro National League was the top black league, but the Negro Southern League considered itself to be on a par with the NNL. The matter was to be resolved on October 2, when the NNL Champion Chicago American Giants played the Southern League Champion Knoxville Giants.

The game was a pitching duel of young left-handers, as Dave Brown faced Knoxville ace Steel Arm Dickey. The game was closely contested but Brown allowed only three hits and his teammates scored twice in the final inning to give him a 2–1 win over the southern champs. This was the American Giants' 14th straight victory and sealed their status as the best black ball club in the country.

The next season, 1921, the Chicago American Giants again played the Negro Southern League champions. This year it was the Montgomery Grey Sox, and it proved to be the second straight year that Brown matched up with Steel Arm Dickey, who had switched teams and brought the southern championship with him.

The showdown between league champions on September 11 played out like a replay from the previous season. The American Giants scored an unearned run in the last inning to win, 1–0, on Brown's brilliant shutout pitching, making the second straight year that the American Giants had won by one run in the last inning.

Later that fall, the American Giants also defeated the two top teams in the east, where there was no league. On October 2 Brown pitched a 3–1 win over the Atlantic City Bacharach Giants, the first of his three victories in the October playoff against the Bacharachs. The American Giants then defeated Hilldale, the other top eastern club, to claim the Negro World Championship.

While the American Giants were still in the east, another interesting autumn sidelight to Brown's extraordinary season came when he tossed a 6–2 win over former New York Giants pitcher Jeff Tesreau and his team, the Tesreau Bears.

In 1922, in what was to be his last year with the American Giants, the team started strong in their successful pursuit of a third straight pennant behind their superlative southpaw. In late summer Brown achieved a measure of immortality when he became the central character in a historic marathon game.

On August 22 the American Giants defeated the Bacharach Giants, 1–0, in a 20-inning battle. Brown entered the game in the fifth inning with no outs and a runner on base. During his extended relief stint, he struck out ten, walked two and allowed only five hits in 16 innings of shutout ball to get the win, when Cristobal Torriente led off the 20th inning with a walk, was sacrificed to second, and scored on Dave Malarcher's game-winning single.

Dave Brown's "relief appearance"— almost the equivalent to pitching a doubleheader shutout— earned him the accolades. Meanwhile, the Bacharachs' unfortunate Harold Treadwell, who went the entire distance, suffered the loss and received only disappointment.

However, Treadwell still fared better than Brown's earlier adversary, Steel Arm Dickey. Only a little more than six months after mysterious Dave Brown's triumph in the marathon game, Dickey was stabbed to death in Etowah, Tennessee, while trying to break up a fight.

The First Dark October: A Look at the Inaugural Negro World Series

When baseball aficionados see the leaves painted in autumn colors and feel the chill of an October wind, they have no need to check the calendar to know that it's time for America's biggest sporting event — the World Series. Even casual fans get excited about the "Fall Classic," which was first played in 1903 and has been virtually a continuous part of baseball tradition ever since.

Seventy Octobers ago, a smaller segment of the American sporting scene was equally enthusiastic about a lesser known baseball advent. The historic occasion was the first Negro World Series, pitting two outstanding and evenly matched teams that induced an electric atmosphere of anticipation among black Americans all across the country.

The Kansas City Monarchs of the more established Negro National League faced the Hilldale team from the Eastern Colored League, which had just completed its second season of existence. Coincidently, both ballclubs were to become "three-peat" league champions and, in 1924, each was in the middle year of its triad.

The Monarchs, owned by white businessman J. L. Wilkinson, finished the season with a .714 winning percentage (55–22), four games ahead of Rube Foster's famous Chicago American Giants. In the East, Ed Bolden's Hilldale club showed a .681 winning percentage (47–22) to finish a comfortable seven games ahead of the slugging Baltimore Black Sox.

The newer league's raiding tactics had precluded a showdown the previous season, but pressure from the press and fans made the event a reality and the players welcomed the chance to play the champions from the rival league.

A total of 45,857 paying customers witnessed the first Negro World Series, which unfolded like an Indiana Jones serial full of action and excitement, each game a new cliffhanging episode and the outcome of the last eight games determined in the winning team's last time at bat.

The best-of-nine Series opened Friday, October 3 at Shibe Park, the home park of Connie Mack's Philadelphia A's, with 5,366 paying fans in attendance. The partisan eastern crowd gave the visitors a cool reception but riveted their attention on the Monarchs' ace right-hander, Wilbur "Bullet" Rogan, as he warmed up on the sideline.

The selection of Phil Cockrell to oppose Rogan immediately generated controversy when the plate umpire objected to him throwing his trademark spitball. After heated discussion, an appeal was made to Rube Foster, Chairman of the Commission, who ruled that Cockrell could use his spitball.

Foster tossed out the ceremonial first pitch, and the

In the inaugural Negro World Series, Hilldale's ace left-hander Nip Winters won three games against the Kansas City Monarchs.

historic contest started a few minutes after two o'clock. The Monarchs' leadoff batter, Lem Hawkins, slammed a double to left field for the first base hit in a Negro World Series, but Cockrell retired the side without allowing him to score. Rogan reciprocated, retiring Hilldale in the bottom half of the inning without allowing a run. The game remained scoreless until the sixth inning, when Kansas City blew the game open with five unearned runs, and Rogan cruised to a 6–2 victory.

Increased newspaper publicity and the arrival of more Kansas City supporters swelled attendance to 8,661 for Saturday's game, and the crowd filled the Shibe Park grandstands an hour before game time. Hilldale gave the home fans something to cheer about, pounding 15 hits behind star left-hander Nip Winters' masterful four-hitter for an 11–0 rout to even the Series.

The third game was played at Bugle Field in Baltimore, and extra bleachers were put in the outfield, with balls hit into these overflow seats being ground-rule doubles. Fans from all along the Atlantic seaboard attended the 13-inning marathon encounter, which was ended by darkness in a 6–6 stalemate, leaving the Series still deadlocked.

Rescheduled for the next day, only 584 fans turned out in the miserably hot weather and the start of the game was delayed an hour due to an incorrect listing in the newspaper. Reporters, using empty beer boxes as tables for their typewriters, were forced to sit in the boiling sun to watch the game. Amidst the multitude of empty seats and the heat, Hilldale made the most of four hits and three Kansas City errors to eke out a 4–3 decision by pushing across the winning tally in the bottom half of the ninth inning without the benefit of a hit.

After a five-day interval, Hilldale carried their one-game edge to foreign soil for a three-game set at Muehlenbach Park in Kansas City. The first contest featured the first confrontation between the top pitchers in each league, as hometown favorite Bullet Rogan faced the invaders' Nip Winters.

As expected, the game developed into a pitchers' duel and Rogan nurtured a 2–1 lead into the last stanza before Hilldale, keyed by future Hall of Famer Judy Johnson's triple, scored four markers for a 5–2 victory to give the eastern champs a two-game lead.

The next game produced the largest turnout of the Series, as 8,885 rabid hometown fans saw the Monarchs win a 6–5 seesaw slugfest that produced 22 hits in a Sunday thriller filled with excitement from beginning to end. The outcome was not decided until the bottom of the eighth inning, when the frenzied hometown crowd was brought to their feet by George Sweatt's game-winning triple. Hilldale's lead in the Series was now cut to a single game.

After a day off, the teams resumed their epic struggles with a 12-inning cliffhanger. As the bottom of the 12th inning opened, the exuberant partisan crowd began stomping their feet and yelling, and the noise was deafening. With two outs, nobody on base and the shadows reaching towards the horizon, it appeared that the contest was going to be another extra-inning deadlock.

The din of anticipation abated somewhat until George Sweatt poled a triple into the right field corner. The crucial play of the game came when Rogan hit a ground ball into the hole at shortstop and Judy Johnson made the play, pegging the ball to first. Touissant Allen, stretching for the long throw, pulled his foot off the base and the winning run crossed the plate for a 4–3 victory. Nip Winters, who pitched valiantly for the entire game, suffered the loss. The Series was once again dead even.

With the remaining games scheduled to be played at Schorling's Park in Chicago, play resumed after a three-day rest. The first game in Chicago proved to be the pivotal contest in the Series, and fate played an important part in the game.

Bullet Rogan and Rube Currie had matched goose-eggs until the sixth inning, when Hilldale took the lead. Down 2–0 in the last of the ninth, the Monarchs staged an improbable two-out comeback rally.

The game appeared to be over when Currie induced slugger Dobie Moore to hit a bounder toward shortstop. But fate smiled on the Monarchs. The ball took a big bounce and deflected off the top of Judy Johnson's glove when he went up for the grab, much like the ground ball that hopped over the head of New York Giants third baseman Fred Lindstrom in the major league World Series that fall against the Washington Senators.

Two batters latter, the bases were loaded, and Frank Duncan fouled a ball back towards the screen. Catcher Louis Santop circled under the ball and, as the high pop fly descended, the Monarchs fans' hearts were in their throats and their hopes in their pockets. If Santop made the catch, it would end the game. But fate laughed out loud.

The ball hit the mitt and dropped to the ground, much like the easy foul pop-up that Hank Gowdy had dropped after tripping over his mask during the 12th inning of the seventh game of the 1924 World Series. In that scenario, when given new life, Muddy Ruel doubled past third base and scored the Series-ending run two batters later, when Earl McNeely came through with a ground-ball single that careened over Lindstrom's head to give the Senators a fairy-tale finish to win the Series.

Now Frank Duncan was also given a second chance.

Hollywood could not have scripted a more thrilling climax: bottom of the ninth, down by a run, the bases loaded, two outs, two strikes on the batter, and tension mounting as Duncan carried Currie deeper into the count.

The next pitch was slammed right at third baseman Biz Mackey, but the ball went through into the outfield and two more runs scored to snatch victory from the jaws of defeat and give the Monarchs their third straight one-run victory. The jubilant crowd swarmed onto the field and hoisted Duncan on their shoulders, parading him around the field amidst the cheering throng.

Contrasting with the Monarchs' thrill of victory on the field was the agony of defeat in the Hilldale locker room afterwards, where the big, strapping Santop was devastated and reduced to tears by a profane tongue-lashing by manager Frank Warfield.

Although the Monarchs had reclaimed the Series lead for the first time since the opening game, Hilldale remained resolute. Despite the demoralizing loss and facing a large, hostile crowd, they fought back Sunday afternoon, scoring twice in the final stanza to give Nip Winters his third Series victory. The 5–3 win evened the Series and kept Hilldale's hopes alive.

After nine games, the teams were still dead even, with four wins, four losses and one tie. The Championship came down to a final game and the tension mounted. Monarchs skipper Jose Mendez, a Cuban pitching ace of the deadball era, took the mound for his club. In earlier years, it had been reported that Mendez had once killed a teammate during batting practice with his deadly fastball. Now he relied on guile, and still had enough of the old-time magic in his ancient arm to weave a three-hit masterpiece and paint a 5–0 whitewash on Hilldale.

Mendez never allowed a runner past first base and, for seven innings, Hilldale hurler Scrip Lee matched him, allowing only one hit. Then in the bottom of the eighth inning, the Monarchs scored five runs to put the game away. With the five-run cushion, Mendez retired the eastern champs in the ninth inning, and when shortstop Dobie Moore squeezed the final out, the ecstatic Monarchs fans rushed the field in a wild demonstration.

After 18 days, 2,614 miles and ten games, the Kansas City Monarchs entered the record books as the first Negro World Series Champions.

Series stars for the Monarchs were Bullet Rogan, who contributed a pair of complete game victories and a .310 BA, while playing as an outfield regular when not toeing the slab; slick fielding second baseman Newt Allen, who led all batters with a .344 BA; and Jose Mendez, who earned two victories with his clutch pitching.

Hilldale's stars included Nip Winters, who captured three games against a single loss that came in a hard-fought 12-inning contest; and Judy Johnson, who had a team-high .341 BA and topped all hitters with 15 base hits in the Series.

After the Series, Rube Foster wrote to the *Chicago Defender* that, discounting the first two games, the match-up had produced "eight of the best played games of ball that I have ever witnessed."

This article was written in 1994 on the 70th anniversary of the first Negro World Series, but has not been previously published. That year the major league World Series was cancelled for the first time in 90 years.

During the interim, two of the Monarchs key pitchers, Bullet Rogan and Jose Mendez, have been inducted into the National Baseball Hall of Fame.

A summary of the games appears below:

1924 Negro World Series

GAME	DATE	LOCATION	ATTND.	SCORE
1	Friday, Oct. 3	Shibe Park, Philadelphia	5,366	Kansas City 6, Hilldale 2
2	Saturday, Oct. 4	Shibe Park, Philadelphia	8,661	Hilldale 11, Kansas City 0
3	Sunday, Oct. 5	Bugle Field, Baltimore	5,503	Kansas City 6, Hilldale 6 (13 inn.)

GAME	DATE	LOCATION	ATTND.	SCORE
4	Monday, Oct. 6	Bugle Field, Baltimore	584	Hilldale 4, Kansas City 3
5	Saturday, Oct. 11	Muehlenbach Park, Kansas City	3,891	Hilldale 5, Kansas City 2
6	Sunday, Oct. 12	Muehlenbach Park, Kansas City	8,885	Kansas City 6, Hilldale 5
7	Tuesday, Oct. 14	Muehlenbach Park, Kansas City	2,539	Kansas City 4, Hilldale 3 (12 inn.)
8	Saturday, Oct. 18	Schorling's Park, Chicago	2,608	Kansas City 3, Hilldale 2
9	Sunday, Oct. 19	Schorling's Park, Chicago	6,271	Hilldale 5, Kansas City 3
10	Monday, Oct. 20	Schorling's Park, Chicago	1,549	Kansas City 5, Hilldale 0

Duel of Two Dark Aces: The Showdown Between Willie Foster and Bullet Rogan

In 1926 the defending Negro National League Champion Kansas City Monarchs won the first half of the league's split season and faced the Chicago American Giants, winners of the second half, in a best five-of-nine playoff for the league championship.

The Monarchs were attempting to extend their consecutive streak of pennants to four, while the American Giants were playing their first season in the franchise's 17-year history without Rube Foster at the helm. Foster, who had suffered a nervous breakdown the previous year, was replaced by his trusted lieutenant, David Malarcher. The new skipper's ace pitcher was Rube's younger half-brother, Willie Foster. The Monarchs' ace hurler was manager Bullet Rogan.

These two dark aces were to play vital roles on the final day of the Championship play-off to determine which team would face the Eastern Colored League Champion Atlantic City Bacharach Giants in the Negro World Series.

Beginning September 18, the first four games of the playoff were played in Kansas City, where the Monarchs won the first three games in front of the hometown fans, by scores of 4–3, 6–5, and 5–0, before the visitors finally salvaged the last game in KC, edging the Monarchs, 4–3.

The series moved to Chicago's Schorling Park for the remainder of the games. In the Chicago opener, played Saturday, September 25, Rogan and Foster opposed each other for the first time in the Series, and the red-hot Monarchs won convincingly, giving Rogan an 11–5 victory over Foster, who "was unable to survive a barrage of base hits in the fourth" inning and was relieved by George Harney and Willie Powell. The win moved the Monarchs to within one game of claiming the pennant.

With their backs to the wall, the American Giants fought back to take the Sunday game, 2–0, behind Rube Currie's two-hit shutout. Rain washed out the Monday game, which would eventually have an unforeseen effect on the outcome of the Series.

When play resumed Tuesday, the hometown fans watched enthusiastically as their American Giants eked out another 4–3 victory with a walk-off run in the ninth inning. Kansas City's failure to nail the game down forced the two teams to the final day and — due to the Monday rain-out — the scheduling of a doubleheader on Wednesday in order for the winner to travel east to play the ECL champion Bacharach Giants in the Negro World Series, beginning October 1.

After the Monarchs had won the first three games and four of the first five, the American Giants had clawed back, but now entered the final day still needing to win both games of the twin bill to advance to the Negro World Series and make that trip to Philadelphia.

The 1926 Negro National League pennant race came down to a doubleheader between the two contending teams on the last day of the season. The Chicago American Giants' Willie Foster (pictured) faced the Kansas City Monarchs' Bullet Rogan with the championship hanging in the balance.

In the first game of the doubleheader, Chicago ace Willie Foster took the mound. Monarchs ace Bullet Rogan decided to oppose him in a showdown between the two future Hall of Famers. The two dark aces battled evenly for eight innings, each whitewashing the other team to send the game into the ninth inning in a scoreless deadlock.

The left-handed Foster took the mound for the ninth frame and retired the side to continue his scoreless skein of innings. The right-handed Rogan took the mound in the bottom half of the inning and was within one out of matching Foster's scoreless streak.

The potential winning tally reached base when diminutive speedster Stanford Jackson beat out a slow roller to third baseman Newt Joseph. Willie

Foster then aided his own cause with a sacrifice bunt, moving Jackson into scoring position. Rogan bore down and fanned Jelly Gardner for the second out, but the left-handed swinging Sandy Thompson stepped into the batter's box and connected with a two-out base hit down the left-field line that landed fair by two feet and chased home Jackson with the winning run. The walk-off hit kept the Chicago hopes alive for a victory in the second game and the championship.

Both pitchers yielded seven hits, but Foster exhibited better control, issuing only one base on balls, while Rogan walked five. The *Chicago Defender* called the matchup "a helluva pitchers' battle," which was truly an apt description.

The outcome was uncertain until the very end, and both teams had earlier opportunities to seize the day. In the eighth inning, both teams threatened to break the scoreless deadlock.

In the top half of the inning, Wade Johnston led off with a double and was sacrificed to third by Newt Allen, bringing up the Monarchs' two top hitters.

Next up was future Hall of Fame slugger Cristobal Torriente, who hit a team high .381. The burly outfielder had played with the American Giants for eight years before this season and had been traded, in part, because of his predilection for the nightlife.

The temperamental Cuban had quit the Monarchs in mid-August over a dispute with ownership about the lack of reimbursement for a lost diamond ring. His time out of the lineup probably cost the Monarchs the second-half title, which would have negated the need for this playoff.

Now was his chance for atonement. The left-handed batter faced the left-handed Foster, who had been his teammate before the trade. Undaunted, Foster fanned the dangerous Torriente, who would finish the playoff with a .407 batting average. Next up was the clean-up hitter Newt Joseph, and Foster coaxed him to pop up to end the threat.

In the bottom half of the inning, Monarchs first baseman Lem Hawkins saved a go-ahead run with a shoestring catch and a "fast double-play."

In the top of the ninth inning, the Monarchs mounted another rally in an effort to break the scoreless deadlock. With one out, switch-hitter Dink Mothel singled and Bullet Rogan connected for his fourth base hit in the game, sending Mothel to second, but he overran the base and left fielder Thompson's "lightening throw" [sic] caught him off the base to kill the threat.

Then came the dramatic finish in the bottom of the ninth, when the American Giants scored the winning tally, as described earlier.

The boxscore of this classic showdown follows:

BOXSCORE

KANSAS CITY MONARCHS	AB	R	H	O	A	E	CHICAGO AMERICAN GIANTS	AB	R	H	O	A	E
Johnston lf	3	0	1	2	0	0	Gardner rf	4	0	1	1	0	0
Allen ss	3	0	1	0	2	1	Thompson lf	4	0	2	3	0	0
Torriente cf	4	0	0	0	0	0	Brown 1b	3	0	0	12	0	0
Joseph 3b	3	0	0	2	1	0	Hines c	3	0	1	3	1	0
McNair rf	4	0	0	0	0	0	Sweatt cf	4	0	2	0	0	0
Mothel 2b	4	0	1	2	2	0	Malarcher 3b	3	0	0	4	5	0
Rogan p	4	0	4	0	3	0	Williams 2b	4	0	0	3	3	0
Hawkins 1b	3	0	0	13	0	0	Jackson ss	4	1	1	1	1	1
Duncan c	3	0	0	7	1	0	Foster p	2	0	0	0	1	0
Totals	31	0	7	26*	9	1	Totals	31	1	7	27	11	1

*Two out when winning run scored.

	1	2	3	4	5	6	7	8	9		
Kansas City Monarchs	0	0	0	0	0	0	0	0	0	=	0
Chicago American Giants	0	0	0	0	0	0	0	1		=	1

Errors—Jackson, Allen. Two-base hit—Johnston. Runs batted in—Gardner. Stolen bases—None. Hit by Pitcher—None. Bases on balls—off Rogan 5; off Foster 1. Struck out—by Rogan 7; by Foster 3.

This was the most critical game of the series. Momentum was now on the side of the Chicago American Giants, with the showdown looming ominously.

By mutual agreement, the second game had been shortened to a five-inning contest to enable the winning team to leave in time to make the opening game of the World Series in the east.

With the championship on the line, Foster chose to attempt an iron-man performance and pitch both ends of the doubleheader. When Rogan saw him warming up before the game, he picked up the challenge and attempted the same iron man performance.

Thus, the team's respective aces — Rogan and Foster — faced off again in the second game with the championship hanging on the outcome. Rising to the occasion again in the deciding game, Foster hung a second shutout on the Monarchs, limiting the visitors to two hits in taking a 5–0 victory in the abbreviated five-inning game. The Chicago hitters wasted no time in reaching Rogan, scoring three times in the first inning and adding another pair of runs in the second frame, while piling up eight hits in their four innings of batting.

After spinning two shutouts in the same day to claim the NNL pennant, Willie Foster and the American Giants left Chicago Wednesday evening in order to arrive in the east Friday morning and prepare for the opener of the Negro World Series, which was played at Shibe Park in Philadelphia.

The American Giants went on to win the best five-of-nine Negro World

Series, defeating the Atlantic City Bacharach Giants, five game to three, with two ties.

Willie Foster pitched the clinching victory.

This account of the dramatic duel to determine the 1926 Negro National League Championship, which was waged between the two greatest black pitchers in the league's history, has never before been published.

The 1933 East-West All-Star Game: The First East-West Classic

Billed as the "Game of Games" the first East-West All-Star Game was played Sunday, September 10, 1933, at Comiskey Park. Promptly at 2:30, on a dark, dreary day and amid a drizzle that threatened to escalate into a storm, the umpires emerged from the home dugout "like groundhogs searching for that proverbial shadow" and set the historic game in motion with a stentorian call of "Play Ball!"

After the ceremonial first pitch was tossed out by *Chicago Defender* attorney Nathan K. McGill, 20,000 howling fans watched as Chicago American Giants ace lefthander Willie Foster took the mound for the West, hitched up his pants and delivered the game's first pitch to Cool Papa Bell, the East's leadoff batter. The first game of what was to become an annual All-Star classic was under way.

In an exciting contest, the lead changed hands five times in the game. Mule Suttles hit the first All-Star home run, and counted the game-winning hit among his three RBI, but the choice for the game's MVP would have to be Willie Foster. Although he had been suffering from a sore arm for the previous two weeks — with no rule prohibiting pitching more than three innings — the gritty left-hander pitched the entire game for the victorious West squad in the inaugural contest.

Following is a complete play-by-play account, the corresponding box score, and additional information about this historic game.

1933 East-West All-Star Game Play by Play

First Inning

East — *Foster pitching for the West.* Bell flied out to Davis; Dixon was out on a pop fly to Wells on the outfield grass; Charleston lined out to Morney, who made a leaping catch. *No hits; no runs; no errors; none left on base.*

Mule Suttles hit the first home run in All-Star history in the inaugural East-West Game. Two years later he again rose to the occasion with a walk-off, three-run homer off Martin Dihigo in the 11th inning.

West — *Streeter pitching for the East.* Stearnes struck out; Wells also fanned; Davis flied out to Bell. *No hits; no runs; no errors; none left on base.*

Second Inning

East — Mackey was called out on strikes; Wilson singled sharply to left field; Lundy grounded into a double play, Wells to Morney to Suttles. *One hit; no runs; no errors; none left on base.*

West — Radcliffe flied out to Dixon; Suttles rolled out, Lundy to Charleston; Morney struck out. *No hits; no runs; no errors; none left on base.*

Third Inning

East — Harris walked; Russell sacrificed, Foster to Suttles, Harris going to second; Streeter fanned; Bell flied out to Stearnes. *No hits; no runs; no errors; one left on base.*

West — Bankhead singled with a deep grounder towards the hole at shortstop that Lundy could not come up with; Brown sacrificed, Wilson to Charleston, Bankhead going to second; Foster struck out; Stearnes lined a screaming single to right field, Bankhead scoring; Stearnes was out attempting to steal second, Mackey to Russell. *Two hits; one run; no errors; none left on base. West leads, 1–0.*

Fourth Inning

East — Dixon walked; Charleston was hit by a pitched ball; Mackey fanned, while Dixon and Charleston executed a perfect double steal; Wilson reached first on a fielder's choice, when Morney fumbled his grounder and threw wildly to the plate in a hurried attempt to get the runner, allowing both Dixon and Charleston to score on his throwing error, with Wilson advancing to second; Lundy walked; *Cornelius begins warming up in the bullpen for the West.* Harris reached first on Morney's error, loading the bases; Russell squeezed Wilson home, with a bunt down the first base line, Foster to Suttles, with Lundy and Harris also advancing; Streeter rolled out, Morney to Suttles. *No hits; three runs; two errors; two left on base. East takes the lead, 3–1.*

West — Wells doubled to left field; Davis rapped a double to left-center, scoring Wells; Radcliffe fouled out to Mackey; Suttles hit a scorching home run into the upper deck of the left-center field stands, scoring Davis ahead of him; Morney flied out to Harris; Bankhead grounded out, Lundy to Charleston. *Three hits; three runs; no errors; none left on base. West regains the lead, 4–3.*

Fifth Inning

East—Bell was out on a hard grounder, Wells to Suttles; Dixon beat out a perfect bunt down the third base line; Charleston was hit by a pitched ball, Dixon advancing to second; Mackey's Texas Leaguer to center field loaded the bases; Wilson singled to left-center field, scoring Dixon and Charleston, Mackey going to third; Lundy hit a long, high fly out to Bankhead, and Mackey was called out for leaving third too soon on an attempt to score (when Brown relayed Bankhead's throw home back to Radcliffe, who had called for the ball to make the appeal). *Three hits; two runs; no errors; none left on base. East regains the lead, 5–4.*

West—Brown drove a hard triple to center field over Bell's head, but Lundy threw him out at the plate on a relay from Bell, with Mackey making the tag; Foster rolled out, Lundy to Charleston; Stearnes also grounded out, Lundy to Charleston. *One hit; no runs; no errors; none left on base. East leads, 5–4.*

Sixth Inning

East—Harris fouled out to Brown; Russell was out on a hard grounder, Wells to Suttles; Streeter flied out to Bankhead near the wall. *No hits; no runs; no errors; none left on base. East leads, 5–4.*

West—Wells singled to center field; Davis sacrificed, Wilson to Charleston, Wells taking second; Radcliffe hit a terrific double down the third base line to left field, scoring Wells; *Hunter relieved Streeter for the East;* Suttles singled to deep right, advancing to second as Radcliffe scored; *While Suttles was batting, a drizzling rain began to fall and fans in the bleachers were allowed to scamper into the grandstands for cover;* Morney singled over second base, scoring Suttles; Bankhead was safe on a fielder's choice when he grounded to Lundy, who forced Morney at second base; Brown slapped what should have been a hit to right-center field, but Bankhead was out when he missed second en route to third base, Bell to Lundy to Russell, with Brown being credited with a fielder's choice. *Four hits; three runs; no errors; one left on base. West regains the lead, 7–5.*

Seventh Inning

East—Bell struck out; Dixon flied out to Davis; Charleston flied out to Stearnes. *No hits; no runs; no errors; none left on base. West leads, 7–5.*

West—Foster singled to center; *Britt relieved Hunter and Gibson replaced Mackey as catcher for the East. Manager Lloyd held a conference on the mound with Gibson, Charleston and Lundy.* Stearnes doubled to right, Foster taking third; Wells flied out to Bell, Foster scoring and Stearnes taking third; Davis doubled to right-center field, scoring Stearnes; Radcliffe singled to left, and went to second on Harris' error, Davis scoring; Suttles struck out; Morney popped out to Lundy. *Four hits; three runs; one error; one left on base. West leads, 10–5.*

Eighth Inning

East — Gibson singled to center; Johnson, *batting for Wilson,* also singled to center, Gibson stopping at second; Lundy lined out to Davis; *Cornelius and Bailey begin to warm up for the West.* Jenkins, *batting for Harris,* grounded out to Suttles unassisted, Gibson and Johnson advancing; Russell fouled out to Suttles near the dugout. *Two hits; no runs; no errors; two left on base. West leads, 10–5.*

West — Bankhead singled to right, stole second, then scored when Gibson's throwing error went through into short center field and he beat Bell's throw to the plate; Brown flied out to Jenkins; Foster grounded out, Lundy to Charleston; Stearnes was out on a foul pop fly to Johnson. *One hit; one run; one error; none left on base. West leads, 11–5.*

Ninth Inning

East — Britt singled softly to left-center; Bell made first and then went to second on Morney's throwing error, Britt advancing to third on the error; Dixon flied out to deep right-center, Stearnes making a fine running catch of the hard drive, with Britt scoring and Bell going to third; Charleston flied out to Davis, Bell scoring on the play; Gibson lined out to Davis in left field for the final out. *One hit; two runs; one error; none left on base. West won, 11–7.*

1933 East-West All-Star Game
Date: September 10, 1933
Score: West 11, East 7
Location: Comiskey Park, Chicago, IL
Attendance: 20,000

Boxscore

EAST

	AB	R	H	BI	A	PO	E
Cool Papa Bell cf	5	1	0	0	2	2	0
Rap Dixon rf	3	2	1	1	0	1	0
Oscar Charleston 1b	2	2	0	1	0	7	0
Biz Mackey c	3	0	1	0	1	6	0
x — Josh Gibson c	2	0	1	0	0	1	1

WEST

	AB	R	H	BI	A	PO	E
Turkey Stearnes cf	5	1	2	1	0	3	0
Willie Wells ss	3	2	2	1	3	1	0
Steel Arm Davis lf	3	2	2	2	0	5	0
Alex Radcliffe 3b	4	1	2	1	0	1	0
Mule Suttles 1b	4	2	2	3	0	8	0

	AB	R	H	BI	A	PO	E		AB	R	H	BI	A	PO	E
Jud Wilson 3b	3	1	2	2	2	0	0	Leroy Morney 2b	4	0	1	1	2	2	3
y — Judy Johnson 3b	1	0	1	0	0	1	0	Sam Bankhead rf	4	2	2	0	1	2	0
Dick Lundy ss	3	0	0	0	7	2	0	Larry Brown c	3	0	1	0	1	5	0
Vic Harris lf	2	0	0	0	0	1	1	Willie Foster p	4	1	1	0	2	0	0
z — Fats Jenkins lf	1	0	0	0	0	1	0								
John Henry Russell 2b	2	0	0	1	0	2	0								
Sam Streeter p	3	0	0	0	0	0	0								
v — Bertrum Hunter p	0	0	0	0	0	0	0								
w — George Britt p	1	1	1	0	0	0	0								
Totals	31	7	7	5	12	24	2	Totals	34	11	15	9	9	27	3

v — relieved Streeter in 6th inning
w — relieved Hunter in 7th inning
x — replaced Mackey in 7th inning
y — batted for Wilson in 8th inning
z — batted for Harris in 8th inning

BATTING
2b: none
3b: none
hr: none
sb: Dixon, Charleston
cs: none
hbp: Charleston (2)
bb: Harris, Lundy, Dixon
so: Mackey (2), Streeter, Bell
sh: Russell (2)
sf: Dixon, Charleston
lob: 6
Fielding
dp: None

BATTING
2b: Stearnes, Wells, Davis (2), Radcliffe
3b: Brown
hr: Suttles
sb: Bankhead
cs: Stearnes (by Mackey)
hbp: none
bb: none
so: Stearnes, Wells, Morney, Foster, Suttles
sh: Brown, Davis
sf: Wells
lob: 2
Fielding
dp: Wells, Morney & Suttles; Bankhead & Radcliffe

PITCHING	IP	H	R	ER	BB	HP	SO	PITCHING	IP	H	R	ER	BB	HP	SO
Streeter (L)	5.1	7	6	6	0	0	4	Foster (W)	9	7	7	2	3	2	4
Hunter	0.2	4	2	2	0	0	0								
Britt	2.0	4	3	1	0	0	1								
Totals	8.0	15	11	9	0	0	5	Totals		9	7	7	2	3	2	4

	1	2	3	4	5	6	7	8	9		
EAST	0	0	0	3	2	0	0	2	=	7
WEST	0	0	1	3	0	3	3	1	x	=	11

The concept of a Negro League All-Star Game patterned after the Major League All-Star Game was the brainchild of two Pittsburgh sportswriters, Roy Sparrow and Bill Nunn, but the driving force behind making it a reality was Pittsburgh Crawfords owner Gus Greenlee, who enlisted fellow owners Tom Wilson of the Elite Giants and Robert Cole of the Chicago American Giants in the venture.

Barely more than two months after the Major League All-Star Game was inaugurated, Greenlee had shepherded the concept to fruition and the inaugural East-West All-Star game was played at Chicago's Comiskey Park, the same venue as the Major League game.

Playing under the direction of managers John Henry Lloyd (East) and Candy Jim Taylor (West), the first East-West Game featured ten stars who would eventually be inducted into the National Baseball Hall of Fame. The winning West squad featured four future inductees—Willie Wells, Turkey Stearnes, Mule Suttles, and winning pitcher Willie Foster. However, the East team, with six players who would be enshrined—Josh Gibson, Oscar Charleston, Cool Papa Bell, Judy Johnson, Biz Mackey and Jud "Boojum" Wilson—featured a preponderance of the future Hall of Famers.

An appropriate addendum to this game is a mention of the gritty performances of two starting players, one from each team. The West squad's Willie Foster had been suffering from a sore arm for two weeks prior to the All-Star classic—yet pitched a complete game. For the East, Dick Lundy played the entire game with an injured hand, which was not made known until revealed by another player after the game.

This summary, play-by-play account and box score of the inaugural East-West All-Star game was written in 1992 in anticipation of the upcoming 60th anniversary of the historic event, but has not been published until now.

It is an amalgamation of the accounts in several different period newspapers, including the Pittsburgh Courier, Kansas City Call, Chicago Defender, Baltimore Afro-American, *and* Philadelphia Tribune, *and is as complete and accurate as possible, considering the plethora of conflicting information that survives from the contemporary reports.*

The Baltimore Baseball Nobody Knows

In 1887, five years before the brawling Baltimore Orioles entered the National League, there existed a black team in the city called the Lord Baltimores. The league they played in survived barely a week, but the club's presence shows how Baltimore's black baseball roots reach much deeper into the past than is generally known.

Several decades later, the Harbor City boasted two of the most prominent black franchises of the halcyon days of America's Negro Leagues, between 1920 and 1950. Such legendary names as Roy Campanella, Satchel Paige and Leon Day put on the Baltimore uniform, and the end of each decade was punctuated by a championship arriving in Baltimore, the honors coming in 1929, 1939, and 1949.

In the following pages we'll take a look at these important contributors to Baltimore's baseball heritage. The first black ballclub to capture the city's attention was organized in 1916 as a regional semi-pro team under the ownership of two white businessmen, George Rossiter and Charles Spedden.

The Black Sox played most of their games at Bugle Field, a park on Biddle Street that was named after the Bugle Coat and Apron Supply Company. They also occasionally played at Westport Park (a.k.a. Maryland Park or Black Sox Park), or a third field called Druid Hill. The most notable characteristic of Bugle Field was an eight-foot-high embankment that ran up to the fence and made outfield play somewhat adventurous.

The franchise first commanded respect when it acquired spitballer Doc Sykes in 1920, and their ace hurler remained with the team until 1924, when he was released because his dental practice prevented him from traveling with the team. Sykes' best season was 1922, when he posted a 22–4 record and the Black Sox were named "Champions of the South."

That year also marked the debut of a young player from the sandlots of the Foggy Bottom section of Washington, D.C. His name was Jud Wilson and he became the greatest player in Black Sox history.

Behind Wilson's bat, the Black Sox immediately reeled off a dozen consecutive victories. The new kid was christened "Babe Ruth" Wilson by the press, but the players preferred to call him "Boojum" (pronounced "bu-ZHOOM) because of the sound the ball made when his line drives hit the fence. Wilson finished the 1922 season with a .390 batting average and led the team in home runs. The Sox had found the cornerstone for constructing a championship ballclub.

Filled with optimism, the Black Sox became charter members of the Eastern Colored League in 1923, but finished in last place. Undaunted, but unhappy with his team's performance, Spedden hired veteran Pete Hill as manager the following year and bolstered the team by signing shortstop John Beckwith, who had been released by the Homestead Grays, along with former Indianapolis ABCs third baseman Henry Blackman and outfielder Crush Holloway. The Black Sox moved into contention, but suffered a tragic setback with the premature death of Blackman.

The slugging Beckwith brought tremendous excitement to games. He hit .417 in 1924 and tied Oscar Charleston for the league home run title, while teaming with Jud Wilson, who hit .385, to provide a powerful offensive tandem. The Sox rose all the way to second place.

Beckwith became one of the highest paid players in the league, as well as

Pictured are three sluggers who appeared with the Baltimore Black Sox at some point during their careers: Jud "Boojum" Wilson, Oscar "Heavy" Johnson, and John Beckwith. The player partially pictured on the extreme left is unidentified.

one of the most popular with the fans, but the moody superstar was as temperamental as he was talented. The Black Sox had appointed Beckwith team captain to keep him in Baltimore, and even acceded to his demand that he be appointed manager before signing for the 1925 season. But his players soon began to voice their disenchantment with his performance at the helm. After facing a fine and suspension by the league for assaulting an umpire, Beckwith was removed as manager and left the team, demanding an unconditional release. This wasn't necessarily good for Black Sox fans. At the time of his departure, the slugger was leading the league in both batting (.429) and home runs (13).

In 1926 legendary first baseman Ben Taylor was appointed playing manager, and he dispatched Beckwith to the Harrisburg Giants. Taylor also replaced other established stars with younger players and, as the team dropped in the standings, his managerial decisions attracted even greater criticism from the media. Taylor spent three troubled years in charge.

The league was having its troubles, too. It suffered from a lack of organization and poor cooperation between owners, and collapsed altogether in the spring of 1928.

But the Black Sox survived. During the winter the American Negro League was organized and the Black Sox fielded their best team ever, winning the 1929 pennant in the league's only year of existence. Key to the championship was the acquisition of three outstanding infielders — second baseman Frank Warfield, shortstop Dick Lundy, and third baseman Oliver Marcelle. With Wilson at first, they became known as "The Million Dollar Infield."

Warfield, who had been appointed playing manager, provided the aggressive leadership that was responsible for much of the team's success. A few years later, during a game in Cuba, he and Marcelle — who were opponents at the time — engaged in a ferocious fight. Fortunately a relatively harmonious atmosphere prevailed between them during their only season together in Black Sox uniforms.

The Black Sox finished with a record of 49–21. Laymon Yokely, who had spun a no-hitter two years earlier, led the pitchers with a 15–6 mark. Offensive leaders were Rap Dixon (.432 BA, 16 HR, 25 SB) and Wilson (.405 BA, 11 HR, 22 SB). Dixon's 14 consecutive hits remains a Negro Leagues record.

The high cost of transportation, not to mention the anticipated poor attendance, prohibited a World Series, but the Black Sox won seven of nine post-season exhibition games played against the white All-Star team organized by major leaguer Fritz Maisel. These contests had become an annual tradition since Rossiter first arranged with Connie Mack to bring his Philadelphia A's to town for an exhibition against the Black Sox. The teams would play an autumn series until the weather grew too cool to continue, and many major league stars played. On the mound for the A's in 1929, for instance, were pitchers Howard Ehmke, coming off his record-setting 13-strikeout World Series performance, and Eddie Rommel, completing a 12–2 season with the World Champions. Other greats to have taken part at some point included Lefty Grove, Jimmie Foxx, Al Simmons, Mule Haas, and Hack Wilson.

Returning to independent status in 1930 — when there were no leagues, teams organized their schedules among themselves — the Black Sox added slugger Mule Suttles, star outfielder Fats Jenkins, and pitching sensation Satchel Paige. As the season progressed, however, the Sox began to suffer from an attrition of talent, losing the three new arrivals as well as Dixon and, in 1931, Wilson.

As the Depression deepened, the Black Sox' performance level declined and they ran into financial trouble. To restore prestige and solvency, the team installed Lundy as manager, began playing under the lights at Bugle Field — the Major Leagues would not play night games until 1935 — and in 1932 joined the ill-fated East-West League. The league folded in mid-year, forcing the Black Sox, who were in first place at the time, back to independent play.

A final attempt to salvage the franchise was made under new owner Joe Cambria, who entered the Black Sox in the new Negro National League when it was resurrected in 1933. The players were taken off salary and the ballclub operated on a percentage basis, but things didn't go well. The Sox played poorly, and eventually dropped out of the league and disbanded.

The first East-West All-Star Game was played that year, as was the first National League-American League Game, but not a single Baltimore player was selected, although several former players were.

A new edition of the Black Sox was organized by Jack Farrell, the club's only black owner, in 1934. Despite the signing of such promising new youngsters as Leon Day, the franchise put on a dismal showing and was terminated. The Baltimore Black Sox name was never again used by a major league black team.

Following the demise of the Black Sox, Baltimore went without a black professional team until, with the help of Dick Powell, the Elite Giants franchise moved from Washington, D.C. to Baltimore in 1938. The Elites had started in Nashville, Tennessee, and moved to Columbus, Ohio, before locating in the nation's Capital. After arriving in Baltimore, they remained a fixture for 13 years.

The Homestead Grays dominated the league back then, and although the Elites' first season in Baltimore was inauspicious, it was the Grays that the Elites overcame in winning the 1939 championship.

That year, under Felton Snow, the Elites finished third and proceeded to a four-team playoff tournament. In the final series, spitball ace Bill Byrd and lefthander Jonas Gaines won as the Elites took the Jacob Ruppert Memorial

Trophy — named for the New York Yankees owner and emblematic of the Negro National League Championship — by beating the Grays in Yankee Stadium.

In the middle of 1939, a 17-year-old by the name of Roy Campanella took over the regular catching assignments. Other acquisitions were shortstop Pee Wee Butts and first baseman Red Moore. The Elites' offense was headed by Bill Wright, who led the league with a .488 average.

In 1940, the Elites finished second behind the Grays, but in 1941, with Wright and Sammy T. Hughes gone to the Mexican League and Henry Kimbro traded, they fell to third place. Two Elites achieved significant individual accomplishments. Gaines struck out 19 batters in an inter-league contest with the St. Louis Stars, and Campanella won the Negro League All-Star Game's MVP award.

In 1942, with Wright, Hughes, and Kimbro back in the fold, the Elites were in contention again with the Grays. But during the stretch drive, Campanella was showcased in an exhibition game in Cleveland and, because he'd left the team without permission, was fined $250 and suspended indefinitely by owner and league president Tom Wilson. Campanella then played in Mexico for the rest of the season and, without their clean-up hitter, the Elites finished behind the Grays.

Over the next five years, the ballclub suffered a series of setbacks. They lost Hughes to military service during World War II. Upon his return, he retired after only one season. Wright stayed in Mexico for the remainder of his career, except for the 1945 season when he hit .371 with the Elites. After his year in Mexico, Campanella returned to the Elites, where he posted averages of .350 and .365 before being grabbed by the Brooklyn Dodgers in 1946.

Byrd's clutch pitching, Butts' stellar fielding, and Kimbro's solid hitting (.371 and .363 in 1946 and 1947) provided stability during these years. But it was not until 1948, the year before the demise of the Negro National League, that the Elites challenged again. Rallying behind Byrd (11–6) and Gaines (9–4), the team won the first half of the split season, before being swept by their old rivals, the Grays, in the playoffs.

In the off-season, playing manager Lennie Pearson and veteran pitcher Leon Day were obtained from the Newark Eagles and helped win the Elites their final championship. Following the demise of the Negro National League, the Elites had joined the Negro American League and won the Eastern Division title before sweeping the Western Division's Chicago American Giants in four straight games to capture the pennant.

The next year was the Elites' last in Baltimore. Future Brooklyn Dodgers stars Joe Black and Junior Gilliam represented the club on the All-Star squad, bringing the total who had worn the Elite Giants uniform in the All-Star Games during the years when the franchise was based in Baltimore to 20.

The Elite Giants and the city of Baltimore proved a good mesh, and the team's identity remained affixed with their home city through the 1950 season, when the trickle of black ballplayers into organized baseball turned into a spate and the quality of play in the Negro Leagues deteriorated accordingly. Both media and fans abandoned the Negro Leagues teams and the owners suffered severe financial losses. Powell sold the Elites to William Bridgeforth in the spring of 1951. After returning to Nashville for a final season, the team was dissolved.

Less than 20 years after the Black Sox had closed up shop, the Elites were gone as well. Baseball's color barriers were soon to fall, while the Negro Leagues which had spawned so many great players had become little more than a treasured memory.

This article first appeared in the 1993 All-Star Game Yearbook, *which featured the black teams in Baltimore's baseball history.*

Since this article appeared, five players mentioned have been elected to the Hall of Fame. Jud Wilson, who was identified as "the greatest player in Black Sox history," was inducted in 2006, along with Pete Hill, Mule Suttles and Ben Taylor. Leon Day, who was featured in a sidebar titled "Baltimore's Living Legend" in addition to being mentioned in the main article, was elected in 1995. The author submits that the exclusion of Dick Lundy, who was passed over in 2006 by the special committee, constitutes a travesty.

Two other Baltimore Black Sox players later achieved a degree of notoriety. Rap Dixon, while a member of a black All-Star team touring the Orient, is credited with hitting the longest home run in the history of Japanese baseball and was presented with a cup by the emperor of Japan honoring him for his diamond exploits. Doc Sykes became a witness in the infamous Scottsboro Trial.

Boojum: The Most Ferocious Hitter and Fiercest Competitor Ever to Play the Game

They called him "Boojum" because of the sound his line drives made when they hit the fence during batting practice. In later years he was described by the press as "probably the hardest hitter Negro baseball has seen." His name was Jud Wilson and he was a savage, pure hitter who hit with power and was at his best in the clutch.

Homestead Grays owner Cum Posey, whose baseball career (1911–1946) spanned virtually the entire existence of the Negro Leagues, considered Boojum to be the most dangerous and consistent hitter in black baseball, and selected him to his All-Time All-American team for a national magazine in 1945.

The 5' 8", 185-pound, left-handed slugger demonstrated a disdain for all pitchers and, when in the batter's box, he sometimes taunted opposing hurlers by daring them to throw the ball. He hit both right-handers and left-handers, regardless of pitching styles, repertoires or exalted reputations. This included the legendary Satchel Paige, who considered Boojum one of the two best hitters ever in black baseball.

Smokey Joe Williams is generally paired with Satchel as the two top pitchers in the history of black baseball. When Williams selected the three top hitters that he had faced during his career, Boojum was at the top of the list.

Other former Negro League players also concur with the recognition of Wilson among the all-time greatest hitters in baseball. Two of these are Hall of Famers Monte Irvin and Buck Leonard, who were also highly regarded hitters in the Negro Leagues.

"On the field he was poetry in motion as a hitter," Irvin said. "He was smooth and he could really hit that ball. He could hit *any* kind of pitching. *And* he was a fierce competitor."

Leonard recalled, "When Josh Gibson jumped to the Mexican League

Satchel Paige called Jud Wilson one of the two best hitters he ever saw. The ferocious slugger earned the nickname "Boojum" from the sound his line drives made when they hit the outfield fences.

in 1940, Sam Bankhead went with him and we also lost Henry Spearman, our third baseman. Losing those ballplayers weakened our team quite a bit, but we added Boojum Wilson to help make up for some of the hitting that we lost. He could hit, even then, and he was in the evening of his career. He helped us with his bat. *And* he liked to win."

The records bear this out as he consistently hit in the high .300s and even topped the .400 level on occasions. His lifetime statistics show an impressive .345 batting average in the Negro Leagues, a .455 average in the East-West All-Star games, a .372 average and two batting titles in the Cuban Winter League, and a .442 ledger against major leaguers in exhibitions.

The human hitting machine was a physical oddity, with a big upper body, a small waist, slightly bowed legs and a pigeon-toed gait. He earned his baseball reputation with his hitting prowess but, although he was awkward, he was fast and sure afield and could play adequately at either infield corner.

Boojum was a rugged competitor and played third base by keeping everything in front of him, knocking the ball down with his chest and then throwing the batter out, and was described as "a crude but effective workman." Although lacking grace, he studied the art of defense and was generous with sharing the knowledge that he had acquired with younger ballplayers — even those on opposing teams.

One of the beneficiaries of Boojum's experience was a rookie infielder with the 1933 Detroit Stars named Ray Dandridge, who is regarded as the greatest defensive third baseman in the history of black baseball and was inducted into the Hall of Fame in 1987. Dandridge discussed those early days of his professional career:

> When I was a rookie we would sit outside the hotels at night, and I'd hear the old-timers talk about each ballplayer around the league. You know, talk about what *this* ballplayer could do and what *that* ballplayer could do.... I'm sitting there, a rookie, and I ain't saying nothing. But I say to myself, "I'm going to see if that can happen." And it *could* happen. That's where I learned a lot about fielding and everything else.
>
> And I had a couple of guys who helped me. I used to wait for the ball to take another hop, and a lot of those guys would beat it out. Jud Wilson, who played at Philadelphia when I was a rookie, used to tell me, "When the ball makes a big hop, always come in on it." I tried and it came out good and I was getting those guys out. Now, this guy on another team is telling me how to field and I'm listening and learning. And that's the reason I don't doubt anything. If anybody wants to teach me anything, I'm going to try it out and see if it works. I ain't doubting anybody's word. Not those old-timers. Because some of those old-timers were *great*. Believe me, if I tell you!

One of those old-timers who were "great" was Boojum. With a hunger for hitting and a thirst for victory, on the playing field Jud Wilson took a back seat to no one. He could hit anything thrown to him, and his strong will to win and aggressiveness on the diamond added another dimension to his team value.

Boojum's intensity at the plate carried over to every aspect of his play on the baseball field, where he was a fierce competitor, hard loser, and habitual brawler. The bull-necked battler was fearless, ill-tempered and equally known for his batting and his fighting. Teammates, opponents and umpires all feared the fury of the fiery-eyed, quick-tempered strongman, who was considered one of the "big four of the big badmen" of black baseball.

Although his on-field conduct improved slightly as he got older, he never eliminated his need to exercise greater restraint in his behavior. He had the reputation as "the toughest man to handle in baseball." In 1925, this led to his arrest on a "frame-up" assault charge, which was just one of many incidents that resulted from his temperament.

Boojum was mean and nasty on the field but, when the uniform came off, he was a genial person away from on-the-field competition. In addition to helping young players with batting and fielding tips, he developed a fast friendship with one youngster — Jake Stephens, a little shortstop, who became his roommate on three different ballclubs: the Homestead Grays, Pittsburgh Crawfords and Philadelphia Stars. Although the roomies were very good friends, the feisty infielder sometimes caused problems for Boojum in various ways, and the response varied accordingly.

One incident occurred in Chicago after the East-West All-Star Game, when Stephens returned to their hotel room around two o'clock in the morning after a night of carousing, and roused Boojum, who was sound asleep. Awakened and angry, the brawny Boojum grabbed his boisterous little roomie and held him out of the 16th-story window by the leg while Jake kicked his arm with his free foot. Boojum simply changed hands, like a gunfighter's "border shift," with Stephens kicking and screaming 16 stories above the pavement. The next morning Boojum's arms were covered with bruises where Jake had kicked him trying to loosen his grip. Fortunately, the efforts were unsuccessful or Stephens would have dropped 16 floors to his death.

Another time, when the pair were playing together with the Philadelphia Stars, Stephens was arguing with an umpire about a call, and Boojum intervened by positioning himself between the two parties as a buffer, keeping his "buddy" behind him and away from the ump. But the scrappy Stephens reached around him and hit the ump in the face, and the arbiter thought it was Boojum and put him out of the game. The volatile Boojum exploded, and the police had to come out onto the field to subdue his fury. It took three policemen, freely using their blackjacks, to put him inside the patrol wagon and take him to jail. After being released he threatened to kill his little friend, and Stephens was so scared that he left town.

Hall of Fame pitcher Leon Day remembered another occasion, from the days when he had watched the Black Sox as a youngster in Baltimore, when he witnessed the police using nightsticks on Boojum. Boojum was one of the roughest players in the league and nobody messed with him. Or, as Leon phrased it: "Nobody living!" Then he added:

Not even the police. Boojum used to fight them in Baltimore. It would take the whole police department to lock him up. He'd knock them down just as fast as they'd get up, and they'd hit him in the head with that 'billy' and he wasn't feeling nothing. Boojum was crazy. He was *crazy*! I ain't kidding.

Day wasn't kidding. On the field, Boojum was vicious, and especially rough on umpires. In fact, he was a devil from an umpire's worst nightmare. The men in blue didn't want Boojum mad at them. His fights on the field are legion, and sometimes they carried over to the clubhouse. Once the menacing strongman, still incensed over what he thought was a bad call by umpire Phil Cockrell during the game, followed the former-pitcher-turned-umpire into the locker room where he grabbed the arbiter by the skin of his chest and lifted him off the floor, berating him for cheating them out of the game. His fury did not abate until his teammate Crush Holloway picked up a bat and interceded on behalf of the ump. Only then did Boojum gain control of his temper and release the umpire. An umpire's physical safety was always in jeopardy — especially when Boojum was involved.

Monte Irvin recalls the perils that Negro League umpires faced on a regular basis:

> Players and fans in the Negro leagues got on umpires worse than they did in the white major leagues. It got so bad that a couple of the umpires carried pistols. Big Fred McCreary started carrying a pistol in his pocket, and Phil Cockrell had a gun, too, because somebody was always threatening him. They had to protect themselves because some players would come after them with a bat. And those guys would hit anybody.
>
> The worst incident I ever saw was when the Eagles were playing the Grays at Griffith Stadium in Washington, D.C. We had an umpire in the league by the name of Pop Turner, who was a graduate of North Carolina Central University in Durham, North Carolina, and he was umpiring the game. Boojum Wilson came up to bat for the Grays in the ninth inning, with the bases loaded and the winning run on base. Turner called Boojum out on strikes on a questionable pitch for the last out.
>
> Both teams and the umps were dressing in the same clubhouse. After the game, Pop was over in a corner of the clubhouse getting dressed. Boojum came in and confronted him. 'Why didn't you call the goddamned play right, you blind son-of-a-bitch?' Then Boojum picked up a bat and said, 'I ought to take this bat and bust your goddamn brains out.' And he drew back with the club end of the bat and was going to hit Pop with the butt of it. Pop Turner just happened to have the presence of mind to duck under it, and the bat splattered all the plaster off the wall.
>
> If Boojum had hit the man he would have killed him! We all grabbed Boojum and tried to cool him down. And somebody brought the cops into the locker room and escorted Turner out. That shows how dangerous it was sometimes. Some of the guys were really crazy and that's why some of the umpires got in a habit of carrying a small gun in their pockets to protect themselves from some of those big bastards.

Boojum was a tough character. I've heard a lot of stories about him hitting players, fans, umpires, and even cops. He was bad, but you could kid with Boojum. You could cajole him a little bit. But Boojum was no piece of cake.

Even during his declining years, Boojum's predilection for fighting continued to manifest itself at home games, at away games, and even on the road between games. Buck Leonard, who played with Boojum for six years with the Homestead Grays, recalls some of these incidents — both on the field and off the playing field — from Boojum's last years in the Negro Leagues:

> I *do* know that he was called one of the 'four big badmen' of black baseball. I *don't* know how he got that reputation but I would say he earned it. In one game against the Bushwicks, he got mad about the umpire's decision and chased the umpire, and the police had to come out there and chase him off the field.
>
> Now, he hit a fellow one time when we were on the road traveling. We went down to Butler, Pennsylvania, to play one night. We were on the bus and a white fellow passed us in a one seat, two-door Ford and as soon as he got his front end against us he cut in too soon and ran us off the road. Our bus driver, a fellow named Johnny Maynard, was driving the bus. We got back on the road and tried to catch up with the car but we couldn't overtake him until we started going downhill. Then we outran him and cut over in front of him and run him off the highway.
>
> And we stopped and three or four of us got out because we didn't know how many were in the other car. Boojum Wilson was one of them that got out with us. We didn't know the other driver was white when we got out, and we went back there and was asking him what did he mean by cutting over in front of us and running us off the road. And he said, well, he was sorry that he cut in front of us. And Boojum knocked him down just with these few words. Boojum didn't say a word. He let us do the talking and he did the hitting. That's why we were so surprised. We didn't intend to do no hitting.

The powder-keg hostility that Boojum exhibited late in his career with the Grays was rooted early in his career and extended to anything that he disliked. He disdained being out of the action and hated the bench almost as much as he hated umpires.

Often he refused to leave the lineup, even continuing to play with injuries that should have kept him inactive. In June of 1924, he was playing first base for the Baltimore Black Sox and was hobbled by a bad ankle, but insisted on playing. The same was true with other injuries.

Boojum defiantly crowded the plate when batting and was frequently hit by pitches. In the late summer of 1926, he was hit by a pitched ball and suffered a cracked bone in his right elbow, and was declared to be out for the season. But, against his doctor's advice, he was back in the lineup two weeks later and slammed two hits. A year later, in 1927, he suffered cuts when he and other Baltimore Black Sox players were in an automobile accident, but he refused to stay out of the lineup.

Ten years later, in June of 1937, his luck finally ran out when the Philadelphia Stars' team bus was hit by a car and his injury necessitated him missing an extended amount of playing time. Consequently, his swing was impaired from then on through the early part of the 1938 season.

However, his distaste for being away from the action never abated and, on another occasion, he played with three broken ribs. As late in his career as May of 1940, he was injured and impatiently hurried his return to the lineup.

Eventually, the accumulation of injuries from car wrecks, pitched baseballs, wild brawling and blows to the head from police batons took their toll, and coupled with the affliction of epilepsy, both his physical and mental health deteriorated.

In the latter stages of his career, he had to be hospitalized because of his diminished condition. In one World Series contest, while with the Grays, the game had to be halted because he was in the field at third base, drawing little circles in the dirt with his finger and completely oblivious to his surroundings.

Buck Leonard recalled the psychological breakdown and the circumstances leading up to it:

> He was in the evening of his career at that time, and he had spells — epileptic fits. Sometimes he would be right out on the field when it happened, so we would have to watch out for him. Sometimes he would have one and he would get down on his knees and start to making marks on the ground while the game was going on. We had to call time and go over there and get around him. Then we'd get him off the field and carry him into the clubhouse. Once he was drawing circles in the dirt during the game, and his wife came in the clubhouse after the game and took care of him. And he did things like that.
>
> And sometimes we'd be riding along on the bus and he would have a fit. But his wife had told us how to treat him when he had one. And sometimes we'd have to put a spoon or something in his mouth to keep him from biting his tongue. And his eyes would look glassy and blurry and look like he couldn't see so good. The spells would last about five or ten minutes and afterwards he would be weak. He would just get limp. Then for the next half hour or so he was kind of down. I think he anticipated a weakness. Sometimes we didn't let him play when he would have one on the day before a game. We never knew when he was going to have one.
>
> Once we were on the Jamesville ferry up in the top deck just to look out. And we looked around and he was standing there with his pants off. We had to gather around him and bring him back down to the bus on the lower deck and put his pants back on him. And we had to make him sit down and calm him down. When he had them spells it took something out of him. It took a half hour or so for him to settle down.
>
> We were in a restaurant one morning in Homestead and he had one of those spells. He was strong as hell. When he was in that kind of shape he was even stronger than ordinary. All of us were his friends, but a boy named Robert Gaston, our second string catcher, was closest to him. He was his friend and his roommate. We

called him Rab Roy. Rab Roy Gaston would get on one side and hold his hand and someone else would get on the other side and hold his hand to keep him quiet and try to relax him.

His wife used to tell us to not let him use salt and black pepper in his food but you can't keep a grown man from putting salt and black pepper in his food. We told him not to, but so far as preventing it we just couldn't do that.

If those spells bothered him he didn't show it. I don't know if he had them before he got with us or not. I never did find out. But he was having them from the beginning with us. But other than that, I didn't know of any problem that he had. He wasn't a heavy drinker that I know of. I never did know him to drink, but Jud Wilson played ball a long time before I was with him. I don't know what he did back then.

Buck's words, "back then," would extend back in time — before Boojum's second stint with the Grays began in 1940 — to his tryout with the Black Sox, when he first earned his nickname by booming line drives off the outfield fences.

In 1922, Boojum's first year with the Baltimore Black Sox, they were the Champions of the South with a record 49-12, and he peppered the walls with base hits, batting a fantastic .522 through mid–August. Although the youngster was homesick and wanted to go back to Foggy Bottom at one point in the season, he stayed with the club for nine years. During those years he matured as a baseball player, and terrorized pitchers, umpires and any others who inflamed his passions.

The Black Sox became charter members of the Eastern Colored League in 1923, Boojum's second season with the franchise, and remained in the league until it dissolved early in 1928. During these years Boojum's batting averages were .373, .377, .395, .346, .469, and .376.

After the ECL folded, the Black Sox joined the American Negro League, which was basically the same teams but in a league with a different name and under different leadership. With Boojum contributing a .350 batting average, the Black Sox won the pennant in 1929, the league's only year of existence. The following year the Sox played as an independent ballclub and Boojum batted .372 in his last full season in Baltimore.

The esteem that Boojum was accorded as a player is shown by a rumored trade that gained credibility in 1929, which would have sent him to the Homestead Grays in exchange for *both* Martin Dihigo and John Beckwith, two of black baseball's premier players.

During this time, Buck Leonard was still playing semi-pro ball in Rocky Mount, NC, but was learning about the Negro Leagues teams from reading African-American newspapers. He explained how he first learned about his future teammate:

> I was aware of the Negro National League's existence because I used to read about it in the Negro papers, but none of us had been up there and looked at it at that time.

My favorite player from the Negro Leagues was Boojum Wilson. He was a home run hitter, and played first base with the Baltimore Black Sox. I never saw him play when I was a youngster, I just read about him.

But in the latter years of his career he played with us on the Grays.

After leaving the Black Sox, Boojum was grabbed by Homestead Grays owner Cum Posey, and in 1931 he batted .323 and joined the other members (Chippy Britt, Oscar Charleston and Vic Harris) of the "big four badmen" of black baseball, who shared the same temperament, battling spirit, and fervent drive to win. Also on that team were veteran pitcher Smokey Joe Williams, rookie slugger Josh Gibson, and the colorful Ted "Double Duty" Radcliffe, who earned his nickname by playing on both ends of the battery.

In 1932 Boojum batted .356 and divided his playing time between the Homestead Grays and Pittsburgh Crawfords, with a brief interlude back with the Black Sox. The demand for his baseball talents were exemplified by that 1932 season, when he began the year as the playing manager of the Homestead Grays but switched in turn to the Baltimore Black Sox and the Pittsburgh Crawfords in the regular season. Then in the latter part of the season, he played with the Black Sox again in a series of exhibitions against a major league all-star team, while being sought by the Kansas City Monarchs to go with them on their Mexican tour.

He joined the Philadelphia Stars in 1933, and remained there for seven seasons, during which he was voted to the East-West All-Star team in the first three years and served as playing manager for the final three years.

As would be expected, in his capacity as manager after his appointment in 1937, he was a strict disciplinarian who did not tolerate loafing or grandstanding on the field. He hit a home run off the center field fence to break a tie and win his first game as manager. As a player he gave his best performance regardless of who was the manager, and he expected the same from the players under his authority.

That season he out-polled future Hall of Famer Ray Dandridge by a narrow margin in the All-Star vote, but he did not play in the contest due to an injury. His batting averages for the first five years in Philly were .354, .342, .324, 315 and .386 through the 1937 season, his first year at the helm. He remained in that capacity through the 1939 season when, after three seasons under his belt as a manager and a .373 batting average in his final season, he left the Stars and joined the Homestead Grays during their glory years of the 1940s.

At age 41, the grizzled veteran was well past his prime when he returned to the Homestead Grays for a second stint with Posey's ballclub that extended through the last six years of his career. Although he didn't play full-time during the latter seasons, he still hit for averages of .282, .340, .255, .350,

.417, and .288 for the years 1940–1945, and the Grays captured Negro National League pennants every year after his arrival.

During his career, he was an integral part of teams which are easily identifiable as some of the greatest teams in black baseball history. During a six-year stretch he starred with the 1929 Baltimore Black Sox, the 1931 Homestead Grays, the 1932 Pittsburgh Crawfords and the 1934 Philadelphia Stars.

All four teams were championship teams, with the Black Sox winning the American Negro League pennant, the Stars taking the Negro National League pennant, the Crawfords claiming an unofficial championship and the Grays winning a play-off for their championship.

Boojum captained this Grays team that is considered by many to be the greatest black team of all time. One prominent player from the team who concurred with this assessment was Ted "Double Duty" Radcliffe, who proclaimed loudly and proudly, "The 1931 Homestead Grays is the best team that I ever saw."

Boojum closed out his 24-year career at the age of 46, after his second stint with the Grays. Buck Leonard remembered his old teammate well, but lost contact with him after he left the Grays: "He lived right in the city limits of Washington, D.C., and they said he was originally from a neighborhood in Washington called Foggy Bottom. But I don't know what he did after he retired from baseball. He left us before we broke up and I lost track of him."

His baseball career began as a product of the Foggy Bottom sandlots, and after leaving the game, Boojum returned to the city of his roots and worked for a road crew building Washington, D.C.'s Whitehurst Freeway.

For 18 years after leaving baseball, the old warhorse remained in the city of his youth, battling the ravages of a hard life that eventually would take the ultimate toll on both his body and his mind. When he was in the last days of his life, Boojum was visited by his old teammate and best friend, Jake Stephens, and while unable to recognize anyone else, he recognized Jake by name.

On June 26, 1963, Jud Wilson, the most ferocious hitter and fiercest competitor ever to play the game, died in Washington, D.C., at the age of 64.

Buck Leonard was not the only one who lost track of Boojum. The world of baseball had also forgotten him until he was ultimately re-discovered and, in 2006, inducted into the National Baseball Hall of Fame at Cooperstown, New York.

The information contained in this article was gleaned from several sources, including period newspapers and personal interviews with Ray Dandridge, Leon

Day, Monte Irvin and Buck Leonard. Much of the biographical and statistical data can be found in The Biographical Encyclopedia of the Negro Baseball Leagues *(1994). Some quotes from my interviews with the players were included in my books* Dandy, Day and the Devil *(1987),* Buck Leonard: The Black Lou Gehrig *(1995), and* Monte Irvin: Nice Guys Finish First *(1996). However, this is the first time this account has been published.*

Biz Mackey: The Man Who Made Campy a Catcher

"If you saw Campy, you saw Biz Mackey."

The speaker is Hall of Famer Monte Irvin. Before joining the New York Giants, he starred in the Negro Leagues, where he played with and against the man acknowledged by Roy Campanella as his mentor. "Campy was a clone of Biz Mackey," Irvin continues. "When they were both with the Baltimore Elites, people used to say, 'Here comes big Biz and little Biz.'"

When Campanella joined the Baltimore Elite Giants in the Negro National League, he was an enthusiastic 15-year-old "wannabe" who was green enough to march in a St. Patrick's Day parade. Assessing the youthful catcher's backstopping skills when he first joined the team, the Elites' veteran spitball ace, Bill Byrd described the way that Campanella handled his spitter. "He would walk back to the backstop and pick it up and throw it back to me," Byrd laughed, with only a slight exaggeration. Recalling the first time he saw the plump youngster behind the plate, Byrd remembered the advice that he imparted to manager Felton Snow. "I said, 'Get that boy out of from behind there before he gets killed.'"

But that was before Biz Mackey took the boy under his wing. Campanella was a quick learner and he had the best master. Within a short time, he had learned to handle Byrd's "wet drop" and a decade later, after he had joined the Brooklyn Dodgers, he was experienced at both handling and hiding Preacher Roe's illegal pitch.

Whenever an umpire asked to look at the ball, Campy knew how to "toe" the ball just as he was reaching down to pick it up, and make it look accidental. Meanwhile, by the time he retrieved the horsehide rolling in the grass, any residual evidence of expectoration on the horsehide had been sufficiently eradicated.

One summer afternoon at Cooperstown, sitting on the veranda of the Otesaga Hotel overlooking the lake that James Fenimore Cooper used as a model for Lake Glimmerglass in his Leatherstocking tales, Campy quietly confided with a twinkle in his eye, "We never had a sign for the spitball, but

I always knew when Preacher was going to throw it." Biz Mackey's protégé had learned his lessons well.

"They had the same style and technique," Irvin emphasizes. "Mackey taught him how to think and taught him how to catch. Campy had Mackey's actions *and* he thought like Mackey. Campy was just a kid when he joined their team. He was just like a clean slate, and Mackey was a great teacher. Biz was a nice guy and had a lot of patience.

"Mackey showed him how to shift, how to frame pitches and all the other inside things that a catcher has to know. And he explained why he would do things, and why he would call a certain pitch. More than anything else, Mackey taught Campy how to set up a hitter, how you can throw a batter his favorite pitch in a certain situation and get him out because he'll take it or he'll miss it because he's not expecting it.

"Campy was just brash enough. Both of them had rifles for arms. Both of them had real quick actions. And Mackey taught him to be accurate with his throws. He said, 'It's all right to have a great arm, but you've got to be accurate, too.' All that inside stuff was taught to him by Mackey."

Another Hall of Famer who played against Mackey in the Negro Leagues was Homestead Grays slugging first baseman Buck Leonard. "Biz Mackey was the best receiver I ever saw," he says unequivocally. That is indeed high praise, when considering that Leonard's teammate on the Grays for nine years was Josh Gibson, also a catcher. "Josh was a better hitter," says Leonard, "but he couldn't compare to Mackey as a receiver."

The fans agreed. In 1933, the first East-West All-Star Game was held at Comiskey Park. When the final votes were tabulated, Mackey was selected over Gibson by a margin of 37,883 to 35,376. Mackey was then 36 years old and past his prime, while Gibson was just beginning to hit his full stride. However,

A master behind the plate, Biz Mackey was voted to start the first East-West All-Star Game ahead of Josh Gibson. Later in his career, with the Baltimore Elite Giants, he became mentor to a teenage Roy Campanella.

his defensive skills were still so far above other catchers that he played in four of the first six all-star classics.

A decade later, Negro League veteran Jake Stevens picked an all-time team and picked Mackey over Gibson. The little pepper-pot shortstop, who played with Mackey in the mid–1920s on the championship Hilldale ballclubs and played with Gibson on the Grays' championship team in 1931, cited his reasons. "Biz was tops in catching, throwing, getting the most out of pitchers, and he was always at his best when the going got tough. I rate Mackey's combined attributes as the deciding factor in my choice."

Leonard concurs that Mackey was a master at handling pitchers. "Biz was past his prime when I saw him, but even though he was old, he could still get a lot out of a pitcher. He had more advice for the pitcher than any catcher I ever saw.

"He was a jovial fellow, full of fun, full of life, and always had something funny to say," Leonard laughs, remembering some of Mackey's efforts to distract batters. "You'd go up to bat and he'd say, 'Well, you're hitting over .400, let's see how much you can hit today.' Or he'd say, 'You're standing too close to the plate.' He'd say anything to throw the batter off. 'What kind of bat are you using?' Then he'd tell the umpire, 'Look at his bat there. I don't believe his bat's legal.' Just anything to upset you.

"He'd ask, 'How'd you all do last night? Where'd you all play last night? Aren't you tired? Don't you need no rest? Where'd you all sleep last night? I know you all slept in the bus. You mean you rode all night last night and you all think you're going to win this ball game?' In other words, he was trying to get hitting off of your mind. Get your mind on something else. Use psychology, you know."

Irvin agrees with Leonard about Mackey's ploys to distract batters, and adds that he passed those pointers on to his pupil, too. "He told Campy how to say certain things to a batter to upset or distract him," Monte laughs. "I remember Mackey used to always say, 'Campy, if you tell a batter the truth, he won't believe you.' In other words, you get in there in that crucial situation, and say, 'Well, we've tried everything else, maybe we'll try a fastball right down the middle.' And then you could throw the ball right down the middle and he wouldn't believe it, because he wasn't used to being told the truth."

Campanella was not the only player to benefit from Biz Mackey's expertise and instruction. Although he was barely literate, Mackey was intelligent and had a good baseball mind. And the ballpark was his classroom. Long after he had left professional baseball, Mackey continued to work with youngsters on the sandlots of Los Angeles. One of those recipients of Mackey's knowledge was Earl Battey, who was taught how to catch by Mackey.

"He taught me how to halve a mitt," Battey recalls, while ticking off a list of catching techniques that he learned before he ever signed a professional contract. Battey credits Mackey's tutoring as the reason that his minor league apprenticeship was short. He had already been taught by the master.

Mackey's reputation was known outside of the Negro Leagues, too. Battey recalls when he first came up to the major leagues with the Chicago White Sox. Manager Al Lopez, who caught 1,918 major league baseball games, watched him for awhile, and asked, "Who taught you how to catch?" "Biz Mackey" was Battey's response. "Well, I guess I don't have to tell you anything about catching then," Lopez said, and walked away.

Mackey was the premier catcher in black baseball for a decade, and the big, husky receiver was surprisingly agile behind the plate. This unexpected quickness, coupled with soft hands, enabled the versatile athlete to often play shortstop, third base or in the outfield and, although lacking noteworthy range, he proved adept at any position. He was also a smart baserunner and, although not fast, pilfered his share of bases.

Because of his superlative defensive skills, Mackey's offensive production is often overlooked. The big Texan was a switch-hitter and, in his prime, was one of most dangerous hitters in baseball, with power from both sides of the plate. For a decade he consistently hit well over .300, with his best marks even passing the .400 level. In 1923, the Eastern Colored League's inaugural season, he finished with a .423 batting average, 20 home runs and a .698 slugging percentage to lead Hilldale to the first of three consecutive pennants. The third flag was capped by a victory over the Kansas City Monarchs in the 1925 Negro World Series. In that Series, Mackey led the team with a .375 batting average.

The big Texan with the competitive spirit learned the rudiments of baseball in the Lone Star State, and began playing professionally with the San Antonio Black Aces in 1918. When the team folded in 1920, he was sold to C. I. Taylor's Indianapolis ABCs of the Negro National League. When the Eastern Colored League was organized in 1923, Mackey was pirated away by Hilldale owner Ed Bolden.

A decade later, after joining Bolden's new team, the Philadelphia Stars, Mackey teamed with the Stars' young left-handed fireballer Slim Jones to form a superb battery, and together, they provided the impetus for the Stars' 1934 drive to win the Negro National League pennant with a come-from-behind victory over the Chicago American Giants in the seven-game League Championship Series.

Mackey's career eventually led him to the helm of the Baltimore Elite Giants, where he took the teenaged Roy Campanella under his wing. By that time, Mackey was already a 20-year veteran and past his prime, but what Campy saw, even then, was vintage Biz Mackey. In July of 1939, Mackey relinquished the managerial reins to George Scales and the starting spot behind the plate to Campanella, and signed with the Newark Eagles to handle their young pitching staff. The *Newark Herald* applauded his acquisition, "He has long been known to be the best developer of young hurlers in the league."

After taking the helm of the Eagles the following August, Mackey continued his work grooming young players. Monte Irvin, Larry Doby and Don Newcombe were all beneficiaries of the Mackey touch during his stint as player-manager at Newark, and he directed the Eagles to the 1946 Negro World Championship with a victory over the Kansas City Monarchs in the Negro World Series.

After retiring from baseball, he lived in Los Angeles. On a special day for Roy Campanella at the Coliseum in 1959, Campy introduced Mackey for a final bow in baseball. Shortly after he heard the applause of the crowd for a last time, the great catcher passed away.

When talking about Negro League players, if Campanella disagreed with an assessment of a player, he would just sit quietly, without comment. But if he agreed, he would nod his head in assent. Any time Biz Mackey's name came up, Campy's head would begin bobbing animatedly. It was clear that Biz Mackey was in the top three or four players from the Negro Leagues that he felt belonged in the Hall of Fame. "With the exception of home run power," Campanella asserted, "Biz Mackey was a better player than I was in every phase of the game."

That is high praise from an impeccable source. If you ever saw Campy, the image burned into your memory forever. So it was with his mentor.

"If you saw Campy, you saw Biz Mackey."

This article was written in 1994 for The Diamond: The Official Chronicle of Major League Baseball. *Unfortunately, this quality publication, considered the Cadillac of baseball magazines during its existence, ceased production earlier than projected. Thus, this is the first time that this article has appeared in print.*

In 2006 Biz Mackey was inducted into the National Hall of Fame. Monte Irvin, who has just passed his 93rd birthday, applauded Mackey's election to Cooperstown's elite. Roy Campanella (1993), Buck Leonard (1997) and Earl Battey (2003) have all passed away since sharing their memories of this great athlete.

Slim Jones: A Season in the Sun and a Winter in the Cold

In winters past, all across the country baseball fans would gather at the local country store, turn a Coca-Cola case on its end and sit around a woodburning stove to talk about the upcoming baseball season. These informal meetings were called "hot stove leagues" and, albeit the stove has now been replaced by an interfaced computer network, that great tradition still lives on.

Prospects of the coming season, arguments about who was the greatest whatever whenever, and discussions about baseball in general are staples at these gatherings. When debating the merits of the greatest left-handed pitcher of all time, names like Lefty Grove, Warren Spahn and Sandy Koufax are inevitably mentioned. If Herb Score had not been injured by Gil McDougald's line drive in 1957, his name would also be among those under discussion.

Talk of the greatest left-hander from the Negro Leagues always includes Willie Foster, Dave Brown and Slim Jones. Jones, like Score, had an abbreviated career but, unlike Score, his end did not come as the result of a line drive. His downfall came from looking at the bottom of too many whiskey bottles. But let's talk about what might have been.

"I faced Lefty Grove and I faced Slim Jones," says one ex–Negro Leaguer, "and I think Slim Jones was faster." The speaker is Buck Leonard, the Hall of Fame slugger who jumped on a fastball like "a chicken on a June bug." Trying to sneak a fastball past Buck was like trying to sneak a sunrise past a rooster. "You could put a baseball in a shotgun and you couldn't shoot it past Buck Leonard," asserted New York Cubans ace Dave Barnhill, who often faced the Homestead Grays' star during his playing career. Buck Leonard is like the E. F. Hutton of black baseball — when he speaks everyone listens. So when he talks about a left-handed pitcher faster than Lefty Grove, it grabs a listener's attention.

Both hurlers were towering, temperamental Marylanders with an overpowering fastball that produced high strikeout ratios. However, there are two major differences in the careers of the two southpaws. First, Slim Jones was black and, therefore, locked out of the established major leagues. Second, Lefty Grove did not get to the major leagues until he was 25, finishing the season about halfway to his 26th birthday. When Slim Jones was the same age, he was dead.

Yet, for a single season in his brief and tragic career, Slim Jones was the best pitcher in baseball. In 1934, during the heart of the Great Depression, Slim Jones had his season in the sun. Recognized as the dominant pitcher in the league, he was selected to start in the East-West classic, the Negro League All-Star Game, and hurled three shutout innings as his East squad took a 1–0 victory. The laurels for the winning pitcher, however, went to Satchel Paige, who pitched the last three innings and was on the mound when the East pushed across the winning run in the eighth inning.

The flamboyant Paige had already earned a reputation that made him a legend in his own time but, when he and Slim met eyeball-to-eyeball, Satchel found that he had met his match on the diamond. One classic duel between the two stringbeans occurred at Yankee Stadium that season with 30,000 fans on hand to witness the encounter. The game was ended by darkness after ten innings in a 1–1 deadlock, and is generally considered the greatest game ever played in black baseball. Slim pitched six innings of perfect ball before finishing with a three-hitter and nine strikeouts. Satchel was almost as stingy, yielding six hits while fanning an even dozen batters.

Three years earlier, Lefty Grove had a career season, recording a 31–4 mark while pitching the Philadelphia A's to the 1931 American League pennant. The Hall of Famer added another pair of victories in a losing World Series against the St. Louis Cardinals. Then, after seven straight seasons with more than 20 wins, Grove left the A's and suffered an off-year in 1934, falling to an 8–8 mark in his first season at Fenway Park

Slim Jones, the Philadelphia Stars' ace lefthander, pitched his team to the Negro National League pennant in 1934. Buck Leonard, who faced both pitchers, considered him to have a better fastball than Hall of Fame great Lefty Grove.

with the Boston Red Sox. This left the spotlight to Slim Jones, who fashioned a season much like Grove's masterful 1931 season.

In 1934, Jones almost single-handedly pitched the Philadelphia Stars to a championship, finishing the season with a 32–4 record, including a 22–3 mark against league teams. He capped the season with a 2–0 whitewash of the Chicago American Giants in the deciding game of the National Negro League Championship Playoff Series.

While Slim was performing his heroics in the Negro Leagues, Dizzy Dean forged a 30–7 mark with his famous fastball to lead the St. Louis Cardinals to a National League pennant. For good measure, "Ol' Diz" then added another pair of wins in their World Series victory over the Detroit Tigers. The two hurlers, who would have won the Cy Young Award in their respective leagues if the award had existed, faced each other in a post-season exhibition game, with the elongated Jones coming out victorious.

At 6'6", Jones stood tall on the mound and, now, he stood even taller atop the world of black baseball, surpassing even the much-heralded Satchel Paige. But while Satchel would continue in an illustrious career and a long life, the view from the top for Slim was short and the slide from the summit a rapid and bitter decline.

Still regarded as the premier pitcher in black baseball in 1935, despite being winless in league competition at the All-Star break, he started and pitched three shutout innings in the East-West game, duplicating the previous year's performance. Unhappy with his contract soon afterwards, he jumped the team until being promised an increase in his paycheck. Jones continued to be plagued with problems, adding arm woes to the combination of contract and drinking difficulties that led to the tragic end of what could have been a great baseball career.

Following the 1938 season, Slim Jones asked for an advance on his salary but, knowing of his propensity for drinking and the probability that the money would go to this end, the Stars' officials refused his request. During the ensuing winter, the once proud pitcher sold his overcoat to buy a bottle of whiskey. The booze kept him warm on the inside but he was unable to fight off the ravages of the bitter cold on the outside. While the rest of the world bustled with the spirit of the Christmas season, Slim Jones, one of the greatest left-handers ever to wear a toe-plate, caught pneumonia and died.

As the new year approached, all across the country baseball fans gathered at the local country store, turned a Coca-Cola case on its end and sat around a wood-burning stove to talk about the upcoming baseball season. Invariably, there were arguments about who was the greatest whatever whenever. And, somewhere, there was talk about what might have been.

Slim Jones

This article was written in 1992 and was one of three submitted to Oldtyme Baseball News *for the feature* Forgotten Heroes *that were not published prior to the business ceasing operation. Thus the article has not appeared in print until now.*

Jones' baseball career was like a comet, shining brilliantly before a rapid burnout. Buck Leonard, who shared his evaluation of Slim Jones' dominant presence when he was at the top of his game, passed away five years (1997) after the article was written.

Jimmie Crutchfield: Small and Proud

"The thing I'm most proud of in my life is that I never did hate nobody."

The speaker was Jimmie Crutchfield, and it was the last time that I saw him. Less than a year later, only six days after his 83rd birthday, the man called "the black Lloyd Waner" passed away. For a man who played 16 years with top ballclubs, appeared in four All-Star games and was a member of one of the greatest baseball teams ever assembled, those words carry a powerful impact. It is even more significant when considering that, despite his exceptional baseball skills, the speaker was denied the opportunity to play in the major leagues, and his country even consigned him to a second class status throughout most of his lifetime. Most people would have been embittered, but not Crutch. "I never did think about things like that," he said, quickly dismissing such thoughts. Crutch was too big to harbor ill will against anyone.

On a good day he could stretch his wiry frame enough to claim 5' 7", and with a brick in each hip pocket, he might push the needle on his scales to 150 pounds. During his playing days, he was called the "Mighty Mite," and was constantly having to prove himself because of his size. "A little man had to always be better than a big man," Crutch explained.

Even when he left home in late March of 1930 to become a professional player, there was widespread doubt about his ability to make it. "When my friends among the people around my hometown, Mobley, Missouri, heard that I was leaving, they said, 'Hey Crutch, you got your bus fare back?' and things like that. Because the rumors were about 100-to-1 that I couldn't make it. But they didn't know the love that I had for baseball."

That love came from his father, who loved the game and passed that passion on to his son. "My mother said that, even before I could walk, my father used to sit me in the corner of the room and roll baseballs to me," Crutch related. And when the coal miners would come by, they would say, 'Hey come in and look at the baseball player.'"

As a youngster, he learned to play the game on the sandlots of his hometown from Bill Gatewood, an old-time pitcher in the Negro Leagues, who helped him transform the inherited love of the game into a baseball career.

While the others in his hometown were building the odds against him making it, Gatewood encouraged him and arranged a tryout for him with the Birmingham Black Barons. In 1927, the wily veteran had managed Satchel Paige during his rookie season at Birmingham. Just as he had seen something special in Satchel, Gatewood's experienced eye saw something in the little outfielder that the others did not. The kind of things that can't be measured or quantified, and are called "intangibles."

"He told me I had a good chance," Crutch remembers appreciatively, "even as small as I was." Gatewood's encouragement fell on fertile soil. Crutch, perhaps the only other person who shared Gatewood's optimism, spoke about his confidence that he carried with him on the trip to Birmingham. "With the love I had for baseball and, as small as I was, I thought I could play baseball. I was young, my eyes were clear and I was looking forward to it. I believed I could play any place."

Satchel Paige raved about the Pittsburgh Crawfords' outfield of Sam Bankhead, Cool Papa Bell, and Jimmie Crutchfield. The diminutive Crutchfield, the least celebrated of the trio, appeared in three consecutive All-Star games (1934–1936) while with the Crawfords.

"When I arrived in Birmingham, they laughed at me. I would walk down the street and I would hear the guys say, 'Hey, here's this kid trying to make the Birmingham Black Barons team.' When I passed, I'd hear them laughing, but I didn't pay any attention to them. The owners were very much upset, too. They said that the man who sent me down there must have been drunk. I was a little guy and they thought that those big pitchers like Ted Trent, Chet Brewer and Willie Foster would knock the bat out of my hands. But the fact that Bill Gatewood sent me down there was all in my favor."

"When we got down to Fort Benning, Georgia, to train, it was the same way there. The guys down there all laughed at me, at first. But after ten days in the training camp, the manager called me over and said, 'Hey, Crutchie, when the season starts, you're going to be my center fielder. That was about the biggest thrill I had."

"It wasn't the money, because the money wasn't there. It was just the recognition that came with being a regular baseball player on a big-time colored baseball team. Just to walk down the street and know that you had made it." And Crutch made it in a big way. In the first game of his professional career with the Birmingham Black Barons, he played center field behind Satchel Paige, and hit a home run to give Paige the victory.

Crutch was reunited with Satchel a few years later, when he was one of the first players signed by Gus Greenlee for the Pittsburgh Crawfords, as they were making the transformation from a semi-pro team to a great professional ballclub. The team had stars at every position, and the lineup included five future Hall of Famers — Satchel Paige, Josh Gibson, Oscar Charleston, Cool Papa Bell and Judy Johnson.

The Crawfords had a great outfield, comprised of Crutch, Cool Papa and Sam Bankhead. Crutch loved to repeat his "Satchel story" about Paige's tribute to the trio. "Satchel said that he looked out towards center field and a storm was blowing in and it started to rain, but we caught every raindrop before they hit the ground," the little fielding genius laughed.

To earn his spot in the Crawfords' outfield, Crutch had to prove himself to manager Oscar Charleston. In his prime, Charleston was compared to Tris Speaker as a center fielder and set a high standard for his outfielders' defensive play. "He didn't like me much at first because he didn't know anything about me," Crutch recalled, "and he didn't like little men."

Charleston was not prone to giving praise to ballplayers, and Crutch savored the rare and reluctant praise from his skipper. "Charleston wasn't the kind to pat nobody on the back," Crutch explained. "During spring training, he put me in the outfield and a guy hit a ball to the outfield and I made a running catch. It was one of the few times he had anything to say. He said, 'Hey little fellow, you can field a little bit, can't you?' I said, 'Yessir.'"

Another time near the end of the season in Monroe, Louisiana, Charleston was forced to admit admiration for the skills of the little man who made the big plays. "The bases were full and two outs," Crutch recalled with relish, "and I was playing this particular hitter to hit to right-center. Charleston came out in front of the whole crowd and moved me over to left-center. And the guy hit a long line drive where he had just moved me from. I was young then and I caught the ball running away from home plate to retire the side. Everybody rushed off the field and into the clubhouse. Charleston came in the dressing room and he didn't even look at me. He just looked straight ahead and said, 'Crutchfield, you are a fielding ass.' From that time on I had it made. From then on I played outfield for the Crawfords."

No outfielder had better hands, or better eyes in judging a ball than the mighty mite from Moberly. He practiced catching fly balls behind his back to entertain the crowd and the fans loved it as much as he loved doing it. Later, while playing with the Newark Eagles, he would sometimes liven up routine outfield plays by making one of his patented behind-the-back catches in a game. "And," he emphasized with a twinkle in his eye, "I never missed one."

But the time came when the thrill was gone from the game and he knew it was time to hang up the spikes. "I was 35 years of age and I was worn out from the traveling, and all the worst of conditions." There was nothing left to prove. "I had made a name for myself," he says.

Fans, teammates and opponents all appreciated his qualities as an all-around ballplayer and recognized his team contributions. He could move a runner around with a well-placed bunt, a perfectly executed hit-and-run play, or a timely base hit. And he could manufacture a run with a stolen base or taking an extra base on a hit. Or he could kill a rally cutting down a baserunner with an accurate throw or by making a sensational catch in the field.

But more than the ballplayer, I remember the man. He may have been small, but he had the soul of a giant. I'll never forget the special sparkle in his eyes, and I'll always remember the one thing that he was most proud of in his life — he "never did hate nobody."

This article was written in 1992 and was one of three submitted to Oldtyme Baseball News *for the feature* Forgotten Heroes *that were not published prior to the business ceasing operation. Thus the article has not appeared in print until now.*

I had known "Crutch" for over a decade when I wrote this article and, only a scant three months earlier, I had been with him when he was one of the players invited to the White House for special recognition at a ceremony in the East Room.

He was truly honored to meet the President that day, and an article about that event is included later in this anthology.

Less than a year later, on March 31, 1993, Jimmie Crutchfield died in Chicago, Illinois. The fact that he "never did hate nobody" was no secret to anyone who ever really got to know him. For a little man, he cast a big shadow and left a big impression. All that's left of him now is the memory of that special sparkle in his eyes, and the teardrops in the eyes of those who miss him.

Not the Only Game in Town: Pittsburgh's Other Teams

Pittsburgh's identification with the Pirates franchise dates back to the nineteenth century, when they were called the Alleghenys and played in the American Association. However, the Pirates were not always the only team in town, nor were they always the best. This was especially true during the two decades following the onset of the Great Depression, when the Smokey City was home to two dark dynasties that rank among the greatest baseball clubs of all time — the Pittsburgh Crawfords and the Homestead Grays. During this time, while the Pirates were in the midst of a 32-year pennant drought, their black counterparts brought 15 championships to the city during a 19-year span (1930–1948). Most of these titles were won by the Grays, sandwiched around a half-decade of dominance by owner Gus Greenlee's Crawfords.

The Crawfords

The Crawfords basked in a meteoric spotlight during the heart of the Depression (1932–1936) and were considered the New York Yankees of black baseball, fielding a team that boasted five future members of the Hall of Fame: Satchel Paige, Josh Gibson, Oscar Charleston, Cool Papa Bell and Judy Johnson.

To build this powerhouse, Greenlee first signed Satchel Paige and then raided his town rivals, the Homestead Grays. By the beginning of 1932, he had acquired the services of slugger Josh Gibson, signed Oscar Charleston as playing manager and built a new ballpark for the team. The first game played at Greenlee Field, one of only two black-owned ballparks in the country, was on April 29, 1932, and the Crawfords, playing as an independent team, finished the season with a 99–36 record.

With Judy Johnson and Cool Papa Bell added to their lineup, they claimed a disputed Negro National League title in 1933 and finished with a

.630 winning percentage in 1934. Then the Crawfords captured successive pennants in 1935–1936, with the 1935 club being regarded as the greatest black team of all time.

The colorful Paige bragged that the Crawfords' outfield trio (Cool Papa Bell, Sam Bankhead and Jimmie Crutchfield) "could catch the raindrops before they hit the ground." After Satchel jumped the team to play with a semi-pro team in Bismarck, North Dakota, left-hander Leroy Matlock became the ace of the staff during his absence and finished with an 18–0 ledger in 1935.

The end of the Crawfords' dominance began in the spring of 1937, when Satchel Paige, Josh Gibson and Cool Papa Bell were among the players who jumped to Santo Domingo. Although the Crawfords remained in Pittsburgh through the 1938 season, the franchise never again reclaimed its previous glory.

During those halcyon years, the Homestead Grays retained a share of popularity in town, and Gus Greenlee and Grays owner Cum Posey had an ongoing rivalry.

The Grays

The Grays' origins date back to 1910, when they were organized to provide weekend recreation for workers in the U.S. Steel Mill in Homestead, Pennsylvania. Posey, a former basketball star at Penn State University, joined the Grays in 1912 and under his leadership, the team made the transition from a regional attraction to national prominence.

Posey signed legendary pitcher "Smokey Joe" Williams in 1925 and by the onset of the next decade, the Grays fielded its strongest teams since the franchise's inception, winning consecutive Eastern Championships in 1930–1931. The 1931 Grays featured Josh Gibson, Oscar Charleston,

Cool Papa Bell played for both of the Smoky City's two great black franchises, the Pittsburgh Crawfords and the Homestead Grays. Cool Papa is generally conceded to be the fastest runner ever to play the game of baseball.

Jud "Boojum" Wilson (one of baseball's greatest pure hitters) and the colorful Ted "Double Duty" Radcliffe, who played on both ends of the battery.

However, the next season Posey felt the impact of the Depression and lean years followed for the Grays, as Greenlee took advantage of Posey's economic condition to lure some of his best players to the Crawfords. In the aftermath, Posey restructured the franchise, forming a partnership with Rufus "Sonnyman" Jackson to rebuild his decimated ballclub. When Greenlee found himself in economic straits in 1937, Jackson opened his checkbook and brought Gibson back to the Grays, where he teamed with Buck Leonard to form a power tandem that earned them the appellation "The black Babe Ruth and Lou Gehrig."

The Grays shared Greenlee Field with the Crawfords until 1939, when they began playing their games at Forbes Field, the home field of the Pirates. A year earlier, *Pittsburgh Courier* sportswriter Chester Washington had sent a telegram to Pirates manager Pie Traynor guaranteeing a pennant if he signed five of Pittsburgh's black stars: Satchel Paige, Josh Gibson, Buck Leonard, Cool Papa Bell and Ray Brown. The Pirates made no response and subsequently lost the flag by a single game when the Chicago Cubs' Gabby Hartnett hit his famous "homer in the gloaming." Without question, the addition of four future Hall of Famers and another ballplayer of equal potential would have made the difference in the pennant race.

At this time, Gibson and Leonard were dubbed the "Thunder Twins" and Raymond Brown was the Grays' perennial pitching ace, while they were dominating the Negro National League, winning nine consecutive pennants (1937–1945). The Grays added a tenth flag in 1948, the league's last season, and also played in five of the seven Negro World Series between the Negro National League and the Negro American League. The last Series was a victory over the Birmingham Black Barons, who featured a young center fielder named Willie Mays. Playing manager Vic Harris was at the Grays' helm each year except 1943–1944, when Candy Jim Taylor guided the team to back-to-back World Series Championships while Harris was engaged in defense work.

The Grays' last hurrah came a year after Jackie Robinson broke baseball's color line, and the demise of the Grays followed in 1950, but the legacy of black baseball in Pittsburgh did not begin with the Grays and Crawfords.

The Keystones

Black ballclubs were a part of Pittsburgh's baseball history, beginning in the nineteenth century. In 1887, the League of Colored Baseball Clubs was formed and the Pittsburgh Keystones were one of the charter members, but the league collapsed after only a week.

Another club, also called the Pittsburgh Keystones, joined Rube Foster's Negro National League 35 years later. Playing their home games at Ammon Field, they finished in sixth place with a 16–21 record and dropped out of the league after a single season.

The Negro League teams were able to co-exist with the Pirates because of the support of the black populace, where earlier black teams had failed in their efforts to establish a following in Pittsburgh.

This is an excerpt from an article that first appeared in the 1994 All-Star Game Yearbook, *which featured all of the major league teams in Pittsburgh's baseball history — other than the Pirates. Only the portion relating to the black teams is included in this anthology.*

In addressing the Pittsburgh Crawfords, the article stated that they fielded "a team that boasted five future members of the Hall of Fame: Satchel Paige, Josh Gibson, Oscar Charleston, Cool Papa Bell and Judy Johnson." Since that time, two other players who were short-term members of the Crawfords have been elected to the Hall of Fame: Willie Foster (1996) and Jud Wilson (2006). However, the regular lineup never exceeded five future Hall of Fame players during the same season.

Similarly, in discussing the proposed addition of five black players to the Pirates in 1938, it was stated that "the addition of four future Hall of Famers and another player of equal potential would have made the difference in the pennant race." The fifth player mentioned here — Ray Brown — was inducted into the Hall of Fame in 2006, making the statement even more powerful.

Buck Leonard: He Could Do It All

During his Hall of Fame career with the Homestead Grays in the Negro Leagues, Buck Leonard was called the "Black Lou Gehrig." Hall of Famer Monte Irvin, who saw Buck in his prime, concurs with the comparison but suggests a different perspective on the appellation. "If he'd gotten the chance to play in the major leagues, they might have called Lou Gehrig the white Buck Leonard," says Monte. "He was that good." Sportswriter Bill Burk, who also watched Buck at the top of his game, wrote, "Buck Leonard is one of the finest hitters we have ever watched in action. For slugging ability he reminds one of the late Lou Gehrig."

These comparisons are valid. Both players demonstrated the same skill on the diamond and the same strength of character off the field, and a description of either player would fit the other like a tailored suit.

Buck was a left-handed, power-hitting first baseman who was especially tough when the game was on the line. Homestead Grays owner Cum Posey, who witnessed black baseball for most of its existence, called his slugging star "one of the greatest clutch hitters in Negro baseball." Since Buck led the Grays to nine consecutive pennants during their halcyon years (1937–1945), Posey could be forgiven if he was not entirely impartial. Sportswriter Lem Graves, Jr., a more objective observer, echoed Posey's assessment, writing that Buck was "at his best when the chips are down."

Opposing pitchers learned that pitching to Buck with men in scoring position was like looking into the barrel of a cannon. When asked how he pitched to the slugging first sacker, one pitcher suggested that the best way was to "throw it and duck." Newark Eagles ace Leon Day, who rode his fastball to the Hall of Fame, described Buck as an outstanding hitter with a lot of power and insisted, "I would rather pitch to Josh Gibson than to Buck." Perhaps part of the reason for Day's preference was that Buck Leonard was a notorious fastball hitter. "You could put a fastball in a shotgun and you couldn't shoot it by him," said Dave Barnhill of the New York Cubans, another hard thrower who was burnt by Buck's bat on more occasions than he cared to remember.

Future Brooklyn Dodgers superstar Roy Campanella, who had a catcher's eye view of Buck's batting prowess while with the Baltimore Elite Giants, agreed with the pitchers. "He had a real quick bat. You couldn't get a fastball by him. Buck was one of the best hitters I've ever seen."

Buck's proven propensity for fastballs led many pitchers to resort to an assortment of off-speed pitches in an effort to neutralize the thunder in his bat. One of these was Ted "Double-Duty" Radcliffe, who bragged before the 1941 East-West All-Star Game that he was going to get Buck out on slow balls. When Radcliffe tried to make good on his boast, Buck blasted one of his change-ups over Comiskey Park's right field fence. After the game a chagrined Radcliffe vowed never to throw Buck another changeup. And he never did.

That home run was only one of three that Buck hit in All-Star competition to establish the all-time record for the East-West Game. During his tenure in the Grays' flannels, Buck became a fixture in the annual classic (missing only two years from his first appearance in 1935 through the last game in 1948) and compiled a lifetime .317 All-Star batting average.

Buck's smooth, powerful swing produced major league home runs on a regular basis, and he was a dead pull hitter. His favorite major league park was Yankee Stadium, whose right field dimensions favored left-handed pull hitters, but regardless of the speed or location of a pitch, Buck could pull it. Former Commissioner Bowie Kuhn, who watched Buck play at Griffith Stadium as a youngster working the scoreboard, once joked, "I remember one time when a pitcher tried to pick a runner off third base and Buck pulled the ball down the right field line."

Kuhn was not the only person to see Buck play at Griffith Stadium. Josh Gibson and Buck formed a formidable power tandem and were dubbed the "Thunder Twins" by the press. Washington Senators owner Clark Griffith watched them hit more home runs at his park than his entire team, and considered the prospect of signing them. After one Sunday doubleheader, he sent for the pair of sluggers to come to his office. "So we went up there," Buck recalled, "and he said, 'We have seen you fellows play and we'd like to have you in the major leagues with us. But nobody wants to be the first one to hire you fellows. That's where the problem is right now.' So that was that. We told him we were interested, but nothing ever came of our meeting."

Like many others, Griffith had the vision but not the courage to implement that vision, and it was years before Branch Rickey signed Jackie Robinson and the doors to the major leagues were finally opened to black Americans. "We thought it would just be a matter of time until they signed black ballplayers," Buck affirmed, "but I knew when it came, it would be too late for me." When the time did come, it was as Buck had envisioned, and the loss was baseball's because fans all across the country were denied the opportunity to see the "Thunder Twins" and others who were among the greatest talents to ever play the game.

Buck and Josh usually flip-flopped in the heart of the batting order depending on whether a right-handed or left-handed pitcher was starting. "When Josh came to the team I started getting a lot of good pitches to hit," Buck said modestly, "because they were pitching around him." While Josh was slugging tape-measure home runs, Buck was smashing screaming line drives off the walls and over the walls.

Although best noted for his hitting, Buck also excelled defensively and was a smooth, consistent and heady player afield. "His play at first base is graceful and steady," wrote sportswriter Bill Burk, who had compared his hitting to Gehrig, "for poetry of motion, he is a closer counterpart afield of onetime kingpin George Sisler."

For 17 years Buck Leonard was the one constant presence in the Homestead Grays lineup. Virtually a perennial all-star, he is the greatest first baseman in the history of the Negro Leagues.

Two members of the Hall of Fame, Ray Dandridge and Cool Papa Bell, who competed against Buck, both used exactly the same words to describe his all-around ability: "Buck was the best first baseman we had in the Negro Leagues." Cool Papa added, "Nobody deserves to be in the Hall of Fame more than he does."

Personal pride and professionalism permeated Buck's play, and sportswriter Lem Graves, Jr. paid him the coveted tribute, "Buck is a ballplayer's ballplayer." He commanded the respect of his teammates and provided leadership by example. Homestead Grays pitcher Wilmer Fields explains, "Everybody looked to him for leadership, guidance, and stability." Even-tempered, Buck's consistency and dependability were a steadying presence on the Grays, especially the younger players. Josh Gibson, Jr., who played briefly with the Grays during their last two seasons, describes Buck's influence. "He was respected by everybody, and was sort of a father image for the younger players on the team."

Off the field, Buck demonstrated impeccable character and a quiet dignity that belied his competitiveness on the diamond. Buck O'Neil, first baseman for the rival Kansas City Monarchs, touched on this dichotomy. "He is one of the best hitters I ever saw *and* one of the nicest guys I ever saw." O'Neil's view is virtually unanimous among Buck's contemporaries. He was one of the most admired and best liked players in the game by teammates, opponents and fans. Sportswriter Bill Burk observed, "Leonard is a perfect gentleman on and off the field." Even to this time, most descriptions of him include the phrase "class guy."

Buck, like Gehrig with Ruth, was less flamboyant than the other half of the power tandem and always seemed to play in Gibson's shadow until Josh's death during the winter before Jackie Robinson's first spring with the Dodgers.

Buck enjoyed a last hurrah in 1948, when he won the batting title with a .395 average and tied for the league lead in home runs, while leading the Grays to another Negro World Series Championship. Over a 17-year career in the Negro National League, his lifetime stats show a .341 average in league play.

Buck recently passed away at age 90, on Thanksgiving Day 1997, in his hometown of Rocky Mount, North Carolina. Still, his name is inevitably linked with that of Josh Gibson. "It seems like we were always doing everything together," Buck once recalled. "We even went into the Hall of Fame together." That was at Cooperstown in 1972. Now, with Buck's induction into Ted Williams' Hitters Hall of Fame, the "Thunder Twins" are together again.

This article was first published in the 1998 Ted Williams Museum Yearbook, *the year that Buck Leonard was inducted into Ted Williams' Hitters Hall of Fame. Buck's widow, Lugenia Leonard, accepted the award on his behalf. I was in attendance at the ceremonies and was pleased to see that Buck's autobiography,* Buck Leonard: The Black Lou Gehrig, *which I had done in collaboration with him, occupied a prominent place in his display case at the museum.*

Don't Forget About Josh

When Mark McGwire smashed his 62nd home run of the 1998 season, breaking Roger Maris' 37-year-old record, America celebrated. With one swing of his bat, the new home run champ wiped away the residual fallout from the 1994–1995 strike and baseball was once again America's game — our National Pastime. McGwire graciously embraced the Maris family and Sammy Sosa, including them in the spotlight. McGwire and Sosa, currently tied with 62 home runs, have done more for race relations than a hundred million-men marches or the rhetoric of a thousand politicians. To watch these two superstar sluggers embrace and see the genuine respect and friendship between them conjured up a vision of two past superstar sluggers — Babe Ruth and Josh Gibson (who was called the Black Babe Ruth). Wouldn't it have been great if Ruth and Gibson could have been afforded the same opportunity to chase the home run record together, rather than having been separated by a color line?

While Ruth will never be forgotten — as Maris and Hank Aaron discovered — Gibson may never be completely rediscovered. He was fashioned in the same mold as Ruth and McGwire, standing bigger than life and hitting majestic home runs with almost unbelievable consistency. Gibson, who spent his career in the Negro Leagues with the Homestead Grays and Pittsburgh Crawfords, was 6' 1", weighed 210 pounds, and had powerful arms and shoulders. The muscular catcher personified power, and his towering home runs electrified crowds. Washington Senators pitching great Walter Johnson considered Gibson to be worth $200,000 — twice the value placed on the New York Yankees' star catcher, Bill Dickey. Indeed, many baseball historians pick Gibson as the best player ever at his position.

Off the field, Gibson carried himself with a quiet confidence and was a charismatic presence. He was to black kids what Ruth was to white kids. They were always crowding around wanting just to touch their hero or maybe to get an autograph. The same thing happened with adults in hotels and restaurants — everyone wanted to meet him. Gibson handled his celebrity status with grace and always accommodated fans of all ages.

Much of black baseball history consists of oral accounts, and former Negro Leaguers invariably talk about two things: Satchel Paige's strikeouts and Josh Gibson's home runs. In every ballpark where Gibson played, fans would point to the furthermost corner and say "Josh hit one over there." Gibson was a natural and his home runs are legendary, as are some of the stories told about him.

One such story tells about a home run that he hit in Pittsburgh that went over the center field fence and completely out of sight. The next day the team was playing a game in Philadelphia and while Gibson was at bat, a ball came out of nowhere and dropped down out of the sky right into the center fielder's glove. The umpire was left with nothing to do but to stab his thumb upward into the air and proclaim to Gibson, "You're out yesterday in Pittsburgh."

Other stories about Gibson, although sometimes embellished, are based on true events. One of these concerns a prodigious home run that Gibson hit, which one eyewitness contends went completely out of Yankee Stadium, a feat that no one else has ever accomplished — including the Bambino. Another former player addressed the controversial home run by saying, "It's the only ball hit out of Yankee Stadium that I ever *heard* of." Whether the ball actually went out or just barely missed is still in dispute, but either way, Gibson's gargantuan power has never been in dispute.

Monte Irvin calls Gibson "the best hitter I ever saw, black or white." Irvin adds, "I think he would have broken Babe Ruth's single-season record for home runs if he had been given the chance to play in the major leagues." Ray Dandridge, who played against Gibson in the U.S. and with him in Mexico, agreed succinctly, "That man was a great hitter. None was better."

Nobody in baseball ever hit the ball farther than Josh Gibson. Had it not been for the color line, he definitely would have challenged — and possibly surpassed — Babe's Ruth's single-season home run record.

Newark Eagles ace Leon Day said that he pitched harder against the batters who came up before Gibson, so that when he hit a home run there would be less damage done. In one game Day was not afforded the opportunity to keep runners off the base. He was rushed into a 2–0 game in the ninth inning with two runners on base and Gibson at the plate. Day blazed two quick fastballs past Gibson but his third pitch ended up in the center field stands for a game-winning three-run homer. After the game, Eagles owner Effa Manley chided Gibson, "You should be ashamed of yourself. You spoiled our day." Gibson responded, "Mrs. Manley, I've been known to spoil a lot of days for a lot of people."

Gibson also made believers of a lot of pitchers. New York Cubans ace Dave Barnhill said the only way to pitch to the big slugger was to "throw and duck." Another hurler who had several days spoiled by Gibson echoed these sentiments, saying it was best to "just throw the ball and hope your third baseman didn't get killed."

Gibson's 17-year career was too short to have challenged Babe Ruth's lifetime 714 mark, which was the record at that time. Although accounts of the era credit him with 962 lifetime homers, this total should be regarded in the same category as Sadaharu Oh's Japanese mark of 868 because they did not all come against major league competition. The Negro League schedules were unbalanced and varied from year to year but generally consisted of between 40 and 60 games. The remainder of the games came primarily against lesser opposition. This, however, should not detract from Gibson's accomplishments. Had he played in the white major leagues there is no doubt that he would have challenged, if not surpassed, Babe Ruth's total of 60.

Black newspapers of the era credit Gibson with 75 home runs in 1931 (his first full season), 69 home runs in 1934, and 84 home runs (170 games) in 1936. It should be reiterated that most of these home runs came against semi-pro competition. The *Pittsburgh Courier* and *Baltimore Afro-American* credited Gibson with 18 home runs in 45 Negro National League contests in 1936. The pitching in these games was major league quality, and this home run percentage projects to 62 home runs in a 154-game schedule and 65 homers for 162 games.

During Gibson's short tenure in the Mexican League his home run production (44 in 116 games) would have yielded 61 homers in 162 games. Another indicator of his home run prowess comes from a winter in the Puerto Rican League where his pace over the short season would have produced 62 homers in 589 at-bats.

Like Ruth, Gibson had a teammate with whom he formed a dynamic power tandem. Ruth had Lou Gehrig, while Gibson had Buck Leonard. The black press called them the "Thunder Twins" and the pair also earned the appellation of "the black Babe Ruth and black Lou Gehrig." Washington Senators owner Clark Griffith, who watched the pair hit more home runs in Griffith Stadium than his entire team, once called the pair of sluggers to his office and asked them if they were interested in playing for the Senators. Griffith, like many owners, had the vision but lacked the courage to implement it. According to Leonard, Griffith told the dark duo that "nobody wanted to be the first" to sign black players.

Leonard had nothing but praise for the other half of the dynamic duo, "Josh Gibson was a big, strong, right-handed power hitter like Jimmie Foxx (who twice hit more than 50 home runs in a season with a high of 58), but he had more power than Foxx." Leonard also noted that he got better balls to hit with Gibson in the lineup, emphasizing his value to the team. "Josh made the whole team better. He put life into everybody."

Also like Ruth, Gibson's home run totals far exceeded those of the player who finished in second place. Reporter Ric Roberts kept his own statistics for the Homestead Grays' home games in 1943. The Grays played their home games in Forbes Field when the Pirates were on the road and in Griffith Stadium when the Senators were on the road. Both of these parks were considered pitchers' parks. Roberts' record showed the Grays with a total of 16 homers in those parks. Gibson hit ten, Leonard hit five and the rest of the team combined accounted for only one dinger.

Eyewitness accounts and available statistics indicate that Gibson's stature as a slugger was commensurate with the Babe and Big Mac. I cheered along with the rest of the country at 8:18 PM on 9-8-98. But I also wondered: If there had never been a color line, would Big Mac's #62 have been enough? We will never know but, amidst our celebration, let us not forget about Josh.

This article first appeared in 1998 on MSNBC.com. *Since Mark McGwire and Sammy Sosa appeared before the Senate Committee Investigating Performance Enhancing Substances, their images have been tarnished and their status in the nation's eyes has declined dramatically.*

While Barry Bonds was approaching Hank Aaron's career home run total, the country's naiveté had eroded, and when he supplanted "Hammerin' Hank" as the all-time home run king, the response from America's sports world was in direct opposition to their reaction to the McGwire-Sosa race that eclipsed Roger Maris' single-season mark.

More recently, the Mitchell Report has greatly expanded the fallout from fan disillusionment and the information gleaned from the Committee's investigation appears to be only the "tip of the iceberg" in regard to the inflated home run totals from the past two decades.

The Thunder Twins: Black Baseball's Power Tandem, Josh Gibson and Buck Leonard

Washington Senators owner Clark Griffith sat watching the Negro National League Champion Washington-Homestead Grays taking batting practice in the ballpark bearing his name. The batter was a big, strong right-hander, standing over six feet tall and weighing over 200 pounds. His rolled-up left sleeve revealed massive arm muscles and, from beneath a turned-up cap bill, his eyes riveted the pitcher. He awaited each pitch from a semi-crouched, flat-footed stance with a casual confidence. When the ball was released, he lifted his foot and set it back down without striding, as a timing mechanism. Then with effortless grace, he impacted the incoming horsehide projectile with a compact swing that generated incredible power. The crack of the bat was almost invariably followed by a baseball sailing over the fence or seeking the remotest parts of the ballpark.

The batter was Josh Gibson and an observer had reason to be impressed. The left field fence at Griffith Stadium was over 400 feet down the line, and center field was 421 feet away. Yet baseballs were landing in the stands with insistent regularity. As Griffith watched the towering flyballs and sizzling line drives jumping off the big slugger's bat, he shook his head with a mixture of admiration and awe.

The Grays began using Griffith Stadium as one of their home parks in 1937 and Griffith had seen the slugger duplicate his tremendous home runs in numerous Negro League contests. Gibson's indomitable presence in the batter's box personified power and electrified a crowd. During his career, he produced tape-measure home runs with such regularity that it came to be expected as the norm. Twice his blasts cleared the left field bleachers' back wall. Only Mickey Mantle, on a single occasion, ever accomplished the same feat.

When Gibson finished his pre-game slugging exhibition, the next batter stepped into the batting cage. He was a husky, left-handed hitter, standing a shade under six feet tall and carrying 185 pounds on his solid frame. Hitting

Pictured in the dugout at Griffith Stadium is the Homestead Grays' murderers row: Sam Bankhead, Josh Gibson, Buck Leonard, Dave Hoskins, and Jerry Benjamin. Gibson and Leonard were called "The Thunder Twins."

from a slight crouch and with a closed stance against the right-handed pitcher, he continued the assault on the fences that Gibson had begun. The muscular pull-hitter displayed a smooth and powerful stroke, as he began ripping screaming line drives that ricocheted off the walls and whistled over the fences.

This batter was Buck Leonard, the other half of the Grays' power tandem called the black Babe Ruth and Lou Gehrig. The appellation was appropriate and the comparison justified. Although lesser known and often overlooked in baseball history, this dark duo followed close on the heels of Ruth and Gehrig, and shadowed the careers of the New York Yankees greats. Each pair of sluggers played together for a decade, and provided a one-two home run punch in the lineup for a dominant team.

Gibson and Leonard formed the heart of an offensive attack that powered the Homestead Grays to a phenomenal nine consecutive pennants from 1937 through 1945. Without a doubt, Gibson would have challenged Ruth's home run records, and Roger Maris and Hank Aaron might have been chasing his marks instead of the Babe's. Leonard shared with Gehrig the dubious distinction of playing most of his career in the shadow of a more heralded teammate.

Dubbed the "Thunder Twins" by the black press, their value to the team offense is illustrated by records kept by reporter Ric Roberts for the Grays' home games during the 1943 season. For the 40 home games played in Griffith Stadium and Forbes Field, the duo accounted for 15 of the team's 16 home runs, with Gibson hammering ten round-trippers to Leonard's five. "It seems like everybody remembers us together," says Leonard. "We even went into the Hall of Fame together."

Gibson was credited with 962 home runs in his 17-year career, although many of these were against non-league teams. Single season home run marks show totals of 75 in 1931, 55 in 1933 and 69 in 1934. Using only league games as listed in the Macmillan *Baseball Encyclopedia*, his 7.7 lifetime home run percentage is second only to Ruth's 8.5. However, this excludes some of Gibson's most productive years when the Grays were playing as an independent team. In 116 games in the Mexican League, he compiled an .802 slugging percentage and a 9.8 home run percentage.

His power was awesome but he hit for average as well, and is credited with lifetime batting marks of .354 in the Negro Leagues, .393 in Mexico, .353 in Cuba, .480 in Puerto Rico and .412 in exhibition games against major leaguers.

"There's no telling what he could have done in the major leagues in his prime," says Buck Leonard. "One year he counted all of his home runs and he hit 72. But you've got to remember all that wasn't on good pitching. Some of the pitching was just mediocre that he was batting against. We didn't face good pitching day in and day out."

Leonard also compiled impressive credentials during his tenure in the Grays' flannels, finishing with a lifetime .341 batting average in the Negro Leagues. A favorite of the fans, he became a fixture in the annual East-West All-Star Game, making a record 11 appearances in the classic and establishing the All-Star record for home runs.

Following the 1943 season, the press credited Leonard with having averaged 34 home runs per year for the previous eight seasons. "My best home run total was 42 in 1948," the former slugger explains. "We played 84 league games that season, but we played around 210 ballgames during the entire year."

"I didn't claim to hit the ball as far as Gibson," he adds. "Nobody hit the ball as far as he did. I didn't see the one that he was supposed to have hit out of Yankee Stadium. But I saw him hit a ball one night in the Polo Grounds that went between the upper deck and the lower deck and out of the stadium.

It must have gone 600 feet. The longest home run I ever hit was in Newark. It went over the fence and hit up against some oil tanks that were behind right field. I'd say it was about 500 feet."

Clark Griffith had been in professional baseball since 1888, and "The Old Fox" was a keen judge of talent. After watching the two-man barrage on the ballfield in batting practice and in Negro League games, he entertained the idea of signing black Americans for his Washington Senators.

Years before Branch Rickey had even scouted Jackie Robinson, Griffith called Gibson and Leonard into his office to discuss the possibility of breaking the color ban. Sitting in the den of his home in Rocky Mount, North Carolina, Buck Leonard reaches back a half-century into his memory banks to recall the meeting. "One Sunday evening we played a doubleheader in Griffith Stadium, and Clark Griffith saw both of the ballgames. So he told the fellow down there at the gate to tell us when we changed clothes to come up to his office. So we went up there."

Upon arriving at the Washington owner's inner sanctum, the players were greeted cordially and complimented on their playing ability by Griffith, who then broached the subject of them playing in the major leagues. After being assured by the pair that they would welcome the opportunity and were confident that they could make the team if given the chance, Griffith expressed the prevailing mindset among the owners.

"We have seen some of you fellows play and we'd like to have you in the major leagues with us. But if we take you fellows into the major leagues, we're going to take the best ones and it's going to break up the Negro Leagues. That's the hangup now. Nobody wants to be the first one to hire you fellows."

"So that was that," Leonard summarizes. "But we thought that it was just a matter of time until they signed black ballplayers. But it didn't happen back there then. When they *did* start taking blacks into the white leagues," he adds, "the black leagues started going down just like he said it would happen."

Griffith's assertion *was* prophetic. For all practical purposes, the Negro Leagues were killed by the stroke of a pen when Jackie Robinson inked a Brooklyn Dodgers contract. Josh Gibson never lived to see Robinson play in the major leagues, dying prematurely only a month after his 35th birthday and a month before the opening of spring training camps in 1947. Buck Leonard *did* see the beginning of what eventually became a flood tide of black players in the major leagues. But it came too late for him. In 1952 Bill Veeck offered him a chance to play with the St. Louis Browns but Buck declined the offer. "I was 45 years old," he explains. "My legs were gone and I knew I couldn't play every day. I didn't even want to try it. But I would have liked to have played when I was in my prime."

If Clark Griffith had taken the lead and implemented his early vision, one can only wonder how baseball's history and record books might have been changed.

This article was first published in the November 1993 issue of The Diamond: The Official Chronicle of Major League Baseball *under the title "The Thunder Twins: Josh Gibson and Buck Leonard Were Called the Babe Ruth and Lou Gehrig of the Negro Leagues."*

Ray Dandridge: Dandy

Look at Ray Dandridge today and he looks more like a retired rodeo cowboy than one of the smoothest fielding third basemen to ever play the game of baseball. His bowed legs look like he spent the better part of his life with them wrapped around the sides of a horse, and his muscular torso looks better suited for bulldogging steers than for scooping ground balls out of the dirt. When Ray dons his Stetson he looks like he just stepped out of a Marlboro commercial.

But don't let the looks fool you. This man had hands of velvet and was the greatest third baseman of his generation. Some say that he was the black Brooks Robinson. Others say that Brooks Robinson was the white Ray Dandridge.

Presently, Ray is living the leisurely life of a retiree. When not flipping channels on his large screen TV, he spends his time playing pinochle, watching jai-alai, or just sitting in his front yard and tossing pine cones for his German shepherd, Pepper, to catch. She goes back on the pop-fly pine cones just like her master used to half a century ago. Ray has taught her to catch short-hops and grounders as well.

I first met Ray in the summer of 1981 at his home in Newark, New Jersey, that he bought with the big pesos advanced as inducement for him to perform his glove magic under the Mexican sun. Ray popped a few tops while we spent an afternoon talking about a career that spanned 23 years and half of the globe. Later we adjourned to his basement where the memorabilia from his career as a baseball nomad was soon spread out over his pool table. The task of assimilating the mountainous montage of baseball history into a workable document was overwhelming. And even then the surface was barely scratched. What did emerge, however, was a profile of one of the greatest third basemen in the history of baseball.

Monte Irvin, who played with and against Dandy in four different countries, shakes his head in awe when remembering the diamond exploits of the man with the velvet hands. "Dandridge and Wells were two of the finest infielders I've ever seen," he states without reservation. "I'm talking about bar none. I've seen Rolfe. I've seen Robinson. I've seen Graig Nettles. I've seen all the great third basemen. But I've never seen anybody who could make the plays any better than Dandridge."

"And once you saw him you'd never forget him because he was short and bowlegged. But he was quick as a cat and he had an adequate arm. If the ball got to him real quick, he would always time it so that his throw would just beat you. When he had to hurry it was the same way, the throw would just beat you. He was the best I've ever seen on a swinging bunt. Because he was already short and he'd come in full speed, take that ball and toss it underhand and just get you. It was a thing of beauty just to see him come in and flip that ball underhand without even slowing down on it. It was the damnedest thing I've ever seen.

"You know, it's hard to describe his style of fielding. You had to see him play. People would have paid just to see him play third base. He was something! The way that he went after a ball ... the way that he would backhand a ball with that big glove of his ... and the way he would come up with a hard hit ball ... and he'd take it and shake it before he'd throw it to first base.

"I saw him and I have so much respect for him. He was very spectacular but not showy, understand. Certainly not a showman in the way he fielded, like Willie Mays with the basket catch. But something about the way he moved made him separate and apart from all the rest of the third basemen. They loved him in Mexico. They thought he was the best third baseman in the world. They still talk about him." Monte pauses momentarily to reflect, and then concludes with finality, "Dandridge was one of the best ever."

One of the best ever!

Ray Dandridge was the best third baseman in the history of the Negro Leagues. With the Newark Eagles, he was part of their storied "million dollar infield" before he opted to take his magical glove to Mexico, where he earned even greater adulation.

Yet in his playing days, because of his skin of ebony, the doorway to the major leagues was closed to Ray. Now the door to the Hall of Fame also seems to be closed to him. For several years he has missed election by a narrow margin. Baseball authorities who have seen him play agree that he should already be enshrined. The standards for the Hall of Fame are self-defining, but if players of Ray's stature from the Negro Leagues continue to be excluded, the integrity of the institution will be seriously compromised.

This article was extracted from my 1987 book Dandy, Day and the Devil, *a trilogy of biographies about the three players still living that definitely deserved to be in the Hall of Fame. The extract had been utilized as a brief introductory segue to the section titled* Dandy, *which was the one-third of the book on Ray's baseball career.*

Between the completion of the manuscript and the publication of the book, Ray was elected to the Hall of Fame by the Veterans Committee. Since it was too late to change the contents of the book, all that could be done was to put a photograph on the back cover, showing Ray at the press conference when his election was announced, along with a caption that read:

> Ray Dandridge thought baseball had forgotten him. But on March 3, 1987 he was awakened by the ringing of his telephone. When he picked up the receiver, a voice said, "From this moment on, your life will never be the same." The prophetic caller was Ed Stack, President of the Baseball Hall of Fame, informing Ray of his election to this elite group by the veterans committee.

The long wait was over. As the impact of the news was fully realized, tears of joy trickled down Ray's cheeks. The feeling was as he had anticipated long ago—beautiful!

Ray Dandridge and the Newark Eagles' Million Dollar Infield

Gus Greenlee was a "well-heeled" numbers banker who had acquired his wealth through involvement in illegal activities, but he was also a sportsman with a penchant for winners. When Greenlee bought the Pittsburgh Crawfords late in 1931, they were an aggregation of youngsters playing at a semi-pro level. He quickly signed Satchel Paige, Josh Gibson, Oscar Charleston and other outstanding ballplayers to elevate his ballclub immediately to the top tier of black baseball teams. For five years Greenlee's Pittsburgh Crawfords flashed across the sky of black baseball like a meteor, and have been called the New York Yankees of the Negro Leagues. The 1935 Crawfords, a team that fielded five future Hall of Fame players, are generally conceded to be the greatest black team of all time.

When Gus Greenlee divested himself of the Pittsburgh Crawfords in 1936 to pay off a hit in his numbers racket, Cum Posey's Homestead Grays moved to the forefront as the premier team in the Negro National League. But their perch at the apex of the league was not uncontested and a heated rivalry emerged between the Grays and Abe Manley's Newark Eagles for league dominance. Year-in and year-out the Grays and Eagles battled tooth and nail. "We liked to beat the Grays," says former Eagles star Ray Dandridge, "because they had the name. They thought they were the king of the mountains."

Knockdown battles, slashing baserunning, brawls, and near riots were not uncommon occurrences when the two teams squared off. The Grays had the power tandem of Josh Gibson and Buck Leonard, who were called the Babe Ruth and Lou Gehrig of black baseball. But the Eagles had the million dollar infield to counter them. Ray remembers:

> During that time when I played with the Newark Eagles, the Homestead Grays and the Pittsburgh Crawfords were supposed to have been the best black teams, but we thought we were the best because we had a million dollar infield. That was in 1937 that we had the infield together. I was playing third base, Willie Wells was

Pictured are Ray Dandridge, Jimmie Crutchfield, Dick Seay, Leon Day, Johnny Hayes, Willie Wells and Red Moore from the 1937 Newark Eagles. These seven players include their famed "million dollar infield" comprised of Dandridge, Wells, Seay and Moore (going around the diamond from third to first).

playing shortstop, Dick Seay was playing second base and Mule Suttles was playing first base. And that was the greatest! That was the million dollar infield right there. Couldn't nothing get through that infield. We could have played on any team in any league. That was the best team. We had one of the best ball teams ever. We were the only ones that was compared to the Homestead Grays.

The million dollar estimate of the infield's worth is modest compared to what their value would be today. Each member of the infield would command that much alone on the current player market. Their first year together, 1937, three-fourths of the infield was voted to the East squad in the annual All-Star Game. Only Dick Seay was passed over for a starting position.

Homestead Grays owner Cum Posey, who doubled as a writer for the *Pittsburgh Courier,* paid Ray the supreme compliment when the veteran baseball authority selected him to his annual All-America team as the best third baseman in black baseball for three consecutive years, 1936–1938. Obviously the 5'7", 175-pounder stood tall in the eyes of Posey, who had seen virtually everyone who had played in the Negro Leagues since 1910.

A veritable human vacuum cleaner at third base, the right-handed swinger consistently hit over .300 and was a good baserunner. These qualities were also observed by Bill Klem, a National League umpire for 35 years, who regarded Ray as the best third baseman in baseball, black or white. Klem lauded Ray's ability to throw from any angle and to time his throws to make it easy on himself and still get his man. Other accolades from the arbiter acknowledged the superior gloveman as being "a terrific hitter" and running like "a jack rabbit on the bases." Ray's physical stature doesn't create the impression of speed, but he was deceptively fast on the bases. Ray relates an incident while he was still a schoolboy that illustrates his swiftness afoot. "When I was in school I ran a 100-yard dash, fell down and got up and won the race. I guess I moved pretty good for my bowlegs," he laughs.

Willie Wells, Ray's sidekick at shortstop, was also bowlegged and fast on the bases. He was known as a battler and was not shy about going into a base with his spikes high. He was a superlative shortstop whose only shortcoming was the lack of a strong arm, which he compensated for with a quick release. He also consistently hit over .300 with good extra-base power. Ray regards the man that he played beside both in the States and in Mexico as the best that he has ever seen.

> I've seen two or three great shortstops. Lundy was good, but in my opinion Willie Wells was the best. The man didn't have a great arm but he'd throw out everybody. I think I seen Lloyd play. He was going out as I came in. And everybody used to talk about him. But Willie was still the best.

Dick Seay was a player much like an infielder of recent years, the Orioles' Mark Belanger. Seay had a golden glove but was weak at the plate. Ray has high praise for Seay's defensive abilities, "He was a hell of a fielder, one of the greatest second basemen fielding we ever had." Ray adds, "But he couldn't hit." Seay compensated for his lack of offensive punch by moving runners over in other ways. He was a good bunter, could execute the hit-and-run play and was a good baserunner.

But you don't have to be fast to be a good ballplayer. Mule Suttles wasn't fast on the bases and was awkward fielding the initial sack, "but he could hit the ball nine miles." The amiable big first sacker was known as being able to "hit them just as far as Josh Gibson" although he didn't hit them as often and was not as good a contact hitter as was Josh. Mule was a dangerous man to have to face in a pressure situation, and his clutch home runs made him the hero in the All-Star Games of 1933 and 1935. Ray recalls once in Louisville when he saw Mule hit a ball over 500 feet only to have it caught.

When the Eagles needed another gold glove in the infield, they could call on Red Moore, who often spiced up infield practice by taking the throws at first base behind his back. The Eagles also were afforded the luxury of having two quick catchers who were outstanding defensively. First they had Johnny Hayes behind the plate, and a year later Leon Ruffin joined the team. Ray regards both receivers highly but has added praise for Ruffin's throwing arm. "Ruffin couldn't hit a ball out of the infield but nobody ran on him," he emphasizes. "That's why we say we had a million dollar infield."

The superlative infield was complemented by good players at the other positions. Ray recalls:

> In the outfield we had Jimmie Crutchfield, Ed Stone, and Lennie Pearson. Later we had Johnny Davis and Monte Irvin when they came in. Back during that time these guys were rookies. Leon Day was with us. We played Day anywhere that we needed help. He was fast, he could hit, and he could throw. And best of all he could pitch. He wasn't very big but he was a great pitcher. Nobody could throw any harder than he could.

Day didn't lose a single league game during the 1937 season. The Eagles also had Terris McDuffie pitching and, when he was right, he and Day formed a dynamic one-two punch for the Eagles.

Tex Burnett, the manager in 1937, had an easy time because he had so much outstanding talent on the team. "He didn't stay with us but one year," Ray remembers. "You know how it was years ago. Those guys weren't going to stay with you too long."

With Burnett's exit, former shortstop great Dick Lundy, who had originally signed Ray for the Newark Dodgers, again took over the managerial reins. After a few years at the helm his legs were getting bad and he left the team to go back to Jacksonville to work as a redcap at the railroad station. Ray credits Lundy with being a major influence in his development as a fielder. In later years, while passing through Florida to play winter ball in the Caribbean, Ray would often stop and talk to his old mentor.

Following Lundy's departure, Willie Wells and Biz Mackey each managed the club. Ray recalls one particularly fond memory of Mackey. "One year Biz Mackey said, 'I'm not going to manage the East-West Game unless you bring Dandridge to play third base for me.'" The East-West Game was black baseball's most prestigious event, and players were honored to be selected. Mackey's feelings were representative of others who had managed the man with the velvet hands. They appreciated Ray because he always gave a hundred percent no matter who the manager was. "I ain't never had any trouble with a manager," Ray states emphatically. And managers didn't have any trouble making out the lineup with the million dollar infield around.

Unfortunately, that infield didn't remain intact over an extended period of time because, within a few years, the superstars on the left side of the infield, Ray Dandridge and Willie "Devil" Wells, departed for Mexico, and slick-fielding second sacker Dick Seay went to Puerto Rico.

Ray still looks back on those days with the Eagles fondly, "Oh man, back during that time we didn't make any money but we had a lot of fun."

Except for the introductory paragraph and minor editorial changes, the content of this article is excerpted from my 1987 book, Dandy, Day and the Devil.

Willie Wells: El Diablo

Try to visualize the Hall of Fame without Honus Wagner, or imagine Ozzie Smith being passed over when he becomes eligible for inclusion. That is the equivalent of a Hall of Fame without Willie Wells. Easily one of the top ten shortstops of all time, he stood alone as the best at his position during his prime. When considering what constitutes greatness, regardless of the criteria used, Wells definitely qualifies. A complete ballplayer, he could hit, run, field, throw and hit with power. And he played with a competitive spirit that infused his natural ability with a fire that earned him the nickname "El Diablo" and made him a consistent winner.

A superior batter, he hit for average and with power, and was also a skilled bunter and an expert practitioner of the hit-and-run play. Playing with the St. Louis Stars, his hitting sizzled, as he posted averages of .378, .382, .353, .368 and .403 from 1926–1930, annexing a batting title the latter season and a home run title in 1929 with 27 in 88 games. A decade later, with the Newark Eagles, he hit for averages of .357, .386, .396 and .346 from 1936–39. After jumping to Mexico and batting .345 and .347, he returned to the Eagles in 1942 to top the league with a .344 mark. Even in the latter stages of his career, after a second stint in Mexico, he hit .320, .297 and .328 in 1945–1946 and 1948, respectively. He finished his career with lifetime marks of .334 in the Negro Leagues, .320 in Cuba, .378 in Puerto Rico and .392 against major leaguers in exhibition games.

His value to a team was further enhanced by his superlative defensive contributions, and Wells was acknowledged as the best at his position for two decades. He had sure hands, great quickness, and exceptional range, and excelled at turning the double play, utilizing a quick and accurate release to compensate for an average throwing arm. His stellar defensive play made him the hub of the Newark Eagles' "million dollar infield" in the late 1930s.

A smart, aggressive and instinctive baserunner, he consistently demonstrated his expertise in stealing bases, was always alert to take an extra base and quick to assert his right to the basepaths with a hard slide to break up a double play or move a fielder who was trying to block him off a base. His style on the bases was reminiscent of Ty Cobb, and gave him another offensive weapon to help win ballgames.

Always team oriented, Wells also possessed the intangibles that make a player valuable beyond the limits of his raw skills, and he consistently provided leadership and a contagious competitiveness. These intangible diamond attributes made him a winner, playing on Championship teams with the St. Louis Stars (1928, 1930 and 1931), the Chicago American Giants (1932 and 1933), Veracruz in the Mexican League (1940 and 1941) and Cienfuegas in the Cuban League (1929–1930).

His presence on a ballclub was coveted by other teams in the Negro Leagues, and his great baseball talent was recognized throughout the hemisphere, creating a demand for him in the Latin American leagues and in the Canadian Provincial League. Wherever he played, he was a star, earning MVP honors in Cuba and All-Star status in Mexico. Although he had already starred for a decade before the inception of the Negro League's East-West All-Star Game, he was selected to the All-Star team eight times and recorded a lifetime .281 All-Star batting average and a .438 slugging percentage.

He was a dominant player during his prime, was conceded to be the best at his position throughout his career, and sustained his performance for 26 years. Clearly, whether the measure of greatness is a player's dominance in prime years or his longevity, Willie Wells is a certain Hall of Famer.

On the baseball diamond, Willie Wells asked no quarter and gave no quarter. He was imbued with a level of competitive intensity rarely matched, which earned him the nickname "El Diablo" and earned him recognition as one of the greatest shortstops in baseball history.

A slightly shorter version of this article was first published in the Negro League Museum 1993 Yearbook. *I had initially postulated Willie Wells' definite qualification for the Hall of Fame in my 1987 book,* Dandy, Day and the Devil. *Not a person predisposed to champion his own cause, the man known as "El Diablo" (Spanish for "The Devil") thought that it was best to let others speak for him whenever discussions got around to that subject. In his heart Wells* knew that he was worthy of the honor and believed that he would eventually be elected, but he thought that it would come after he had passed away. The passage of time proved him right.

Wells, who died in 1989 prior to this article being written, was posthumously inducted into the National Baseball Hall of Fame in 1997. As anticipated in the article, Ozzie Smith joined him in 2002 when he was elected to the Hall of Fame in his first year of eligibility.

Other honors came to Wells after his induction into the Hall of Fame. In February of 1998 his hometown, Austin, Texas, honored him in a ceremony in which Congress Avenue was renamed Willie Wells Boulevard for the month and 100 eight-foot-high posters of Wells lined both sides of the street all the way to the state Capitol Building at the end of the avenue. In 2004 his hometown again honored him when his body was re-interred to the Texas State Cemetery to rest among the most prominent Texans in the state's history.

The accolades, although belated, kindled many memories from the time that we spent together. My most enduring memory of Willie was following a 1986 visit to his home on Newton Street in Austin. As I was leaving, he followed me to the door. "God bless you," he said as I closed the screen behind me.

God bless you, too, Willie.

Leon Day: A Living Legend of the Negro Leagues

Sunday, May 5, 1946. A new baseball season was beginning. It was the first opening day in five years that was not under the cloud of a World War. An opening day game always kindles a new hope and stirs emotions. But this year, it was more than just another baseball season. It was a homecoming for America. World War II had ended, and the ballplayers who had gone to war had returned along with the peace.

At Ruppert Stadium, in Newark, a slender right-hander walked to the mound. The opening day festivities were over but, for him, this was more than just another opening game. When he took the mound that day, Leon Day felt at home. The Newark Eagles' ace had spent two prime baseball years serving in an amphibian unit that landed on Utah Beach during the Allied invasion of France. "I was glad to be back in baseball and out of the Army," Day explains. "Until spring training that year, the only time I pitched was in 1945 in the G.I. World Series. I hadn't picked up a baseball before that for two years."

After V-E Day, Leon's OISE (Overseas Invasion Service Expedition) team faced General George Patton's Third Army team, predominantly comprised of major leaguers. By contrast, the OISE team consisted primarily of semipro players. In the battle for the ETO Championship at Nuremberg, Germany, with 100,000 American soldiers watching, Day defeated Ken Heintzelman 2–1, yielding only four scratch hits.

Afterward, the two teams were combined and flew to Italy, where Leon easily defeated the MTO Champions in a lopsided game. In a rematch in Nice, France, Leon and Willard Brown, the only two black Americans on the team, were asked to switch sides to make the contest more competitive. Not only did they change teams, they also changed the outcome, as Day defeated Ewell Blackwell, 8–0.

That was his last baseball game until after his return home. "I was discharged in February at Fort Dix, and went home to Newark until spring training. We trained in Tampa that year, but my arm wasn't too good. My arm

Leon Day could hold his own against any pitcher, including Satchel Paige. In head-to-head match-ups with his flamboyant opponent, the quiet, unassuming Day most often came out on top.

never was what it was before I went into the Army," he emphasizes. "It never was the same. My arm never felt right, even on opening day."

Even with two years of athletic rust and an arm not completely rehabilitated, Day was still the ace of the staff and manager Biz Mackey's choice to start on opening day. "I was a little nervous, like I always was at the beginning of a game," he recalls, "but after I got started, everything was all right."

That is a bit of an understatement. Bob Feller, another famous fastballer, is credited with the only opening day no-hitter in major league history, fashioning his gem in 1940. Leon Day's "all right" performance matched Feller's opening day no-hit feat.

Facing manager Oscar Charleston's Philadelphia Stars, Day won the game, 2–0, facing only 30 batters with no baserunner reaching second base. The only baserunners were the result of a walk and two errors, and he struck out six batters in the contest. Yet, Leon does not classify that game as one of his best. "I didn't have good stuff that day," he laughs. "I didn't have nothing on the ball at all. I've had way better stuff lots of times. Anytime I didn't strike out at least ten batters, I knew I didn't have good stuff." Typically, Day shares credit with others. "I had good control, and I had good defense."

Columnist Butts Brown wrote, "Leon showed he has lost none of his effectiveness because of his long stint in the Army." But Brown and other observers couldn't feel the pain in Day's right arm. "I fell on it fielding a bunt during the no-hitter," Leon confides, "but I finished the game." Even with the bad arm, he continued his pitching heroics during the season, topping the league in strikeouts, innings pitched, and complete games. He finished with a 13–4 record for the 63-game season, to pace the Eagles' drive to the Negro National League title. But a price had been paid for the pennant, as the workhorse re-injured his pitching arm late in the season.

Despite the pain, the veteran moundsman started two games in the ensuing Negro World Series. "The New York Giants' trainer taped my arm up before the game at the Polo Grounds," he remembers, "and it felt pretty good for a while. But after about two innings, I couldn't pitch." Unable to continue on the mound in the Series, the versatile athlete was inserted into the lineup in center field and made a game-saving catch to help the Eagles edge Satchel Paige's Kansas City Monarchs in seven games.

Throughout his career, Day delighted in hooking up with Satchel in pitching duels. Before entering the Army, the 1942 Negro World Series had served as a backdrop for one of their classic encounters. After dropping the first three games to the Monarchs, the Homestead Grays added Day to their roster to face Satchel. "I guess they picked me to go against Satchel because they figured I could beat him," understates the modest but tough competitor. When the game was over, Leon had a dozen strikeouts, a five-hit, 4–1 victory, and a double off Satchel. For this sterling performance, he received the princely sum of $100 and a train ticket back home. Today a pitcher gets more than that for picking up a resin bag.

Monte Irvin, a Newark Eagles teammate, recalls another of these classic match-ups. "One day we were playing against Satchel Paige and Leon said, 'Get me a run.' But Satchel had us shut out and we couldn't get the run. So Leon hit a home run and won his own ballgame. That's the kind of player he was."

"If you could have seen this man when he was in his prime," Monte continues, "you would never forget him. He was the perfect pitcher and when the going got tough, you wanted Leon Day on your side. In a must-win situation, the manager always gave the ball to Leon. If we had one game to win, we wanted Leon to pitch."

Day holds the individual game record for strikeouts in both the Negro National League (18) and the Puerto Rican Winter League (19), and the lifetime strikeout mark for Negro League All-Star games (14). In second place on the All-Star list is his favorite rival, Satchel Paige.

Unlike the flamboyant Paige, Day never stood out from the crowd until he got a baseball in his hand. Then everyone took notice. In his prime, his blinding fastball made him the best pitcher in the Negro National League. Today, he is the last living player from the Negro Leagues not enshrined in the Hall of Fame who definitely deserves the honor. When the Veterans Committee met in February, he missed by a single vote. The disappointment from that near miss did not abate the ground swell of public awareness being generated across America. Within the last year the accolades have finally begun to come his way.

On February 19, 1992, Day was one of four ex–Negro League players invited to the White House to meet President George Bush. Two weeks later, on March 3, he was a guest on the "Larry King Show" on the Mutual Broadcasting System. Two months later, Maryland Governor William Donald Schaefer proclaimed May 18, 1992, to be Leon Day day and during ceremonies in Baltimore, he was presented a key to the City. On September 24, baseball got into the act as the ace right-hander took the mound at Camden Yards to throw out the honorary first pitch on Leon Day's day with the Orioles.

But all the hoopla and media attention has not changed Leon Day. The former superstar is still a gracious host with a quick wit and charming sense of humor that belies his status as one of the best pitchers of his generation. He remains modest and soft spoken and, as is his manner, talks more about other players than about himself. When attending reunions or appearing at baseball functions he is satisfied to sit quietly outside the spotlight and let someone else hold center stage. A casual observer would never guess that this quiet, unpretentious man had appeared in seven East-West All-Star Games and in his prime out-dueled the legendary Satchel Paige.

His best season record came in 1937 when, backed by the Eagles' "million dollar infield," he finished league play with a perfect 13–0 record and a .320

batting average. After his perfect season, he injured his arm in the Cuban winter league and missed virtually all of the next season, but through hard work and determination, he rehabilitated the arm and was credited with a 16–4 mark in 1939.

In 1940, he succumbed to the lure of a higher salary and left the Eagles for Latin America. He carved out a 12–1 record, while pitching Caracas' Vargas ballclub to the Venezuelan Championship, and then signed with Veracruz in the Mexican League, where he logged a perfect 6–0 record and contributed a .298 batting average as they captured the Mexican Championship.

After his season in the Latin climate, the Eagles welcomed their star back into the fold in 1941, and issued a publicity release describing Day as "the most versatile and outstanding player on the team." In 1942, he established the league's strikeout mark as he fanned 18 Baltimore Elite Giants, including Roy Campanella three times, and saved the All-Star Game by striking out five of the seven batters that he faced, including the final four in succession. At the end of the season, Homestead Grays owner Cum Posey selected him over Satchel on his All-Star Dream Team, stating, "Leon Day was the best pitcher in Negro Baseball ... despite the fact that he was used daily, either as a pitcher, outfielder or infielder." The following season, his last before entering the Army, he was described by the *Pittsburgh Courier* as "the outstanding moundsman in Negro baseball."

Born October 30, 1916, in Alexandria, Virginia, Day's family moved to Mount Winen, Maryland, where he played sandlot and semi-pro baseball before making his first excursion into professional baseball with the Baltimore Black Sox in 1934. When his father asked him if he really wanted to leave home to play baseball, he responded, "That's the *only* thing I want to do." For the next 22 years, summer and winter in a half-dozen countries, that is exactly what he did.

His love for baseball has not waned but, until recently, he received little in return except a heart full of memories. At the age of 76, Leon has an assortment of ailments that comes with the passage of time. "I've got a bad kidney and gout in my foot," he admits, "but I'm doing all right." If Father Time continues to be kind, maybe Leon can corner that elusive vote necessary to join Satchel Paige at Cooperstown. When that happens, Leon Day will feel at home again.

This article was first published in the August 1993 issue of The Diamond: The Official Chronicle of Major League Baseball *with the title "Make Room for Leon Day: Is the Former Negro Leagues Star the Next Member of the Hall of Fame?"*

Less than two years after this was written, Leon was elected to the Hall of Fame. He was in the hospital when he learned of the vote. "I'm feeling good," he told me when I phoned him. "I'm sick but I'm feeling good." It was gratifying to know that he had been honored, but his health was failing and he died March 13, 1995, only a couple of weeks after being elected.

At the induction ceremonies in Cooperstown, his wife Geri accepted on his behalf, and in her acceptance speech she expressed her wish that Leon could have been able to accept the honor in person. It is a shame that Leon could not have garnered that solitary vote the year before, so that he could have experienced the camaraderie that comes with induction into the Hall of Fame brotherhood.

In the spring of 1989 I wrote an article that was published in Oldtyme Baseball News *in which I stated: "Leon Day was consistently the best pitcher in the Negro National League during his career.... Today Leon is the last living player from the Negro Leagues who—without question—deserves to be in the Hall of Fame." Then I concluded the article with the observation: "Like all old-timers, as the years get more remote, the home runs get longer, the strikeouts become more numerous, and the memories grow sweeter. As sweet as the smell of the roses will be a Cooperstown when Leon is finally permitted to savor the fragrance of the long denied, but richly deserved, recognition of his forgotten greatness."*

Buck O'Neil: The Dean of the Monarchs

He's the Dean of the Monarchs, walking tall and proud, carrying his 80 years with a noble dignity borne from labor in the celery fields of Florida and nurtured on baseball diamonds all across the continent. The measure of success that Buck O'Neil has enjoyed in his baseball career is directly proportional to the intrinsic motivation for him to escape a life of labor in the fields. A generation later, he might have gone to the University of Florida, earned a master's degree in business administration and moved into the front office after the completion of his career in the dugout. But 1934 was a different time socially and economically. Depression lay heavy on the land and black youngsters didn't think about playing in the major leagues, much less about working in an executive position with a major league ballclub.

So a youthful Buck O'Neil, who eventually was to become the first black coach in the major leagues, embarked on a course that would lead him to a more attainable goal and secured his father's blessing to try his hand at earning a living from baseball. He began playing professionally with the Miami Giants — forerunners of the Indianapolis Clowns — and after four years as a vagabond ballplayer with the New York Tigers, Zulu Giants, Acme Giants and Memphis Red Sox, he eventually found a home with the Kansas City Monarchs. Once there, only Naval service during World War II interrupted his brilliant footwork around the initial sack. From 1938 through 1955, he exemplified the spirit of the Monarchs. There were other players who were more colorful and more talented but none had more heart or a keener baseball mind.

As an all-star first baseman he played in the first Negro World Series between the Negro American League and the Negro National League. The series was a classic confrontation — pitching vs. power and youth vs. experience — featuring two great dark dynasties. The NNL Champion Homestead Grays featured the power tandem of Josh Gibson and Buck Leonard, often called the black Babe Ruth and Lou Gehrig, while the NAL Champion Kansas City Monarchs featured a pitching staff headed by the famed Satchel Paige-

Hilton Smith combination. But the Monarchs were not *all* pitching, and fielded a team that demonstrated excellent defense, good baserunning, and a potent offense generated from the bats of Willard Brown, Ted Strong, Joe Greene and Buck O'Neil. The teams were evenly matched but the Grays were accorded the role as slight favorites in the Series. The Monarchs, however, had different ideas, and O'Neil and his compatriots swept the Grays in four

Buck O'Neil was a standout first baseman on the Kansas City Monarchs teams that won five of the first six NAL pennants before his career was interrupted by service in the U.S. Navy during World War II. After his return in 1946, O'Neil captured the league batting title and the Monarchs won another pennant.

straight games. Satchel Paige had a good Series against his former teammate Josh Gibson. But as O'Neil says, "Satchel had a pretty good series *every* year."

Unofficially, the Grays won one game from Satchel when Leon Day bested him in Kansas City, but the game was disallowed because the Grays' owner Cum Posey had picked up the Newark Eagles' ace as a "ringer" and he was not on their World Series roster. Buck O'Neil remembers that game from his Kansas City home.

> I remember mostly the fact Leon Day pitched against us in that Series, but the ball game didn't count. We had beaten them three ballgames and we moved to Kansas City and Posey got Leon and somebody else off of that ballclub to come out and play against us in Kansas City. Leon struck the bat out of our hands on us. We didn't do nothing on him, really. He threw the ball right by us. But the ball game didn't count because he wasn't eligible.

O'Neil spent another season with the Monarchs and was just hitting his stride as an all-star ballplayer when World War II intervened. Many players suffered from athletic rust after their tour of duty but the classy first sacker's self-discipline enabled him to be an exception.

> Well, there's one thing about it. I was in pretty good shape. I was in a stevedore battalion, so I was in good shape. Even when I was in the service I would run, especially after the war was over in '45. So I would run and do a lot of things to get myself in shape because I knew I was coming back to play baseball.

His determination and preparation paid off. After two years in the Navy, he returned to the baseball home front in 1946 to cop a league batting title with a robust .350 average, while pacing the Monarchs to another NAL flag. This thrust them into another classic Negro World Series. This time the Monarchs faced the Newark Eagles, who had ended the Grays' nine-year skein of pennants in the NNL. The Eagles were a young team that featured a keystone combination of future major league stars — shortstop Monte Irvin and second baseman Larry Doby — and a strong pitching staff comprised of Leon Day, Max Manning, Rufus Lewis and Len Hooker. The Monarchs again featured the Satchel Paige-Hilton Smith combo but also had a lot of help with Lefty LaMarque, Connie Johnson and Ford Smith.

O'Neil and his teammates jumped off to a 3–2 lead in games, but with only one victory needed to wrap up the black championship, Satchel Paige and Ted Strong left the team to negotiate a winter league contract, leaving the Monarchs short-handed for the final two games. The sixth game was the turning point in the Series. With scouts from the Brooklyn Dodgers and New York Giants watching from the stands, the game turned into a slugfest. Monte Irvin paced the Eagles with a perfect 3-for-3 day, including a pair of homers. Buck O'Neil, with a grand slam already under his belt as he stepped into the batter's box in the eighth inning with the tying runs on base, tried to match his opponent's power display and blasted a ball towards deep center field that looked like a sure triple to everyone present. But the versatile Leon Day, Newark's ace pitcher who was playing center field in this game, ran the ball down, making a sensational over-the-shoulder catch to rob O'Neil of an extra-base hit and save the game.

> When Leon wasn't pitching Leon had to be in that ballgame someplace. I hit the ball to straightaway center field over Leon's head. I just wish I could have pulled the ball a little because it would have been a home run had I pulled it a little. The center field was deep but in left of center that wall ran down the part of the stands which was a short field there. But I hit it straightaway center field and I thought sure it was going to be extra bases and possibly a home run if that ball had gotten over or by him. But Leon Day ran that ball down and caught it. And really, he actually caught the ballgame.

Literally, Day saved the day. Leon remembers the game too. "My arm was bad and they put me in center field," he recalls. "That was in Newark and center field was 410 feet. Along about the eighth inning O'Neil hit one. I was kinda shading him over and he hit the ball a little to right-center. I had to go a pretty good ways to get it," the modest former superstar says simply. Unlike Willie Mays, who made *the catch* off Vic Wertz in the 1954 World Series and maintains that he knew he had it from the time the ball left the bat, Day did not know if he could catch up with the ball. "I didn't know I had it until I looked over my shoulder and saw it coming down."

After the sixth game fireworks, the finale was close (3–2) but somewhat anti-climactic. O'Neil hammered a homer in the sixth inning to tie the score at 1–1, but the Eagles came back in the bottom half of the inning to win the game when outfielder Johnny Davis doubled home Irvin and Doby to sew up the game and the championship. O'Neil points out a factor that may have made the difference in the outcome.

> What hurt us mostly was we were playing the seventh ballgame without Satchel Paige and Ted Strong. But what happened, they were signing up to go to play ball in Puerto Rico and they thought they would get there on time, but they got tied up in traffic because we stayed over in New York City, and they just didn't get there. That really hurt us, but we still could have lost the ballgame.

Although the Monarchs lost, O'Neil did more than his part, finishing the Series with two homers and a .346 batting average.

The following spring Jackie Robinson, who had played with the Kansas City Monarchs while O'Neil was in the service, made his debut in a Brooklyn Dodger uniform. As the door to organized baseball opened, Buck O'Neil was one among many Negro League veterans who were good enough to play in the big leagues but whose age was against them. "I was too old for that," he emphasizes. At the age of 36, he was past his prime but continued as an everyday player through 1950 and, having taken over the managerial reins in 1948, he relegated himself to only occasional appearances and pinch-hitting duties thereafter.

After leaving the Monarchs, he became a coach with the Chicago Cubs and later a top scout for many years. Today, he remains active in baseball affairs, and is the Chairman of the Board of Directors for the Negro League Museum in Kansas City. And he is *still* the Dean of the Monarchs.

This article was first published in 1992 in Oldtyme Baseball News *(Vol. 6, No. 4) as the feature* Forgotten Heroes, *which spotlighted the greatest black baseball players before 1947.*

In the accounts of the 1942 and 1946 Negro World Series, there are two questions that should be addressed. One is an incident that was not included in this article but was later described by O'Neil where Satchel Paige intentionally walked the bases full to pitch to Josh Gibson and then proceeded to strike him out. This account was disputed by Homestead Grays first baseman Buck Leonard, who stated that he had no recollection of this incident.

The other incident involved the 1946 Series, and involves the reason for the absence of Paige and Strong in the seventh game. Neither player appeared after the fourth game of the Series. Willard Brown's version (as he related it to me) is that the two absent teammates had "picked up a couple of girls" in Chicago (where the fifth game was played) and preferred their company to making the trip to Newark for the final two games.

After the Series, the Kansas City Call *reported that Strong had "deserted the team" and Monarchs owner J. L. Wilkinson stated that Strong had "walked out on his team without giving any reason for his actions." Subsequently, Strong expressed regret for his behavior and offered several exculpatory factors that contributed to his actions, including an attempt by gamblers to bribe him to fix the outcome of the Chicago game.*

Satchel's absence is not addressed in these newspaper accounts, and questions about the official explanation have generated speculative inquiries. One possible contributing factor in his "no show" might be found in his post-season tour with Bob Feller. Satchel's Negro League All-Stars traveled with Feller's All-Stars in a coast-to-coast barnstorming tour that began in Pittsburgh the day after the seventh game of the Negro World Series was played in Newark. This monetarily rewarding tour certainly required much personal attention and might have taken the top spot on Satchel's list of priorities. We may never know the complete truth.

A much different kind of question about an absence surfaced in 2006 with the exclusion of Buck O'Neil from the group of 17 former Negro League personalities elected to the Hall of Fame by the Special Committee appointed for this purpose. Amid the surrounding furor, although in failing health, the popular baseball ambassador spoke at the ceremony honoring those who were elected.

Shortly afterward, on October 6, 2006, Buck O'Neil passed away in Kansas City, Missouri, at the age of 94. Two years later, he was honored by the National Baseball Hall of Fame and Museum when his permanent life-size statue was dedicated in Cooperstown, New York.

Bill Byrd: Baseball's Black Spitballer

The occasion was the 50th anniversary of the National Baseball Hall of Fame at Cooperstown, New York. Roy Campanella sat on the veranda of the Otesaga Hotel and looked out over the calm waters of the lake that served as James Fenimore Cooper's model for Glimmerglass in his classic Leatherstocking stories. The Hall of Famer's eyes were focused on the mist rising from the horizon where the mountains surrounding the lake converge, but his mind saw 50 years into the past when he was a catcher for the Baltimore Elite Giants in the Negro National League.

"We had at least four pitchers on our staff who could have won 20 games in the major leagues," Campy said quietly, "and Bill Byrd was the ace of our staff. Byrd had exceptional control and," Campy added with emphasis, "he had something on the ball! He threw a slow knuckler, fast knuckler, slider, roundhouse curve, fastball and sinker," Campy continued as he took inventory of his old battery mate's repertoire. "And," he understated, saving the best for last, "He had the privilege of throwing the spitball."

Byrd was one of the last black pitchers to have that distinction. When the white leagues outlawed the "spitter" in 1920, the Negro Leagues assumed a position consistent with the decree, permitting only previously identified pitchers to continue utilizing the pitch. Unlike most spitballers, the big Baltimore righthander could spot the pitch. "Most pitchers bounce it in the dirt," Campanella recalled as he gazed out over the lake into the past, "but he would keep it up where you could handle it."

At his home in Philadelphia, Bill Byrd also took a glimpse into the past and described the pitch taught to him in 1932 by Roosevelt Davis when they were teammates on the Columbus Blue Birds. "I could make it come in or out, down, or break it in-and-down, or out-and-down. And I never had any trouble with control."

The old spitball master's "wet one" was only one weapon that he used to cut down enemy batters. In August of 1947, when Larry Doby made the transition from the Negro Leagues to become the first black player in the American League, he compared the pitching in the two leagues. "The pitchers

Bill Byrd was one of the last legal spitball pitchers. The Baltimore Elite Giants ace effectively utilized both a spitter and a "fake spitter" along with a diverse array of other pitches in his repertoire.

in this league (American League) use more head work. They throw a lot of curves and sliders and keep the ball low. They pitch like Bill Byrd."

Doby's teammate on the Newark Eagles that season, Monte Irvin, confirmed this assessment. Joining Campanella on the veranda, the Hall of Famer recalled the first time he faced Byrd in the Negro Leagues. "I was right out of college and I didn't know anything about him. I went five-for-five that day, but I don't remember ever getting another hit off him. He was that tough!"

Byrd was a smart pitcher who kept a mental book on batters and had such confidence in all of his pitches that he would tailor them for each hitter. "It depends on who the batter was as to which pitch was my out pitch," he stated. For major league slugger Joe Gordon, it was Byrd's roundhouse curve. "Every year there would be a bunch come to Baltimore and we would play until the weather would turn bad," Byrd related. "We were playing the All-Stars and Gordon came up to bat. I threw one of them little old roundhouse curve balls and he looked up at me and said, 'Damn, what was that?' I said, 'That was a little old roundhouse.' He said, 'You could throw it around a barrel!'"

But even when Byrd wasn't throwing the spitter, it was still one of his most effective pitches because he had hitters looking for it. "He would go to his mouth with two fingers like he was going to load it up," Irvin recalled, "And you would be looking for it and then here would come that fastball or that roundhouse curve or one of those other pitches." Campanella chuckled and nodded, remembering his old teammate's ploy. Byrd acknowledged that he used to play mind games with the batters to keep them guessing. "They trained me to do that," he explained about the Elites' management. "They made me fake it all the time."

Byrd also remembered the first time Campy got behind the plate after joining the Elites in 1937. "I told them to get that kid out of there before he got killed," Byrd laughed. When reminded of his initial difficulty with Byrd's favorite pitch, Campy looked out at the lake again and smiled, remembering his introduction to the spitter as a 15-year-old rookie. "When I first got up there I didn't really know anything about catching," he said laughing. "I learned to catch in batting practice. They had Biz Mackey and I was just a kid."

Mackey was one of the greatest of all time, and Campanella's apprenticeship as a receiver was accelerated by the presence of the veteran, who took the enthusiastic teenager under his wing. "We all looked after him because he was so young," recalled Byrd. "He always called me 'Daddy.'" The nurturing by the veterans paid off as Campy quickly learned the skills of his position and developed into a premier receiver. By then Campy was ready for the major leagues — if the doors had been open. "He could have gone straight to the majors," appraised Byrd. But while he was awaiting the opportunity, Campy was gaining invaluable experience in the Negro Leagues.

Years later, when he joined the Dodgers, Campy would handle Preacher Roe's spitter without any trouble, having learned about the pitch from catching Byrd. "With Byrd we had a signal," he remembered, "but not with

Preacher." Campy paused for a moment and there was a twinkle in his eye. "We never had a signal for it, but I always knew when Preacher was going to throw the spitter."

Roe was only one of many pitchers who have utilized the outlawed pitch. Gaylord Perry won 314 games with it, a goal that almost automatically qualifies him for the Hall of Fame. When he is elected, he will join the best known of the last legal spitball stars, Burleigh Grimes, who is already ensconced in the marbled halls at Cooperstown. Does Byrd, the black Burleigh Grimes, also deserve a plaque there?

"Bill Byrd should be considered," Campy responded. "He was a good pitcher and he was good for a long time!" The Baltimore spitball artist's career spanned 19 seasons (1932–1950), mostly with the Baltimore Elite Giants. During that span he maintained close to a .600 winning percentage and played in seven All-Star Games.

Today he would be among the black superstars signing multi-million dollar contracts, but conditions a generation ago presented a stark contrast. "Sometimes it seems it never happened, or that it happened in another century," an unembittered Byrd said on behalf of his generation of black players. "Why should we be bitter? We understood how things were. Those were the times."

Today the times are better and Byrd, now 82 years of age and retired from General Electric, lives comfortably with the lady he married 53 years ago. "I've been his number one rooter since 1936," Hazel Byrd adamantly asserts, "and Bill Byrd belongs in the Hall of Fame." If the Veterans Committee agrees, maybe next year the old spitballer could join Campy on the veranda at Cooperstown.

This article was first published in 1989 *in* Oldtyme Baseball News *(Vol. 1, No. 4) as the feature* Forgotten Heroes, *which spotlighted the greatest black baseball players before 1947.*

The following spring I went to Dodgertown in Vero Beach with Ray Dandridge. Dodgers manager Tommy Lasorda, who had played against Ray in Cuba, was a great admirer of Dandridge and had issued a standing invitation for Ray to come down any time he wanted.

We were in Lasorda's office along with Roy Campanella, Sandy Koufax and Joe Ferguson. Ray and Campy had played against each other in the Negro Leagues and in Mexico. Campy said to Ray, "Come over here. I've got something I want you to read. It's the best article that I've ever read." Ray said to me, "Riley, come over here, you'll want to read this too." I looked at it and said, "This is *a good article but I don't have to read it. I wrote it."*

Campy's remark had made my day.

Less than a year later, on January 4, 1991, Bill Byrd died in Philadelphia. On June 26, 1993, in Woodland Hills, California, Roy Campanella joined his old battery mate in eternity.

Sandwiched between the loss of these two great players was the 1992 induction of Gaylord Perry into the Hall of Fame. In contrast, Byrd continued to be passed over by the Veterans Committee each year. In 2006 the Hall of Fame empowered a special committee to make a final determination on all players from the Negro Leagues. Once again, Bill Byrd was overlooked.

Dave Barnhill: Impo

Dave Barnhill was small, weighing only 130 pounds "when it snowed on him." But on the mound he stood tall. Leon Day, a six-time All-Star pitcher with the Newark Eagles and a contemporary of Barnhill's, marvels, "That's what I couldn't understand about him. He was so small but he could throw that ball like he did. Very few people could throw as hard as he did."

A strikeout artist, Barnhill threw so hard that he scared himself. "I was afraid I might hit somebody," he says. Fortunately, his control was as good as his fastball. When he was right he could throw as hard as the legendary Satchel Paige. Hall of Famer Buck Leonard of the Homestead Grays, who faced Barnhill year in and year out, concurs. "He was a humdinger. He was one of the best we had in our leagues. He threw just as hard as anybody. He was right up there with Slim Jones and Satchel Paige, right next to them."

Indeed, there were some who maintained that there really wasn't any difference between Satchel and Dave. This contention was illustrated one year when Dave was recruited to pitch behind Satchel Paige for the Kansas City Monarchs on a barnstorming trip. This particular day the Monarchs were playing the Toledo Mudhens, a AAA white ballclub. Satch shut out the Mudhens over the first four innings, yielding a single hit while striking out ten batters. The slightly embarrassed Toledo manager approached Frank Duncan, the Monarchs' manager, and said, "Hey, how about putting somebody else in so we can kinda even things up. After all we're a major league farm club." Duncan looked down to the bullpen, where Barnhill was warming up, and said, "How about that little guy down there?" The Toledo manager quickly agreed, "Okay, put him in." Dave walked out to the mound, wound up and threw the first pitch — and the batter just stood there with his bat on his shoulder, not believing a little man could throw so hard. And so it went for the rest of the ball game. Dave pitched the last five innings without allowing a hit while striking out 11. After the game Toledo's manager came into the clubhouse and said to Duncan, "You think you're smart, that you pulled a fast one or something." Duncan said, "What do you mean?" Toledo's manager explained, "You said that you'd take Satchel out, but you didn't. You just took him over behind the dugout and cut his legs off and put him right back in." Dave chuckles when recounting the incident.

Satchel figured prominently in Dave's career. As the ace on the New York Cubans' pitching staff, Dave was matched up with Satch every time the Kansas City Monarchs came to town. Dave remembers, "Normally when Satchel pitched against other teams, he would only pitch three innings and if he got

Dave Barnhill was small but he stood tall on the mound and could throw as hard as anyone. He and Satchel Paige were the starting pitchers in the 1943 East-West All-Star Game.

one score ahead, he would come out. But any time he came to play the Cubans, I had to pitch against him so he had to pitch nine innings. He didn't let my team get nothing and I didn't let his team get nothing. We didn't have any of that foolishness about pitching three innings and coming out."

It was the same way in the East-West Game, which was the Negro Leagues' All-Star game. When Satchel pitched, Dave pitched; and when Satchel started, Dave started. This classic match-up provided Dave with his biggest thrill in baseball, as he and Satchel were the opposing starting pitchers in the 1943 All-Star Game at Comiskey Park in front of 52,000 fans.

Some might think that this would make anyone nervous. After all, facing a legend in front of 52,000 screaming fans is a far cry from playing stickball in the streets of Greenville, North Carolina, where Dave learned his baseball skills as a youngster. But Dave was always cool and collected on the mound. He recalls, "When I walked out of the clubhouse and saw all those people, then I wanted to put on my big show. That ain't no time to be nervous."

And the record backs up his claim. In his three All-Star appearances from 1941 through 1943, he pitched a total of nine innings, giving up only two runs while striking out six batters. This was accomplished against the best in the Negro American League, including such stalwart hitters as Cool Papa Bell, Newt Allen, Alex Radcliffe, Neil Robinson, Ted Strong, Buck O'Neil, Parnell Woods, Willard Brown and Jimmie Crutchfield. The veteran Crutchfield, who was then playing with the Chicago American Giants, vouches for what the Toledo players had learned earlier. "There were days when he could throw as hard as Satchel." Johnny Davis, hard-hitting All-Star outfielder of the Newark Eagles (who had to face Barnhill all season long), picks Dave as the pitcher who gave him the most trouble. Hall of Famer Cool Papa Bell is more direct and to the point: "He threw smoke."

It was during these years that Barnhill received the first hope that he might get the opportunity to pitch in the major leagues. In a telegram dated July 24, 1942 (more than three years before Jackie Robinson signed with the Dodgers organization and before any black player had a tryout with a major league team), he received the following message from sports editor Nat Low:

HAVE JUST ARRANGED WITH WILLIAM BENSWANGER, PRESIDENT PITTSBURGH PIRATES, A TRYOUT FOR YOU WITH TEAM IN PITTSBURGH SOON. CONGRATULATIONS. WON'T YOU PLEASE GET IN TOUCH WITH ME SO THAT WE CAN MAKE FULL ARRANGEMENTS?

For whatever his reasons, Benswanger backed out of his commitment, thus denying Dave a chance to be the first black player in organized baseball in modern times. Regarding the incident, Dave remembers, "He [Benswanger] was scared to take a chance."

Dave wasn't discouraged. He knew from his barnstorming trips that he was good enough to play in the major leagues. He continued his winning ways in the Negro National League, coming back from a sore arm to team with Luis Tiant, Sr. and pitch the New York Cubans to a championship in 1947. Neither he nor Tiant lost a game during that season. He also picked up another victory in the Negro World Series that year, shutting out the Negro American League champion Cleveland Buckeyes, 6–0, as the New York Cubans took the Series four games to one.

That winter Dave went to Cuba for the first of three winters that he spent with the Marianao team. He led the league in strikeouts while compiling a 2.26 ERA. One game, played January 10, 1948, was especially noteworthy. In this game Dave locked up with Connie Marrero, who was to spend five major league seasons with the Washington Senators, in a 15-inning, 0–0 marathon. Dave struck out 15 batters while allowing only two walks and five hits before the game was called. In the opposing lineup were future major leaguers Monte Irvin, Sam Jethroe, and Dee Fondy as well as Negro League All-Stars Gene Benson and Pee Wee Butts.

The next winter Dave did even better, leading the Cuban league in victories as well as complete games. The New York Giants organization signed him and Ray Dandridge, veteran black third baseman, to contracts. Buck Leonard states, "Now you take Dandridge and Barnhill, they could have gone right on to the major leagues." Ray Dandridge himself agrees and says of Dave, "He was one of the best pitchers there was. During that time he was great." But the major league powers-that-be thought that black players needed time in the minors to adjust to playing with white players. And although both Barnhill and Dandridge had been playing with white players for years in the winter leagues, they were sent to the Giants' AAA farm team, the Minneapolis Millers. There they pitched and batted the team to the championship in 1950. Dandridge batted .311 and earned MVP honors while Dave compiled an 11–3 won-lost record. This earned him a second brush with the major leagues.

Dave remembers, "The year we won the championship, Leo Durocher was going to bring me up because I had a pretty good year and he was going to call me up like they do a lot of ballplayers at the last part of the season. Let them play with the major leaguers. But we got into a play-off. I told Dandridge, 'My goodness, I could have gone up and got a cup of coffee and come on back.'"

But it was never to be. By then Dave was 36 years old and past his prime as a player. Instead of going to the major leagues he stayed at Minneapolis and helped launch a youngster named Willie Mays. Later the Giants sent him to Oakland in the Pacific Coast League. From there he returned to Florida to be near his family and pitch for Pepper Martin's Miami Beach Flamingos. He closed out his career with Fort Lauderdale in 1953.

After ending his baseball career, he worked for the Miami Department of Recreation and Parks, retiring in 1981. A handsome plaque presented to him by the Miami City Commission upon his retirement reads as follows:

> TO DAVE BARNHILL IN GRATEFUL APPRECIATION FOR YOUR OUTSTANDING DEMONSTRATION OF SKILLS AND DEVOTION TO DUTY WHILE EMPLOYED BY THE CITY OF MIAMI FROM SEPTEMBER 1953 THROUGH JANUARY 1981. YOUR PERFORMANCE HAS BEEN AN EXCELLENT EXAMPLE TO THOSE WHO WORKED WITH YOU.

This vividly describes the qualities that made Dave the ballplayer that he was, as well as the kind of man he is.

This article was previously published in the 1981 SABR Research Journal under the succinct title "Dave Barnhill" and also appeared in the anthology Insider's Baseball, *edited by Bob Davids with a foreword by Bill James and published by Charles Scribner's Sons in 1983.*

The two versions were essentially the same with the exception that the original SABR article included the final sentence "Today, Dave Barnhill lives in Miami with his gracious wife, Suzie, and their lovely daughter, Scherry Lee."

Dave Barnhill died January 8, 1983, in Miami, Florida, at the age of 68.

Edsall Walker: The Catskill Wildman

Beginning in 1937, the Homestead Grays won nine consecutive Negro National League pennants. One of the top moundsmen on eight of those championship ballclubs was a hard-throwing left-hander with a look in his eye that transmitted the unspoken assertion that the inside third of the plate belonged to him. His name was Edsall Walker, but the media called him "The Catskill Wildman."

He earned that appellation for two reasons. First, because he hailed from the area around the Catskill Mountains, and second because he was afflicted with the "left-handers' disease." When he turned loose of a baseball, he had an uncertain idea about what direction it would ultimately take. The ball was about as likely to wind up against the backstop as it was to cut the heart of the plate.

But, while his location was erratic, his velocity was a known quantity. "When I first went to the Grays I could really *throw*," Walker says without any presence of braggadocio. The big Homestead hurler had two pitches — a high hard fastball and a low running fastball. Coupled with the "heat" that he brought to the mound, his peculiar occupational attribute called "wildness" often worked in his favor.

A fastball low and away was his most effective pitch but, when he could control it, his "high heat" also proved expedient, especially when it was aided by an intimidating look in his eye that reflected his propensity to play "chin music" for any batter foolhardy enough to dig in against him. When a batter deigned to "insult" the big, muscular hurler by getting a solid foothold, Edsall would watch from the mound, while sometimes giving voice to his intentions, "Go ahead and dig it deep, 'cause I'm going to bury you in it."

Edsall admits that not even his own teammates were exempted from this intimidation. "If I pitched batting practice and one of them hit the ball back through the box, he would go and sit down and he wouldn't bat no more, because he knew I was going to throw at him."

A favorite story about his inclination to assert himself in this manner traces its origins back to the 1938 East-West All-Star Game. With both Josh

Edsall Walker was the top left-hander on the Homestead Grays' pitching staff during eight pennant-winning seasons. His best year was 1938, when he earned the starting assignment in the East-West All-Star Game. Walker (right) is pictured with Hall of Famers Josh Gibson and Ray Brown.

Gibson and Buck Leonard in their prime, the Grays' squad that year was considered to be the best during their skein of nine straight flags. That season Edsall teamed with right-hander Raymond Brown in a rotation reminiscent of the Boston Braves' "Spahn and Sain and pray for rain" mound corps that carried the Braves to a National League pennant a decade later.

Edsall's personal best performance in 1938 earned him the starting assignment for the East squad in the East-West Game but, unfortunately, he experienced some difficulty with his control and suffered the loss in the contest. On the trip back east following the game, Newark Eagles superstar shortstop Willie Wells chided Edsall, "We can't beat you and you go out there and let them chumps beat you."

"Wells, you better watch yourself!" the big hurler responded. "I'm going to be pitching against you some day."

"That's all right," Wells retorted. "I've got me a helmet."

As fate would have it, when the two teams played their next game at Buffalo, New York, Grays manager Vic Harris handed the ball to his hard-throwing left-hander. When Wells came to the plate, Edsall looked in from the mound and reminded him, "Hey, Wells! Here I am!"

The fiery Wells responded, "*Throw* the ball, sucker."

Edsall accommodated the request. "The first pitch I hit him right between the shoulder blades," he recalls. "I told him, 'That helmet didn't do you any good, did it, Willie?'"

Nailing Wells was nothing new for Edsall, who regularly used Wells as a target, as did almost all of the Grays' hurlers. "Everybody on the team threw at him except Raymond Brown," the former Grays hurler says. Brown's reluctance to knock Wells down was especially exceptional because, when the Grays and Eagles squared off, it was much like the Brooklyn Dodgers–New York Giants confrontations, with each hurler swapping "paybacks" throughout the game.

"When we played Newark, my first pitch hit against the backstop," Edsall says, "and Josh would tell the hitter, 'Man you better watch out, Walker's wild today.'" That was just a little intimidation, and Edsall attributes the intense rivalry to "good baseball" rather than "bad blood." But he remembers one time when it led to a riot.

"One game we played in Newark and their pitcher didn't throw at anybody. So his manager said, 'Throw at 'em! If you don't throw at him, you're going to get fined.' We had a guy named Blue Perez up to bat. So Blue came over to the dugout and says, 'If this man throws at me, I'm going to throw the bat at him and you hurry up and hustle me another one out there.'

"The first pitch didn't brush him back, he *hit* Blue. Blue looks over to the dugout at Vic and says, 'Can I get him?' Vic says, "Go ahead.' And, boy, you talk about a race towards second base, Blue right behind the pitcher. Both dugouts emptied. One of the smallest players on the field jumped on Josh Gibson and Josh throwed him down and sat on him. And the next thing we know there are cops out there with horses.

"The fans and everybody was on the field, but they got things under control. But some people in the crowd said, 'Wait until after the game, we'll get you.' After we got dressed we said, 'Don't put those bats up.' Everybody got a bat and we was ready, but when we got outside there wasn't a soul out there." Such incidents demonstrated the vagaries of black baseball, which was not always played by "the book."

Baseball's "book" says that a pitcher can't get by with speed alone, but Edsall disagrees. "What you talking about?" he asks rhetorically. "I remember one time we played an exhibition game against a white all-star team in the Polo Grounds. I pitched the first five innings and they were wondering where I got the smoke from. I said, 'Wait awhile. I ain't warmed up yet.'

"Another time in Washington, I shut 'em out 3–0, and after the game we dressed in the same locker room. They were saying, 'Man, you're lucky.' I said, 'What you mean?' They said, 'You're not throwing nothing but a fastball and that wasn't fooling nobody.' I said, "I didn't *need* to throw nothing else, you weren't hitting *that*.'"

Eyewitnesses back his assertion. For ten years he threw his fastball by batters and, fortunately for hitters, his control improved somewhat. Again, contrary to the "book," Edsall had more trouble pitching to left-handed batters than right-handed batters. For some reason that he still hasn't been able to identify, the strike zone proved elusive when a lefty was in the batter's box. "A left hander kind of bothered my mind," he says, "I was afraid of hitting a lefthander when I didn't want to."

His concern that he might hurt someone unintentionally was well founded. In 1942, the only season that he did not pitch for the Grays, he accidentally beaned Jud "Boojum" Wilson, one of the game's greatest pure hitters. "When I went to the Philadelphia Stars, Oscar Charleston was the manager," recalls Edsall, "and he told me to 'hug' Boojum. That means to keep the ball inside. The first pitch I hit Boojum right up behind the head and the ball bounced back almost to second base. So I run up to see if he was hurt. I said, 'Boojum! Boojum, are you hurt?' He said, 'I'm all right. I'm all right. Come on, let's play ball.' But the next morning, he couldn't get out of bed."

It is apparent that Edsall Walker's decade in the Negro Leagues was eventful, including appearances in the East-West All-Star Game and the Negro World Series. But he maintains that his biggest thrill in baseball was "just pitching for the Grays. I would have pitched for the Grays for nothing. Playing for the Grays was the best time of my life. The best fun I ever had. I wouldn't change it for nothing. Living was halfway rough, but *we had a time.*"

This article was written in 1992 and was one of three submitted to Oldtyme Baseball News *for the feature* Forgotten Heroes *but which were not published prior to the business ceasing operation. Thus the article has not appeared in print until now.*

Edsall Walker died February 19, 1997, in Albany, NY, at the age of 83.

Gene Benson: Baseball Pioneer

Take a look at Gene Benson today and he looks more like Kirby Puckett's uncle than the sleek, speedy center fielder that a youthful Willie Mays watched making basket catches at a time when the world had never heard of "The Say Hey Kid." There is little doubt in Benson's mind that Mays "borrowed" the idea from him. "I had the basket catch a long time," the former Philadelphia Stars outfielder says. "It was just something that I picked up. It was just something I was comfortable with. I had never seen anybody else do it. I developed it myself. Willie Mays was just a kid. I really don't know where he got the basket catch, but Willie has said that he got it from me."

Mays is not the only baseball great to benefit from Gene Benson's baseball expertise. Jackie Robinson, in preparing for his role as the first black in the major leagues in modern times, was the recipient of Benson's counseling. The pair were teammates on the American All-Star team that toured Venezuela during the winter of 1945-1946, and just before the team left the airport on their exhibition trip, Branch Rickey had signed Robinson to a contract with the Dodgers organization. Heeding Rickey's request, Robinson did not discuss the matter with his teammates until after the official announcement had been made. "He never told us about it," Benson confirms, "We read it in the newspaper."

But after the news broke, Benson and Robinson spent many long evenings together talking about the importance and far-reaching impact of the now historic contract. "Jackie and I were roommates," Benson remembers. "Felton Snow, the manager, gave Jackie to me as a roommate because he thought I could help him. I sat up night after night talking to Jackie, trying to encourage him."

Robinson, with only one season of Negro League baseball under his belt, had doubts about his ability to play at the major league level. "He didn't really have the confidence," Gene confides, "because he was just another ballplayer in our league." But Benson assuaged his anxieties and assured him he could make it in the big leagues. "I used to tell him baseball in the majors is so much easier than what you're playing here. First of all you don't have to worry about nobody throwing at you. And you don't have to worry about no spitballs or other illegal pitches."

Benson's message was based on his own experience. Teams in the Negro Leagues would try to intimidate a young ballplayer, and the Homestead Grays were the hardest on Benson when he first signed with the Philadelphia Stars. "The Grays pitchers would come by and say, 'So you're the one we've been hearing so much about. Well, today we're going to see how good you can hit laying down.'"

"Hell, in our league everything goes," the veteran emphasized to Robinson. "If you can hit these pitchers you can hit anybody in the world." Even today Benson is insistent on the point that he hammered home to Robinson. "Having played so much against major league ballplayers, I know I would rather hit at major leaguers than what I was hitting at in the Negro Leagues."

Philadelphia Stars all-star outfielder Gene Benson utilized the "basket catch" long before Willie Mays introduced it to the major leagues.

How Robinson responded to the challenge after returning to the States has been well chronicled, but Benson's role as Jackie's advisor has been virtually lost to baseball lore. But it was not lost on Robinson, who later expressed his thanks to his benefactor. "Jackie told me I helped him tremendously, and that everything I told him was true," Benson recalls. "He respected me and we became good friends." That friendship remains important to Gene, who is content with Robinson's words of appreciation and in the knowledge that what he did helped in some measure to open doors for the generations of black players who have followed Robinson into the major leagues. "Jackie told me, 'I can't ever repay you for what you did,'" Benson remembers. "'I said, 'You did it on your own.'"

It is conceded that Robinson was not the best player in the

Negro Leagues, and his selection was based on factors other than his baseball ability alone. Among the many proven players who were better on the ballfield was Gene Benson. In addition to being a sterling fielder and excellent baserunner, Benson was a consistent .300 hitter who had been an integral part of the Philadelphia Stars lineup for a decade. When the All-Stars were being selected for the Venezuelan tour, Benson had just completed a .370 season.

There was never any doubt in Benson's own mind that he, too, could play on the major league level. While Robinson was at Montreal in 1946, Benson continued his own career in impressive fashion, rapping the ball for a .345 average. After the season, he joined Satchel Paige's All-Stars to tour the country playing against Bob Feller's All-Stars. "Satchel said, 'I want you on my team because I know as hard as you hit me, you can hit anybody else.'"

Satchel's pronouncement proved prophetic. Feller was in his prime and had led the league in 1946 with 26 wins, 10 shutouts, and 348 strikeouts, but Benson hit him like he was a cousin. He was so successful batting against the Cleveland Indians righthander that Feller asked him if he was tipping his pitches. "After the series was over he came to the hotel and asked me how I knew what he was going to throw," Benson smiles, recounting the conversation. "He said, 'I must be doing something. Nobody hits me as hard as you do.' "I said, 'I know what you're going to throw and when you're going to throw it. When you get in trouble, you go to the curveball.' He said, 'You're right. I think my curveball is good enough to get anybody out.'"

The two all-star teams ended their cross-country tour with Feller's stars only one game ahead, proving that black players could compete on an equal basis with white major leaguers. But for veterans like Gene Benson, the door to the major leagues remained closed, as the establishment moguls decided to take only the younger black players into organized ball.

So baseball fans never witnessed Gene Benson picking baseballs off his shoe-tops to rob a batter of a basehit; and they would have to wait until Willie Mays came on the major league scene to see the basket catch. Players like Gene Benson, who could have been stars in the major leagues, had to be satisfied with the reflected glory of the younger black players for whom they paved the way. Without men like Gene Benson, there would have been no Jackie Robinson. And without Jackie Robinson, there would have been no Willie Mays or Hank Aaron — or any of the other great black players who have contributed so much to the national pastime.

Today's black superstars should be thankful for men like Gene Benson, every time they swing a bat or throw a ball or sign a multi-million dollar contract. For without the Bensons of the past, today's black players would be getting on a bus for a long ride for a short paycheck, playing exhibitions among themselves, whenever and wherever they could, unknown to the majority of America. Baseball historians are just beginning to search for their counterparts from the past.

They have found one in Gene Benson. As we start a new decade, he remains Philadelphia's most gifted story-teller and baseball goodwill ambassador, generously sharing his memories of America's game with baseball fans across the nation and helping America discover the forgotten heroes of yesteryear.

This article was first published in 1990 in Oldtyme Baseball News *(Vol. 2, No. 3) as the feature* Forgotten Heroes, *which spotlighted the greatest black baseball players before 1947.*

Gene Benson, a gifted story-teller who generously shared his time and stories with younger generations, died April 6, 1999, in Philadelphia, Pennsylvania at the age of 85.

Wild Bill Wright: A Mexican League Legend Comes Home

The plane's descent from the grey October skies carried no special significance for most passengers. But when the big jet landed at the Baltimore-Washington airport, Bill Wright breathed the air of his native country for the first time in 32 years. The 76-year-old former outfielder was returning to the city where he had attained stardom with the Baltimore Elite Giants of the old Negro National League before he left to become a baseball legend in Mexico.

Thomas Wolfe's enduring expression regarding a return to one's roots — "You can't go home again" — has become a widely accepted axiom. But proving that there is an exception to every rule, Bill Wright *did* come home! The occasion was a reunion with other Negro League veterans and, although confined to a wheelchair by the crippling effects of advanced arthritis, the 76-year-old former outfielder still carried the same 190 pounds on his 6'3" frame as in his playing days.

His professional baseball career began as a Tennessee teenager with a passion for pitching. "I've played all my life, since I was five," Wright recalled. "But I got into professional baseball at the age of 15, in 1931. At my hometown in Milan, Tennessee, there was a fellow who had played professional baseball. So he phoned around to Nashville and arranged a chance for me to have a tryout, and I got my start from the Elite Giants. I started originally to be a pitcher. We were training in Nashville and it was kinda cold. I threw too hard, like all young kids, and I strained my arm a little. I was always a pretty nice hitter, so I went to the outfield."

During his 12 years with owner Tom Wilson's club, the big Tennessean followed the franchise through a succession of moves from Nashville to Columbus to Washington and finally to Baltimore, where the team found a home until the demise of the Negro Leagues.

Those were the halcyon years for the Elites, with 1939 being especially notable because they defeated the Homestead Grays in a post-season playoff. The team's offensive thrust that season was led by Wright, who copped the batting title with a fabulous .488 average! The big, swift switch-hitter had become a perennial all-star, playing in the Negro Leagues' annual East-West All-Star Classic for five consecutive years (1935–1939) before succumbing to the lure of Mexico. During World War II, due to his draft status, he played an additional two years in Baltimore, making his sixth All-Star appearance (1942) and finishing his career with the Elites in 1945 by stroking the ball for a .371 average.

Counted among his teammates during his tenure with the Elites were some of the greatest players ever to pull on a spiked shoe, including Biz Mackey, Sammy T. Hughes, Roy Campanella and Bill Byrd. But while the players were first rate, the playing conditions were considerably less. "You know," Wright explained, "With the Elites we had to play every day. One time we played in Cleveland, Ohio, on Saturday night and had to be in New York for a four-team doubleheader at one o'clock the next day! And we had to ride a bus, be up all night, and just got there in time to get out and run in the dressing room and change clothes and have about 20 minutes to warm up and that was it. It was a hell of a game against the New York Black Yankees and we beat them, 1–0. But that's what went on back then. We'd go about 600 miles and get out and play a baseball game."

With the Negro Leagues' schedules often demanding as many as eight games a week, it is easy to understand that, in addition to the jingle of the pesos, Wright was beguiled by Mexico's comparatively easy scheduling. "We went to Mexico and found out that we only played three games a week," he explained. "It was kind of a rest, you know." What began as a respite from the rigors of Negro League travel turned into a permanent arrangement with Wright playing in the Mexican League from 1940–1951, exclusive of the two wartime seasons (1942 and 1945) when circumstances required that he remain in the States.

In Mexico he quickly became one of the most productive and most popular players in the country, registering averages of .360, .390, .366, .335, .301, .305, .326, .282, .299, .and 362. Wright's versatility was demonstrated by the diversity of the statistical categories in which he topped the league. In 1940, his first season, he tied for the lead in doubles with Willie Wells (while ranking fifth in batting average). The following season he led the league in stolen bases and batting average (with future Hall of Famers Josh Gibson and Ray Dandridge ranking #2 and #3) and finished third in home runs (behind league leader Gibson).

But his ultimate accomplishment came in 1943, when he won the Triple Crown. The honors did not come easily, as he was embroiled in a heated, but friendly, battle with Ray Dandridge that went down to the wire. In the final analysis, Wright barely edged Dandridge for the batting title and the two ended in a dead heat for the top spot in RBI. Wright was also engaged in a tight race for the league lead in both home runs and stolen bases, surpassing Roy Campanella by one homer to complete the coveted trilogy, while missing the stolen base crown by a single theft.

Wright still savors the sweetness of that Triple Crown season, and delights in recounting how he won the struggle for the batting title. "I could circle the bases in 13.2 seconds," he said, "so you know, I could run fast. I could drag the ball. I could bunt the ball — throw the bat down the left field line and that was it. So, if I needed a hit, just one hit or two hits, I could get them on my own — just *running*."

"That's the way I beat Dandridge out in 1943," he continued. "He was talking about he was going to be the batting champion and I could be the champion home run hitter." Wright paused, choosing his words carefully. "When it came to talking," he emphasized, "I wasn't a talker about what I was going to do. I just went out and did it. When a guy said he was going to do this or do that, or he was going to win a championship, I tried to beat him out." Warming to the story, Wright came to the sweet part. "So I decided to do some running," the human greyhound affirmed. "So I did a little bunting and a little hitting, and I beat him out by a few points. That was in 1943. I won the triple corona that year," Wright repeated with more than a modicum of personal satisfaction.

Bill Wright was an excellent hitter with exceptional speed. The big Baltimore Elite Giants outfielder divided his baseball career between the Negro Leagues and the Mexican League, and was an all-star in both countries.

The man he edged out that season and who later won a batting title of his own, Ray Dandridge, nods, affirming Wright's successful quest for the Triple Crown in 1943. "He was a *good* player, and he could *run*! I played against him several years down there." Both men enjoyed long careers and attained legendary status on the baseball diamonds south of the border, and in recognition have been elected to the Mexican Hall of Fame.

Both were there in 1946, when the flash of Mexican Pesos began to entice white major leaguers to the Mexican League, and Max Lanier, Fred Martin, Sal Maglie, and Mickey Owen were among those traveling south. Upon their arrival, the major league exiles found a much better brand of baseball than they had expected, primarily due to the presence of the black Americans. And the black players remained the best in the Mexican League despite the newly arrived major league pitchers. "I didn't have any trouble with them," Wright stated conclusively. "They couldn't even be compared with Martin Dihigo, Ramon Bragana and Barney Morris."

Major League pitchers were nothing new to Wright. The big switch-hitter faced some of the best white pitchers of the era in the California Winter League. "We had so many guys pitched out there from the major leagues," he recalled. "Bob Feller was tough," he said, leading off the list of the best pitchers that he had faced. "'The Whip,' Ewell Blackwell, was tough, too. His ball ran like a top. Bobo Newsom, when he was a 20-game winner with Washington, was tough, too. And Larry French, who was with the Cubs, and pitched out there many years with us."

There was one more pitcher that he was compelled to mention, even though theirs was only a brief encounter. "Dizzy Dean came out there and played but he only pitched one game. We had a good crowd and the fog was coming in, so we had to rush it through to save the gate receipts. That's the only game he started and then he left. He didn't pitch any more. He knew we had a heck of a team, so I guess he kept himself and his big league winning streak intact."

Wright decided to call it a career after the 1951 season, but was soon prevailed upon to reconsider. "I just decided to quit baseball. But this guy Salazar was managing and he needed an outfielder and he just kept calling. And I decided to come down with him and help him out and we won the championship that year."

Not long afterwards, Wright decided to move from Los Angeles to Mexico to continue a baseball career that spanned a quarter of a century as a player (1931–1956) and an additional three seasons as a coach. After retiring from the game, the popular outfielder opened a restaurant, *Bill Wright's Dugout*, in Aguascalientes, and the sojourn that started as just a rest from the rigors of life in the Negro Leagues became an unplanned permanent home.

Prior to this visit his last time back in the USA was in 1958, shortly after Roy Campanella's tragic accident which left him paralyzed. Television's Ralph Edwards hosted a special *This Is Your Life* show after Campy was able to get around in a wheelchair, and Bill Wright, in respect for his former Elites teammate, returned to be one of the surprise guests.

Now, after 32 years, Bill Wright had come home again.

This article was first published in 1991 in Oldtyme Baseball News (Vol. 3, No. 3) *as the feature* Forgotten Heroes, *which spotlighted the greatest black baseball players before 1947. An accompanying photo in the publication carried the caption "In 1943 the big, swift switch-hitter demonstrated his versatility by winning the Triple Crown and only missing the stolen base title by a single theft."*

Bill Wright died August 3, 1996, in his adopted hometown of Aguascalientes, Mexico, at the age of 82. Three years earlier (June 26, 1993) his friend and former teammate, Roy Campanella, had died in Woodland Hills, California, at the age of 71.

Johnny Davis: Cherokee

Johnny Davis. His teammates called him Cherokee. The Homestead Grays called him Geronimo. In Puerto Rico they called him Chief. But by whatever name he was called, he *was* a ballplayer. There was no doubt about that.

The big, hard-hitting outfielder demonstrated his slugging prowess everywhere he went. From the days when he was a Black-Indian orphan playing with homemade baseballs in the New York Catholic Protectory to the days when he was an all-star in the Negro Leagues, he always excelled.

During his years in the Negro National League Johnny played against the greatest stars of black baseball, including Satchel Paige and Josh Gibson. Johnny selects Gibson as the greatest hitter that he ever saw. He remembers, "He could bust that ball. He was great!" It was Gibson who gave Johnny the nickname "Geronimo." During the first series that Johnny played against the Grays, Josh was ragging him about having such a big reputation as a slugger with the Mohawk Giants of Schenectady. John had gone hitless in eight trips to the plate during their first two games at Ebbets Field, but in the third game at Griffith Stadium he hit one out of the park and after rounding the bases, as he jumped on home plate with both feet in triumph, Josh yelled "Geronimo!" And the name stuck.

Johnny remembers that the first time he faced the great Satchel Paige he was unimpressed. Johnny hit a long drive to center field that the center fielder had to go back about 40 feet to catch. When he got back to the bench, he asked Biz Mackey, "Who's that guy pitching?" Mackey's reply was "Satchel Paige." Johnny was not intimidated. He replied, "Big deal." Now he reflects, "But I got impressed later."

Johnny first joined the Newark Eagles in 1941 and for a decade he was a mainstay on the team, playing with such greats as Ray Dandridge, Monte Irvin, Larry Doby, Leon Day, Dick Lundy, Willie Wells, Dick Seay and Mule Suttles. During his tenure with the Eagles, Johnny was a consistent .300 hitter with power. "He was a good fastball hitter — don't try to throw the fastball by him," says former teammate Leon Day, adding "he hit the ball a long way."

His first big year was 1944 when he hit a robust .345 and was selected to play in the East-West Game, where he got two hits while batting behind future Hall of Famers Buck Leonard and Josh Gibson in the all-star lineup. He followed this performance with another outstanding season, hitting .319 and tying with Buck Leonard for second place behind the slugging Gibson in the home run derby. The best was yet to come, however, as he teamed with Monte Irvin, Larry Doby, and Lenny Pearson to form the "Big Four" that powered the Eagles to the championship in 1946. The World Series against Satchel Paige's Kansas City Monarchs was icing on the cake, as he hit .292 and was the hero of the deciding seventh game. His line-drive double scored Doby and Irvin with the runs that sewed up the 3–2 victory for Rufus Lewis and the Eagles. The following year, Johnny continued swinging a big bat, finishing the season only one home run behind league leader Monte Irvin. In 1949, after the franchise had moved to Houston, Johnny made the All-Star team for the third time.

Johnny's most memorable year was 1946. Not only did he help lead the

Johnny Davis was a hard-hitting outfielder for the Newark Eagles, and also showcased his power-laden swing in the Carribean winter leagues. He is pictured here smashing a home run in Puerto Rico.

Eagles to a pennant and star in the Black World Series, but after the season ended he played on Satchel Paige's All-Star Team as they barnstormed across the country playing Bob Feller's All-Stars. Many teams barnstormed, calling themselves all-stars, but these two were truly all-star teams. Feller's team had Mickey Vernon, Johnny Berardino, Phil Rizzuto, Ken Keltner, Charlie Keller, Sam Chapman, Jeff Heath, Rollie Hemsley, Jim Hegan, Johnny Sain, Dutch Leonard, Bob Lemon and Spud Chandler. In addition to Johnny, Satchel's team had future major leaguers Sam Jethroe, Hank Thompson, and Artie Wilson as well as Negro League All-Stars Gene Benson, Buck O'Neil, Othello Renfroe, Frank Duncan and Hilton Smith.

These two teams played virtually even, with Feller's squad winning a single game more than the Paige aggregation. This series provided Johnny with his biggest thrill in baseball, as he got two hits off of Bob Feller in Yankee Stadium. Another memorable incident occurred in Kansas City during the last game of that series when, with his team trailing by a run in the last inning, Johnny hit a dramatic home run to win the game. Johnny remembers vividly, "They were leading us in the ninth inning with two outs and a man on, and I hit Spud Chandler's fast ball over the left-field fence. As I was rounding the bases, I picked Phil Rizzuto up at shortstop and carried him piggy-back from shortstop to third base and we both slid in at home plate together."

Baseball presented a means for the ex-merchant marine to continue his free-spirited ways, for when the regular seasons ended, John was island-hopping around the Caribbean, playing in the Latin American winter circuits. This included jaunts to Puerto Rico, Cuba, Venezuela and Mexico. Johnny says, "To me, the best thing was just going from city to city. I just wanted to see the next town. I like to go from here and see what's on the other side of the street. That's what intrigued me, going to different places to play baseball. I guess that's why I liked it so much." In the winter leagues he excelled not only as a hitter but also a pitcher. In 1946, while pitching and batting clean-up for San Juan in the Puerto Rican League, he compiled a 7–4 record while earning a highly respectable 2.42 ERA. He did this even though weakened with the flu, which caused him to lose over 20 pounds and a month and a half of playing time.

While with Mayaguez, also in the Puerto Rican League, Johnny hurled a no-hitter in 1944; led the league in strikeouts in 1948; and was voted the MVP in 1947–1948 when he was described in the newspapers as "the magnificent pitcher." His ability to excel both as a hitter and a pitcher was, at the same time, an asset and a liability. Monte Irvin, Johnny's teammate both in the states and in the winter leagues, confirms, "John was a good ballplayer. He could hit the ball. But we felt that if he had concentrated entirely on either pitching or hitting and not had to divide his time, he could have been even better."

Back in the outfield in Venezuela during the winter of 1950–1951, he hit a robust .381 in support of future Dodgers star Clem Labine's sterling 13–1 won-lost record and helped lead Caracas to the championship. The following winter, back in Puerto Rico, this time with Santurce, he led the league in home runs and, assisted by such name players as Ruben Gomez, Dan Bankhead, Junior Gilliam, Valmy Thomas and Bob Thurman, he spearheaded the team to their third consecutive championship.

But ball games were not all that he won in Puerto Rico, for it was here that he first caught the eye of the lovely lady who is now Mrs. Johnny Davis. By coincidence, the same year that he was married was the year that he came closest to getting his chance in the majors after the color ban was broken. Johnny remembers, "I was with the San Diego Padres in the Pacific Coast League in 1952. They wanted me to go to the Chicago White Sox to hit behind Eddie Robinson, but I broke a leg. Before I broke my leg I was hitting about .400 and I was only one home run behind Max West for the league lead. When I came back my average dropped, but the way I started the season, I believe that I could have gone up there (to the majors) and kept on doing what I was doing. I regret not going to the majors ... just a little. I'd love to go up there in August or September just to see what it was like."

In 1953 he took his classic swing to the now defunct Florida International League, where he hit .321 and led the league with 35 homers and 136 RBI while playing for Pepper Martin's Ft. Lauderdale team.

In 1954, the 36-year-old finished his organized baseball career with the Montgomery Rebels in the Sally League. He was still smashing the ball even then, for in one game he batted twice in the ninth inning, hammering a leadoff homer and then later knocking in the winning runs with a two-on double.

After this last hurrah he settled in Ft. Lauderdale, where he still lives today with his wife, Ada, their two daughters and their only grandchild. Looking back on his baseball career, Johnny Davis reflects, "I had a ball. I really had a ball. Baseball has been very good to me."

This article was previously published in the 1982 SABR Research Journal with the succinct title "Johnny Davis." Davis and his entire family were grateful that he was being "rediscovered" after so many years. Shortly afterward, on November 17, 1982, Johnny Davis died in Fort Lauderdale, Florida, at the age of 64.

Piper Davis: The Man Who Made Mays

His hair is salt-and-pepper now, and the spring is gone from his step, but Piper Davis still stands tall and straight, and carries himself with a dignity becoming the three-quarters of a century that he has walked God's good earth. But the sparkle in his eye belies the passage of time.

Four-and-a-half decades have passed since he first wrote the name "Willie Mays" on his lineup card as the left fielder and seventh place batter for his Birmingham Black Barons. The future superstar was then a 17-year-old high school student, and Piper was like a second father to him.

Piper remembers those days when he was Willie Mays' mentor, and even farther back in time when he was a teenager himself. A time when black baseball players were excluded from playing in the major leagues. But as time passes, memories grow sweeter and injustices of the past grow softer. The hardships and indignities are tempered by better days and different times, and it is more constructive to remember the good that came from bad experiences and worse circumstances, than to nurture residual bitterness.

When Piper was a youngster, times were never good for black Americans, but during the heart of the Depression, the accustomed burden was felt more intensely. The increasing scarcity of jobs and their resultant dollars created unwanted choices in many American lives. A youthful Piper Davis was one of those affected.

> After I finished high school, I went to Alabama State College at Montgomery. My father was a miner and the miners were on strike at that time, so he had borrowed money for me to go to school. I had a part scholarship for playing basketball, but it came time for the next semester's money and the miners were still on strike. And I knew he'd have to borrow more money. I don't like to owe anybody anything and I never liked to ask anybody for anything, so I left school. I called my parents and I told them, "Don't borrow any more money, I'm coming home." I was about twenty-some miles from Birmingham, and I told them to come pick me up. So they came out and picked me up. I always wanted to work for myself and to earn my own money, so I got a job in the coal mines. We were poor folks — that's why I went to the mines.

Piper Davis was a versatile player for the Birmingham Black Barons, and could play any position. As manager, he discovered and developed a young player named Willie Mays.

The town of Piper, Alabama, had two separate distinctions. First, it served as the source for Lorenzo Davis' nickname that he would carry through the rest of his life, and secondly, it was the location of two coal mines that provided employment for many of the town's citizens. In the coal mines the work was hard, the pay was low and the danger was always present. And the thought of baseball, home runs and strikeouts was far away. Ironically, it was a strikeout of a different kind that lifted Piper from the coal mines to the baseball diamond.

> I worked for about three or four months, and then we had a series of accidents that was responsible for me getting out of the mines and into baseball. I guess you might say I struck out as a miner.
>
> We had some loose coal where the mules go down in the mines, and as one miner went down, he passed the mule and pushed him over and hit that bank of loose rock and coal and it covered him up. As soon as that mule touched it, he was gone. That was strike one.
>
> The next incident happened when a rock had fallen on the cable and they had a guy following the line trying to find the end of it. Somebody accidentally turned the juice on and when he put his hand on that raw spot, it burned him up. I remember it distinctly. That was strike two.
>
> Then we had a rock with a crack in it and it grumbled and this fellow looked to see what happened and it caved in and broke his leg. And that was the third one. That was strike three. And I was out — out of the mines!

That day in 1936, the Alabama coal mines lost a miner, but baseball gained a diamond star. But the transformation was not immediate. A natural athlete, he had excelled at baseball, basketball and football at Westfield High School, and it was a half-dozen years before Piper presaged Bo Jackson and Deion Sanders by playing two professional sports, starring with baseball's Birmingham Black Barons and touring with the Harlem Globetrotters in the off-season.

After leaving the mines, Piper had gone to Birmingham, working at the Acipco Cast Iron and Pipe Company and earning $3.26 a day as a pipe-fitter. He supplemented his income by playing semi-pro baseball on weekends in the Steel and Industrial League, polishing his diamond skills before getting the call from the black major leagues. His weekend play eventually expanded to include home games with the Black Barons, where he earned $10 for a single game and $15 for a doubleheader. In 1942 Winfield Welch became the manager of the Black Barons and, in the latter part of the season, offered Piper $500 a month to travel with the team.

So he became a Black Baron and his presence in the lineup paid immediate dividends, as Birmingham won consecutive Negro American League pennants during his first two full seasons with the club, 1943–1944. Equally adept at any infield position, the star infielder moved to second base in 1946 to form a great keystone combination with Artie Wilson. The tall, smooth infielder had outstanding hands, a good arm and was a master of the double play. Considered a premier player in the league, that season marked the first of four consecutive starting assignments in the East-West All-Star Game, where he compiled a .385 batting average in the summer classic.

I didn't class myself as a home run hitter. I was a line drive hitter. But I could hit the long ball when I got ready. I played against Jackie Robinson one year in the league and I played with Jackie in one (exhibition) game in California. I was playing with a team called the Birmingham All-Stars and Jackie borrowed me one night to play with his team. Now he hadn't seen me since 1945 and this was about '47. Jackie got on first and I'm hitting behind him, and he got time out. He said, "Can you still hit a fly ball like you used to?" I said, "Yeah." He said, "See if you can wait until I get to third." On the first pitch, he stole second. And after two pitches, he'd stole second *and* third. And I hit a high fly ball to center field and he scored the winning run.

By then Piper was an established veteran and he was appointed playing manager of the Black Barons in 1948. As a manager, Piper had a commanding presence, an abundance of patience and a keen baseball mind. Leading by example, he hit .353 while guiding his team to another pennant, the third flag in his six seasons with the Black Barons. That season was especially gratifying because he was at the helm from beginning to end, selecting the players and shaping them into a team.

At the beginning of the season, prospects were as plentiful and commonplace as the ore that he had dug out of the coal mines of north Alabama in his younger years. Among those trying to earn a place on the Black Barons' roster were aspiring phenoms who were long on promise but short on delivery, and grizzled veterans on the fringe, believing in their minds that they could still play when their bodies could no longer be fooled.

But Piper found one player who was special. Very special. He was a diamond in its rawest form, uncut and unpolished, and unrecognizable to an inexpert eye — but a diamond just the same. It was obvious that he could run and he could throw, but Piper saw beyond the basic raw skills of the kid who was barely 17 years old. When he was the same age, he had played with the youngster's father in the Industrial Leagues around Birmingham and Piper knew what was in the genes. He was a natural.

Piper's prize pupil that season was called Buck by his friends, but his real name was Willie Howard Mays, Jr. Mays' father, who had a great respect for Piper Davis, had taken Willie to meet the Black Barons' star a year earlier, and Piper remembered the youngster when he saw him again.

> We were in Chattanooga and we were at the hotel messing around and I saw him there. He was playing with some semi-pro team. About two weekends later, we were playing in Atlanta, and I saw him again. I said, "If you're still playing ball for money, Sunday morning you tell your daddy to call me." He was about 17, and I told him that if he got permission from his father, then I'd go ahead and let him play. And his daddy called and that's how he came to be playing with the Black Barons. He was an infant compared to the folks he was gonna be playing with, but you could see the talent in him. He had a special something inside.

Willie's first day in a Black Barons uniform was a Sunday doubleheader at Rickwood Field in Birmingham. During batting practice, Piper told his recruit to shag some flies and when the game started, Piper sat him out the first game. While the restless youngster observed, the Black Barons won the first game and then relaxed in the clubhouse between games. The rookie was sitting off to himself in a corner, when Piper went over to where he was sitting. Then the skipper called over the equipment manager, handed him the lineup card, and told him to post it in the dugout. And gave Mays a wink. Listed in the seventh spot in the batting order on the lineup card was 'Mays lf.' "Just give it your best shot," he said to the grateful rookie, and walked away.

When the players assembled for the second game, Piper noticed that the lineup card had attracted both a crowd and more comments than the manager cared to hear. He watched them clustering around the posted lineup and grousing. After observing in silence for a few minutes, he decided that an immediate understanding was essential.

> I went back over there and said, "How's the lineup look to you fellows?" And I said, "If anybody doesn't like it, there's the clubhouse," and I pointed, "and you can go back in there and take off your uniform if you want to. And you can take it with you." I didn't hear anything else. That's how Willie got his start and he did all right for himself. That was in 1948, the year we won the Negro American League Championship.

Willie had two hits in the game off a tough veteran pitcher but, at that time, he was still the fourth best outfielder on the team. Conveniently, fate stepped in and by the first of June, he was the regular center fielder, taking over when starter Norman Robinson broke his leg. Neither of the fielders in the side pastures was noted for his range and, when a ball was hit to the outfield, they would yell, "Come on, Willie! Come on, Willie!" Piper watched as the rookie was running his legs off covering his territory and half of the other fielders' as well, and he was not pleased.

> I was a little peeved. Between innings, I said (to the other outfielders), "Come here right now. You're going to have to earn your money. We can get anybody to stand out there and yell, "Come on Willie." If you can't make the plays, you shouldn't be playing in this league. I said, "I don't want you running him from foul line to foul line. You're not going to run his legs off." That's when we started rolling.

The message that Piper transmitted was received and, consequently, the adjustments helped the rookie save his legs. "Willie can go get it, and Willie can bring it back," Piper said then and still says today, describing how Mays could run and throw, "but he couldn't hit a curveball." Piper saw what the youngster needed and he made sure that Mays learned the right way of doing things that would earn him a ticket to the major leagues.

In the field Mays had all the tools, but Piper taught him to charge a ground ball hit through the infield, to throw the ball on one hop to the plate and to get a quick release on his throws. On the bases Mays was an instinctive runner, but Piper taught him to assert his right to the basepaths aggressively by sliding hard into fielders trying to block him off the base. At the plate, Mays could pull the trigger on a fastball, but Piper taught the youngster to hit a curve by correcting a problem with his stance. Mays had a habit of turning his front shoulder towards the plate, making it harder to see the ball and more susceptible to being hit by a pitch. Piper made him turn more toward the pitcher and straightened him up more at the plate, enabling him to better pick up the spin on a curveball, and also allowing him to more easily avoid a beanball. Mays adopted the stance and used it throughout his career.

Before Piper corrected Mays' stance, the youngster had been getting a steady diet of breaking balls and was having trouble handling the assorted variety of curves, and also was getting hit by inside pitches. In a game soon after having joined the Black Barons, a veteran pitcher tested the new arrival, sending Mays a message that hurt both his body and his pride. Unable to react as quickly as necessary, he was hit on the arm, and as he lay sprawled in the dirt, with his mind on the pain, a shadow loomed over him. He opened his eyes and looked up to see Piper glowering down at him, and the expression on his manager's face quickly dispelled any expectations of sympathy. The emotion mirrored in the eyes boring down on him was anything except approval.

The rookie looked up at the tall, lanky, dark form hovering over him. "Skip, they're throwing at me!" he whined in his high-pitched voice. Mental toughness was an attribute that Piper desired in his players. "Boy, can you see first base?" he asked. "Yessir," Mays said. "Point to it," Piper instructed. "It's right down there," Mays answered, motioning toward first base. "Then get up and go on down there." The rookie scrambled to his feet, and Piper added, "And when you get there, steal second." Then he turned and walked back to the dugout, as the young Black Barons outfielder trotted down to first base without even rubbing. He knew that his skipper would not have approved of that either.

The young ballplayer learned two lessons that day. One from the pitcher and the other from his manager. The pitcher's lesson was that the inside part of the plate belongs to him, and the manager's lesson was not to let the pitcher have the satisfaction of knowing that he has hurt you. Instead, turn the play around on him and make putting you on base come back to haunt him. And that is exactly what Mays did, promptly stealing second base, as Piper had instructed, sending a message to the pitcher that was received just as certainly as the hurler's own had been.

Mays credits Piper as being the most important person in his baseball career. Piper told a player something only once, and expected the instructions imparted to become a permanent part of a player's psyche. The Birmingham rookie learned his lesson well and that was a major reason why the young center fielder matured so quickly.

Jackie Robinson had won the Rookie of the Year honors in the National League the previous season, and things were beginning to change for black ballplayers. The Negro Leagues' death knell had come with the stroke of a pen, when Robinson signed a contract with the Brooklyn Dodgers organization. But the same pen stroke that closed one door opened another, and the door to the major leagues was ajar. Waiting to get a foot inside the door was a multitude of expectant black Americans, and for many, the stepping stone would be the Negro Leagues in their dying throes. Piper's protégé was one of the fortunate ones. Within three years he would be playing center field in the Polo Grounds.

Mays was signed by the Giants organization in 1950 and, after blistering the ball at Minneapolis for the first month of the 1951 season, he was quickly sent to the parent club in New York. But while his prize pupil sizzled his way to major league stardom, Piper Davis was still on the outside looking in, and was destined to sustain his vigil while playing in the Pacific Coast League, waiting for a chance at the "bigs" that never came. Any player of his ability would have been disappointed at the unfulfilled promise, and he was no exception.

Piper was a hardnosed ballplayer and had been considered for the pioneering role in which Jackie Robinson had been ultimately cast. His contract had been acquired in 1947 by the St. Louis Browns at the same time that Willard Brown and Hank Thompson were signed. But the Brownies wanted to option him to Elmira and Piper wanted to play in the major leagues, so the option was not exercised.

After guiding his team to the 1948 Negro World Series with his teenage prodigy in center field, his hope of playing in the major leagues was renewed, when he became the first black player signed by the Boston Red Sox organization. The Red Sox assigned Piper to Scranton in the Eastern League, and he was expected to become the Sox' first black player in the majors.

> I signed with Scranton and we trained in Cocoa, Florida. After we got there, I would stay out in the community with one of the waiters at the Brevard Hotel and I found out I was supposed to eat in the servants' quarters. So I would go 'round in the back door at the hotel and eat in the waiters' quarters and then go 'round out front and get in the bus where it was parked. And when we played spring exhibition games, I wasn't allowed to play in the south.

Piper was waiting for a chance to prove himself in the major leagues, but Walt Dropo's super season in 1950 destroyed whatever hopes the former Black

Barons skipper had for that opportunity with the Red Sox. He knew that he was good enough for the big time, but as the years passed and he remained in the Pacific Coast League, he knew his chance to make "the show" would never come and, even if it did, he was too old to walk through that magic door that led to his field of dreams. His last season, 1958, he hit .282 to wind down his baseball career. By then he was 42 years old and Piper Davis hung up the spikes for a final time.

After his baseball career ended, the old warhorse returned home and still resides in Birmingham, where he stirred the hearts of baseball fans for a decade, and near the place where he first abandoned the dark future of life in the Alabama coal mines for the sunshine and fresh air of the baseball diamond. That choice has proved a good one. Baseball was a good life, and Piper doesn't regret anything about it — except that he was never afforded a chance to play in the major leagues.

He will be honored February 27, 1993, by induction into the Alabama Sports Hall of Fame, where the mentor will join his protégé, Willie Mays, and belated recognition is better than the continued obscurity that has been the destiny of most Negro League players.

When a discussion comes up about an All-Time Baseball Dream Team, the name of Willie Mays almost invariably heads the list of center fielders. Upon reflection it is disquieting to realize that if he had been born only a decade earlier, we would never have known about him. Piper Davis discovered and salvaged this rough, uncut diamond that, when polished, shone with the magnificence of a super-nova.

The question without an answer remains. How many other players of Willie Mays' brilliance have been lost in the shadows of time, existing only as a name in an obscure box score or as bits of dust caught in the cobwebs of an old man's memory?

This article was first published in the July 1993 issue of The Diamond: The Official Chronicle of Major League Baseball *under the title "The Man Who Made Mays: Piper Davis, Coal Miner-Turned Coach, Taught Willie How to Play."*

I had known Piper for a decade and had previously written about him for other publications. Soon after this article appeared, I called Piper. The publisher had sent him a copy of the magazine and he began telling me about a great article that had been written about him. From his description of the story line, I knew immediately that he was talking about mine, and asked if he really liked it. "Yes," he said with much enthusiasm, "I like it a lot!" Then I told him that I was the person who had written the article, and it was apparently the first time that he had taken notice of the byline. I heard him telling his daughter Faye, "This is the man who wrote that article." "Little Piper," as she was called by Piper's teammates, took the phone and was also very complimentary about the article. The most gratifying compliments are those that come from a player and his family.

Piper Davis died May 21, 1997, in Birmingham, Alabama, at the age of 79, only about six weeks short of his 80th birthday.

Felix "Chin" Evans: The Winning Pitcher in the Last Black All-Star Game Before Robinson Broke the Color Line

On July 10, 1990, 40,000 dedicated fans weathered the rain at Chicago's Wrigley Field to witness the nation's best baseball players represent their respective leagues in the 61st All-Star Game. Countless others all across America watched the contest on TV as the stars, black and white, showcased their talents. However, there was a time when not *all* of America's best players were allowed to play in the same game. During the first 16 years after the classic's inception, there were two all-star games played each season — one for the white stars and another for the black stars.

In 1946, the last season before Jackie Robinson broke baseball's color line, the winning pitcher in the Negro Leagues' East-West All-Star Game was a tall, slender curveball artist for the Memphis Red Sox named Felix "Chin" Evans.

Now confined to a wheelchair at his home in Pompano Beach, Florida, Evans has a unique reminder of his only All-Star appearance — the game ball that was presented to him after the victory. Players from both squads signed the spheroid. He turns the ball in his hands as he reads the signatures: Josh Gibson, Buck Leonard, Monte Irvin, Biz Mackey and a host of other stars who were in the lineup when the 6'2", 185-lb right-hander took the mound as the starting pitcher for the West squad.

The conjured memories are still clear, even after more than four decades. Nearly 45,000 screaming fans were on hand at Chicago's Comiskey Park that day for the mid-season classic. But Evans, who carried a 15–1 record into the game, was oblivious to the crowd. "I wasn't nervous when I started," he recalls. "That was one of the biggest crowds I had ever played in front of, but I hadn't noticed the crowd. I didn't even think about it, and people were still coming in."

Fingering the old game ball and taking a glimpse back 44 yesteryears, he adds, "I kept my eye on the opposing lineup. I knew I was playing against the best ballplayers they had in the Negro National League." Included in that power-laden lineup were the Homestead Grays' home run duo of Josh Gibson and Buck Leonard, a combination that had slugged the Grays to consecutive pennants in the preceding nine years. Joining them in the East lineup was a younger combination, the Newark Eagles' Monte Irvin and Larry Doby, who were in the process of leading the Eagles to the championship that year to break the Grays' nine-year domination.

The winning pitcher in the 1946 East-West All-Star Game was a tall, slender right-hander with a tantalizing assortment of curves. Memphis Red Sox hurler Felix "Chin" Evans was best known for his "mountain drop."

But Evans effectively silenced their big bats. "I never had trouble pitching to power hitters," the Atlanta native recalls. "You get a guy off stride and he's not going to have his full strength. I had a pretty fair curve ball, I guess," he understates as he demonstrates the grip he used to get the proper spin to make the ball break the way he wanted. "Some of the boys called it a 'mountain drop.' I got all the power hitters out."

"During the three innings I pitched they didn't get but one hit and that was a pop fly that Buck Leonard hit and the right fielder lost in the sun." But the solitary base hit that he surrendered is not as vivid in his memory as a ball that Monte Irvin hit. "Monte hit a high fly ball that was the darnedest thing I ever saw," the Negro League veteran laughs, shaking his head incredulously. "When the ball went up it looked like I was going to catch it. It was hit in front of the infield and that ball just kept going—you know how that wind is in Chicago. Then the boy playing shortstop, Artie Wilson, called for the ball. He started in and then he kept drifting back and then the left fielder called for the ball. That ball stayed in the air longer than any I ever saw! The left fielder, Bubba Hyde, backed up against the wall in Comiskey Park and that's where the ball landed! And he caught the ball and dropped it—and Monte got to third. That was the highest fly ball I ever saw in my life."

The three-base error would have unnerved some pitchers, especially since the next batter was future Hall of Famer Josh Gibson. But the crafty Memphis hurler changed speeds on the slugger and coaxed a ground ball to shortstop Artie Wilson, who threw Irvin out trying for home. "That was the nearest they came to scoring," Evans affirms, noting that Irvin and Leonard were the only baserunners that he allowed that day.

The difficulty encountered by the East All-Stars was nothing more than a continuation of the frustration felt by the West squad's own sluggers who tried to tee-off on the right-hander's fancy curves during the regular season. "I threw three different speeds really," Evans explains. "I threw it straight overhand to the left-handers and I threw three-quarters to right-handers, and sometimes I would throw three-quarters to break in on left-handers' wrists. The more motion you use, the more you can confuse a batter. I raised my leg up and then I slung my arm around like that before I pitched. I think that helped me, because if a guy's watching the pitcher and his delivery, he's going to have trouble picking up the ball."

Evans pauses in his narrative and chuckles, reflecting. "They used to yell at me all the time—'Throw the ball hard!' They'd cuss me coming off the field. I'd say, 'I'm not trying to make you look good, I'm trying to get you out!'" Once Newark's great slugger Mule Suttles became so infuriated at his inability to hit Evans' tantalizing curves, he wanted to go after the lanky hurler between innings with the intention of doing him bodily harm. But an altercation was averted when Evans laughed off Suttles' efforts at intimidation.

In addition to being a superior curveball pitcher, Evans was also a good curveball hitter, and the right-handed batter sometimes played in the outfield when not on the mound. Like most pitchers, he took pride in his hitting, and like most players from the Negro Leagues, he has a "Satchel story." In a game against Paige's Kansas City Monarchs, the hurler's batting reputation had preceded him. "Hey Felix, they tell me you can hit a curveball," Satchel yelled in from the mound when Evans came to the plate. Naturally, Satchel — the consummate showman — challenged his strength. "I fouled off five straight pitches, all curves," Evans recounts how Satchel set him up. "Then he threw a fastball right down the middle and struck me out! I felt like going over and kicking something, I was so mad."

Although laughing about it now, he still fumes at being victimized by Satchel's trickery, but gives his former antagonist his due as one of baseball's greatest pitchers. "He had the best control of any pitcher I ever saw," emphasizes Evans. "He would set up two bats at home plate and put a ball on them, and two out of three times he would knock it off from third base."

Satchel's old adversary shakes his head in wonderment as he remembers Paige's exhibitions of control. He looks again at the game ball from the past, gripping it the way he did for his big-breaking curve. It is one of only two that he has kept through the years. Signatures scrawled in every direction across the discoloring horsehide cover almost every inch of the sphere that he used to retire some of the greatest hitters the game has ever known. Reading those names from long ago helps to rekindle and sweeten memories of his "day in the sun." Earning that All-Star Game victory was only one thrill among many in a long career, but it is the one that Felix Evans considers to be his most outstanding achievement in baseball.

This article was first published in 1990 in Oldtyme Baseball News *(Vol. 2, No. 6) as the feature* Forgotten Heroes, *which spotlighted the greatest black baseball players before 1947.*

I talked to Chin Evans many times through the years that I knew him, either visiting at his home in Pompano Beach, Florida, or on the phone. One day I received a phone call from him and he asked me when I was coming down again. Then he said that the next time I came to see him, he had a surprise for me. I was surprised indeed — he gave me the game ball from the 1946 East-West Game that is described in the article.

We continued to talk often prior to his death on August 21, 1993, in Pompano Beach, Florida, at the age of 81, only a few weeks short of his 82nd birthday. The last time that I went down to see him was at his funeral, and I was one of only two white people at his "home going." The other was Alan Pollock, whose father Syd Pollock owned the Indianapolis Clowns when "Chin" played for them. Although I didn't know Alan at the time, we later became good friends and I assisted him with his memoir about his father and the Clowns, Barnstorming to Heaven, *which was published by the University of Alabama Press in 2006.*

Red Moore: He Could Pick It!

Whenever a Negro Leagues veteran is asked about James "Red" Moore, the response is almost automatically "He could pick it!" Then the player adds anything else that he has to say. Such is the reputation that the Atlanta-born former baseball star earned during his career in the Negro Leagues.

Described by *Atlanta Daily World* sports editor Ric Roberts as the "most perfect" first baseman ever, Red was expert at handling ground balls, excelled at making a 3-to-6-to-3 double play, and was masterful at digging low throws out of the dirt and gloving other errant throws while making it look easy.

Buck O'Neil, a star first baseman for the Kansas City Monarchs and a contemporary of Moore, said of his rival, "He could pick it! He was quick around first base and had outstanding hands. He could handle that low throw in the dirt better than anybody. Nobody had better hands than Red Moore. Most first basemen back then used two hands but Red was a one-hand first baseman. As far as playing first base, nobody was better. People came to see him play."

And Red, who liked to showboat on occasions, never disappointed them. Frequently, the fancy fielder would take throws behind his back in pre-game infield practice and make other trick catches to entertain the fans. The home folks adored him and he became a crowd favorite everywhere he played.

The second of four children born to James Benjamin Moore, Jr. and Sadie Robinson Moore, Red reflects back over his early years living in the Bush Mountain neighborhood of southwest Atlanta and remembers that he learned his craft the hard way. As a left-handed youngster, he made his first mitt by taking apart a standard right-hander's glove, turning it inside out and re-stitching it. From that rudimentary beginning with a makeshift glove, the aspiring young ballplayer developed into a flawless "one-hand" fielder whose defensive skills would eventually attract the attention of top black baseball teams.

His creativity carried over to his hitting and, early in his professional career, he pioneered the use of a batting glove. Red describes his role in the development of this new piece of equipment: "The pitchers were throwing

Pictured here are Newark Eagles teammates Lennie Pearson, Willie Wells, Dick Seay and James "Red" Moore. Moore was an extremely gifted fielder, and the flashy first baseman often livened up infield practice by taking throws behind his back

me inside and the ball came right in on my fists, right up on my left hand — my top hand — and when I hit the ball it would sting. So I got a glove like we used to use in cold weather — a good leather dress glove we would wear in the winter time — and cut the fingers off. I wore that on my left hand. I could grip a bat pretty good and when I hit the ball it would take the sting out of it. That was in '36 or '37 and I used it the rest of my career."

It was around this same time when Red, as a raw rookie with the Newark Eagles, received an unforgettable welcome to black baseball's big time from Satchel Paige. Red now laughs when he recalls the first time he faced Satchel. Speaking to a group of school children in the Hank Aaron Room at Turner Field in 2006, the aged veteran looked back 70 years to that first encounter with the legendary pitcher.

Actually, it was an encounter with *two* legends. Satchel's battery-mate that day was Josh Gibson, the great slugger who was called the "Black Babe

Ruth." Gibson was noted for talking "trash" to hitters — especially young ones — in an attempt to intimidate them, or at least to shake their confidence and break their concentration. This time was no exception and Gibson bantered with the "green" batter as he stepped up to the plate. Red remembers his initiation vividly. "Josh said, 'Young man, I heard you're a pretty good hitter. Can you hit laying down? When Satchel faces a rookie the first time, he kinda lays 'em down. You better watch, young buck, we're going to have to check you out.' Satchel was on the mound and I'm listening to Josh and then all of the sudden the ball popped like a shot in Josh's mitt. He said, 'That was pretty close and next time it's going to be a little closer. You know you can't hit laying down.' And while Josh is talking, another fastball zipped by me. Then another one. I just kind of waved at 'em."

After Satchel hummed three straight fastballs by him before he had really settled into the batter's box, the rookie had to face his manager's ire in the dugout. A smile creases Red's face as he describes his discomposure at the time: "W. Bell was manager then. When I got back to the dugout he said, 'You've been hitting good 'til now — what happened?' I said, 'Mr. Bell, Josh is back there and he made me nervous. I was listening to him and didn't watch the ball.'"

The old warhorse chuckles, recalling the experience, and adds, "The first time I faced Satchel, I didn't do nothing. And I never did do much against him." Red's rookie experience was not unique. Few players — rookies or otherwise — hit Satchel.

After this disquieting experience, Red settled into his role with the Newark ballclub. The fielding wizard added finesse to a team's defense everywhere he played, but nowhere was it more apparent than with the Eagles in 1937, where he was part of their famed "million dollar infield." Slugger Mule Suttles divided his time between first base and the outfield during his career but, when Red arrived on the scene, the big slugger spent more time in the outfield in deference to the youngster's sterling defensive skills.

Once ensconced at the initial sack, Red teamed with second baseman Dick Seay, shortstop Willie Wells, third baseman Ray Dandridge, and catcher Leon Ruffin to give the Eagles Gold Glove quality at each infield position. Dandridge said, "Now, when *he* was at first base, that was our million dollar infield." Wells echoed that sentiment, praising Red's defensive play lavishly. Dandridge and Wells are now members of the Hall of Fame in Cooperstown, New York. Two of Moore's other teammates at Newark, Leon Day and Monte Irvin, are also among the Cooperstown elite, and both concurred with their former teammates' assessment and added their own high praise of Red's superior defensive prowess.

Following his stint in Newark, Red returned to his hometown in 1938 and helped the Atlanta Black Crackers become the first Atlanta team in any major league sport to win a championship. Although winning his greatest acclaim with his superb defensive skills, the left-handed batsman also had some good seasons at the plate, batting .320 with the 1938 Atlanta Black Crackers when the team captured the second-half championship of the Negro American League's split season. The resulting playoff with the first-half champion Memphis Red Sox was not completed and the NAL president subsequently declared a co-championship.

Although he could pilfer a base when the game situation called for it, Red did not present a base-stealing threat. In fact, a baserunning mishap led to an injury sliding into a base and put him on the shelf for an extended time during the Black Crackers' title run. The irony is that this occurred in an exhibition game. Red describes the incident: "I cracked my left ankle going into second base. I made a late slide and my spikes hung up under the base. I was out about six weeks, and it kept me from playing in the East-West Game. I wore an ankle brace, and that kind of stabilized it. They didn't put it in a cast but I was on a crutch for awhile. I was in the dugout for our home games, but I didn't do no traveling. I was kind of incapacitated. I wasn't a fast man anyway, even before the injury. After I got back in the lineup is when we began our big winning streak and won the second-half championship."

Although Ted "Double Duty" Radcliffe was 102 years old and in poor health, his memory remained sharp about the 1938 Atlanta Black Crackers and one of the best first basemen he ever saw. "They had a heck of a ballclub. I managed the Memphis Red Sox in the championship playoff against them. Red Moore was a great fielder. *He could pick it!* And he was a good all-around ballplayer."

Off the field, Red was quiet, unassuming and practical. Radcliffe also voiced his respect for his opponent as a person and spoke of how well liked he was. "He was one of the best fellows I ever met." Buck O'Neil concurred. "I knew Red on the field and, after he stopped playing, I'd see him every time we would play in Atlanta. Red was always a good person. He was always a churchgoer."

This admiration of the Black Crackers' star was not isolated, and Red Moore's contribution to the team's success did not go unnoticed in Atlanta, where the fans held a special day for him at Ponce de Leon Park to show their appreciation. Despite the restrictive economics of the Great Depression, the grateful fans presented the star first-sacker with $350 worth of gifts and merchandise.

In addition to the fans, another Atlantan who admired the way that Red Moore played the game was Earl Mann, president of the white Atlanta Crackers, who earlier in the season had tried to sign the flashy fielder to a contract with his ballclub and pass him off as a Cuban. Red explains why he declined the offer. "Earl Mann wanted me to learn a little Spanish to help the ruse to succeed, but I knew that wouldn't work. Everybody around Atlanta knew me. They all had seen Red Moore play, and I knew what would happen. They would've been calling me all kind of names, and I didn't want any part of that. I stayed where I was with the Black Crackers."

The press also noted his sterling performance and, at the end of the season, the *Southern News Service* selected Moore to the Negro American League's All-Star team. What more could a young ballplayer ask than to be an All-Star in his hometown?

In 1939, the Black Crackers relocated to Indianapolis and played briefly as the ABCs before disbanding early in the season. Afterward, Red was quickly signed by the Baltimore Elite Giants, where he roomed with Roy Campanella, who later became an All-Star catcher with the Brooklyn Dodgers and subsequently was voted into the Hall of Fame.

Both players were respected by their opponents and well-liked by their teammates, and their similar personalities made them compatible roomies. Red remembers the years with his young roommate fondly. "I was about six years older than Roy. At that time he was just a teenager. He was a nice young fellow, good to be around. He was always telling jokes. He loved baseball — he loved the game. His dad would ride with us on the bus. He loved the game like we did and would be with us. He was Italian, but there was no problem with meals, accommodations or anything — he would go where we would go."

Both young players were easygoing off the field but competitive on it, where the Elites battled Red's old team, the Newark Eagles, and the dynastic Homestead Grays for the Negro National League pennant. In the end, the Elites lost out to the defending-champion Grays. Absent a championship playoff, the top four teams played a postseason tournament, and this time the Elites emerged victorious over the Grays to claim the championship trophy. Photographs snapped after the final game, which was played at Yankee Stadium, show the jubilant young roomies in the front row of the team picture.

When I mentioned his old roommate to Campy one year at Cooperstown, his face lit up and a smile spread across his face. "Yes," Campy agreed emphatically, "*He could pick it!*"

Both Campy and Red returned to the Elites the following spring and, at that point in Red Moore's life, the world looked rosy to the young star. Little did he know what changes lay just around the corner.

Late in 1941 Red was married, but soon afterward the United States entered World War II, and he was inducted into the Army in 1942. During the next three years, he served in England, Belgium and France in a combat-engineer battalion attached to General George Patton's Third Army. After the war ended, he was discharged in 1945 and returned to Atlanta. However, the years of athletic rust had taken their toll and, although he resumed his baseball career on a part-time basis, he never again played at a major-league level.

Leaving baseball in 1948, Red took a job in Atlanta with Colonial Warehouse until retiring in 1981. In retirement he has retained a quiet demeanor and still loves chicken dinners, his favorite meal.

At age 93, Red resides in Atlanta with his wife Mary and remains active in his church and community. He serves as Deacon Emeritus at the Springfield Missionary Baptist Church and has given talks about his baseball career at a wide range of venues, including public schools, colleges, civic clubs and SABR meetings. During the past four years, he has spoken to over 1,000 school children in the Hank Aaron Room at Turner Field, as part of the Atlanta Sports Hall of Fame educational program.

Recognition came late in life for Red Moore. Once ignored to the point of invisibility, the Negro Leagues legend is belatedly receiving honors and recognition all across the country. He has appeared at numerous special functions, and has been featured on television and in newsprint. In his hometown, the Mike Glenn Foundation presented him with a Pioneer Award, and the Georgia House of Representatives honored him at the State Capitol with a resolution acknowledging his accomplishments. All of these recognitions were gratifying to Red, who was genuinely appreciative in accepting the accolades. Only in recent years has he come to grips with the fact that he is truly deserving of the awards.

The honor that was most personally fulfilling for him came when he was inducted into the Atlanta Sports Hall of Fame in 2006. When he received the call informing him of his election, Red shouted with joy. "I was so elated, I just shouted," he explained. "I'm living and I can get to smell the roses. I'm glad that I will be able to do that. A lot of time some of us get awards and everything after we're already gone."

This article was previously published in The National Pastime: Baseball in the Peach State *(2010). The information for this article came primarily from the author's interviews with Red Moore, Roy Campanella, Ray Dandridge, Leon Day, Monte Irvin, Buck O'Neil, Ted Radcliffe and Willie Wells.*

Buck Leonard on Jackie Robinson: The Negro Leagues Superstar Talks About Jackie's Signing and the Aftermath

Buck Leonard, the Homestead Grays' superstar first baseman, was a 12-time All-Star in the Negro Leagues, and was inducted into the National Baseball Hall of Fame in 1972. When baseball's color line was challenged, he was an established veteran who was recognized as a premier player in the Negro Leagues. There is no doubt that he had the skills to play in the major leagues, but his age was against him. However, as fate would have it, he was well-positioned to observe the selection and successful transition of Jackie Robinson from the Negro Leagues to the Major Leagues. Relaxing in the cozy den of his Rocky Mount, North Carolina, home, Buck shared his thoughts about this historic event.

"In the winter of 1945 we took an American All-Star team to Venezuela to play the local teams, and our team included Jackie Robinson. We all met in New York City and we didn't even know Jackie was going to be on the trip until we got to New York and saw him.

"We would rather have had Willie Wells as shortstop instead of Jackie Robinson. That's why we were surprised to see him there. Wells was a veteran all-star, who had been playing for more than 20 years, and Jackie was just a rookie. Wells was past his prime but we still thought he was better than Robinson.

"Jackie came up in 1945 with the Kansas City Monarchs. We had played them and had looked at him play. We just thought that he was a big ol' college boy coming into the league. He was running and ripping and we just said, 'Well, soon as he gets tired, he's going to calm down like the rest of us.' But we didn't have any idea at that time that he would be taken into the major leagues. That's why we were surprised to see him there.

"When we went down to Caracas, we were supposed to leave New York on the 15th of October. But there was some kind of revolution going on down there and we had to delay our departure for about a month. When we got down there we could see where some shooting had been done, and we couldn't go out just anywhere we wanted.

"Jackie Robinson had signed with the Dodgers the day before we left, but we didn't know it. That was the big story about our trip that winter.

"Before we left, Branch Rickey came to the hotel and we had seen him talking to Jackie, but we didn't know why. We thought Rickey was going to try to organize a black team to put into the Negro Leagues and he wanted Jackie to help him get some players so he could have one of the best teams in our league. Or maybe, he'd start a team to be in a new league — the United States League — and put Jackie in charge of it. That's what we thought it was, and we asked Jackie if that was what Branch Rickey was talking to him about. Jackie said, 'No, that's not what it was. He was just talking to me about some business.'

Following the 1945 season, an All-Star team toured Venezuela during the ensuing winter. Buck Leonard (standing extreme right) and the other veteran players were surprised that Jackie Robinson (kneeling extreme left) was selected to be on the team.

"Then, before we left New York, Branch Rickey came down there to the airport when we were getting ready to catch the plane to go to South America, to talk to Jackie again. But we still didn't know what they were talking about. So when we got down to Caracas we asked Jackie again, 'What was Branch Rickey talking to you about?' He said, 'We were just talking about some things. He had something that he wanted me to do.'

"We didn't have any idea what Rickey had in mind. We didn't have any idea that he was trying to get Jackie to go to the white leagues. We never even thought *that* was in the making. We were down in South America when we found out.

"It was about Christmas time when it came out in the *New York Times* that Branch Rickey had signed Jackie Robinson. We asked Jackie about it and he said, 'Yeah, that's what it was. That's what we were talking about.' But Rickey had told Jackie not to say anything about it, and to let him make the announcement.

"By the time when we got the paper, it was four or five days old. And it said, it was thought that Jackie was going to be sent to play with Montreal in the International League. We felt like up there in Canada he had a better chance of not being called 'nigger' than he would down south, and it finally came out afterwards, that was the case and he was going to play in Montreal.

"At that time we didn't think too much of him as a ballplayer. He was a hustler, but he wasn't a top shortstop. He didn't look too good when we got down there, and we noticed that he couldn't hit the inside pitch. He hadn't been playing as long as we had and, at that time, we didn't think he was so good. So we said, 'We don't see how he can make it.'

"We talked among ourselves about Jackie and realized the importance of the situation. We knew that he was an example and that the way he acted was going to have a bearing on who else might be selected. And we thought that if he didn't make it, they would be through with us for the next five or ten years. We also thought that if he did make it, they would keep him in the minors for a long time, but we were wrong about that.

"Jackie Robinson was *not* the best ballplayer we had in the Negro Leagues, but he was what we *needed*. He was a college man and he knew how to take charge of his weaknesses. Branch Rickey made a good selection. I was glad to see Jackie go to the Dodgers. He was the best one for that role.

"I think Rickey looked at his ability first. Jackie was big, fast, strong, a fair hitter, had a good arm, but he wasn't the best of hitters. Of course he was only in his first year in the organized Negro Leagues. And he was intelligent. He had been to college and we felt like a fellow who'd been to college and was intelligent could cope with things better than the average fellow. Situations come up, and he was more able to handle them than some of us who had not been to college. We thought that he was the best man to pick for that particular time and for that situation, which turned out to be right.

"As far as ability was concerned some players could have gone straight to the major leagues. We already knew how to play baseball. What we needed mostly was to learn to play *with* white boys. It's a little different in playing *against* a fellow and playing *with* them. You don't know their actions and they don't know yours.

"Some people thought that black players should have been sent down to the minor leagues for orientation, but I don't think that was as important as just needing to play *with* white players.

"At UCLA, Jackie had played *with* white players and had played *against* white players. And his reactions might have been better than someone else who hadn't played under those circumstances. He grew up with it, so he knew how to cope with the condition. I think Jackie was the right man — the ideal man.

"I don't know anybody that would have been a better pick for the first one. We thought if they had picked some other ones, there might have been a big mess. I think some of them might have done just as good in playing as he did, but they wouldn't have took what Jackie took. Sometimes people will try to excite you, so that you say something or do something. He took it all.

"We had some others that they took later, like Larry Doby and Roy Campanella, who might have been able to do what Jackie did. But I say if they had been taken first, it would have been different. Doby was the first in the American League but if he had been taken before Jackie, knowing Doby like I do, I don't think he would have stayed. I don't think even Campanella would have taken it at first. I know when they took Campanella and Doby and those guys, the heat had died down somewhat, and the pressure wasn't as intense as it was when Jackie first went in. Maybe some more would have taken the pressure but I don't think so. We felt like Jackie took more than most of us would have.

"I don't know if anybody else could have taken the pressure that Jackie Robinson did. I don't think I could have withstood the pressures of being the first black player. I don't *think* so. And I *know* I wouldn't have. Not like that. I don't know anybody else that could have taken it. To stay there and take what he took, day after day.

"Jackie had trouble *off* the field and *on* the field. We heard that Dixie Walker didn't want to cooperate with him, and probably would have done the rest of us the same way if we had been on the field. Of course all of us would have liked to have been in the major leagues, even though the conditions turned out to be like they were. We still wanted to play in the major leagues regardless of the conditions.

"The same time the Dodgers got Jackie Robinson, they got Johnny

Wright from us, the Homestead Grays. Wright was a good pitcher. He had a good curve ball and everything and could throw the ball over the plate. He was as good as Joe Black, or maybe even better. Both of them — Robinson and Wright — went to spring training at the same time in 1946 with Montreal.

"When they reported to camp, they weren't allowed to dress in the clubhouse with the other players. We were training in Jacksonville that year, and the Dodgers came to town to play the Jacksonville team an exhibition game. Since they couldn't take part in the game with the Dodgers, Johnny Wright and Jackie Robinson came over where we were playing on the other side of town. They were not angry, they knew before they got there that they wouldn't be able to play or go in and change clothes in the clubhouse. It wasn't one of those things where it was sudden or anything like that. They understood the conditions and we understood the conditions, too.

"Johnny Wright had the ability to play in the major leagues, but that was only one part of it. There was something else, too. Robinson stood up under the pressure and Wright didn't. He just wasn't able to stand the pressure and couldn't take the things that he had to take. I don't think many people *could* have or *would* have. So he didn't stick with Montreal and later, when they signed (Roy) Partlow, he didn't stick either. I think that, at that time, they didn't want but one black player."

Some former Negro Leaguers filter their stories through a lens of more recent events to tailor them for compatibility with the subsequent outcome. Buck Leonard was not one to engage in such revisionist history. He spoke the same way as he lived his life — straightforward and honest.

This article came from extensive interviews that I conducted with Buck Leonard from 1981 through 1996. This is the first time that it has been published in this form but some elements of my interviews were also used in my collaboration with Buck for his autobiography titled Buck Leonard: The Black Lou Gehrig, *published in 1995.*

Several years before Jackie Robinson signed with the Brooklyn Dodgers, Buck Leonard and Josh Gibson had been approached by Washington Senators owner Clark Griffith about the possibility of them playing with the Senators in the major leagues. However, Griffith said that nobody wanted to be the first to sign black players and nothing ever came of their conversation. Both Buck and Josh wanted to play and told Griffith they thought they could make good in the major leagues, but as Buck candidly describes in this article, he had reservations about whether he could have taken the amount of abuse that Jackie Robinson endured.

Buck Leonard died November 27, 1997, in Rocky Mount, NC, at the age of 90.

Eddie Klep: The Reverse Jackie Robinson

On March 17, 1946, Jack Roosevelt Robinson took the field for the AAA Montreal Royals against the parent Brooklyn Dodgers in a spring exhibition game at City Island Park in Daytona Beach, Florida. This historic occasion marked the end of organized baseball's unwritten "color line." For the first time in this century, black and white Americans were playing together on the same Major League Baseball team. Labeled Branch Rickey's "Noble Experiment," this was a radical departure from baseball's established social structure.

That spring also provided a second challenge to baseball's "color line." The venue was Birmingham, Alabama, where the "separate but equal" doctrine approved by the U.S. Supreme Court in 1896 was an accepted way of life and even more firmly entrenched than in Florida.

The central figure in this second attack on baseball's segregated structure was Edward Joseph Klep. While Jackie Robinson has been lionized and elevated to the status of an American hero, Eddie Klep, by contrast, has been relegated to a mere footnote in the history of our National Pastime.

On March 24, 1946, only a week after Robinson's first appearance, the Cleveland Buckeyes team bus arrived at Birmingham's Rickwood Field for a Sunday doubleheader against the host Birmingham Black Barons. The first game was scheduled to begin at two o'clock in the afternoon, and it would be the first spring training game for the defending Negro World Series Champion Buckeyes.

The players had dressed at their hotel before boarding the bus for the ride to Rickwood. All except one. He was not allowed to sleep in the same hotel or eat in the same restaurants as his teammates. His name was Eddie Klep, he was a lefthanded pitcher — and he was *white*. That was why he had to stay separate from his teammates, just as Jackie Robinson was doing in Florida.

As the Buckeyes took the field for their pre-game workout, two of Police Chief Theophilus Eugene "Bull" Connor's policemen informed the Buckeyes that Alabama laws prohibited blacks and whites from playing together and ordered Klep from the field. The Buckeyes were acquainted with southern mores and, to avoid a threatened cancellation of the game, did not attempt to force the issue. Klep left the playing field as instructed and was not even allowed to remain in uniform or sit in the dugout.

Banished from the ballpark, Klep went back to his hotel and changed into civilian clothes. Upon his return to Rickwood Field, he sat in the box seats behind the Buckeyes dugout, but was rousted again by the police and told that he had to sit in the section reserved for whites. So it was that Eddie Klep's first game with the Buckeyes was spent in the stands as a segregated spectator.

After the confrontation, Klep was sent back to Erie, Pennsylvania, to train with a predominantly black semi-pro team until the Buckeyes began their regular season. Knowing that he needed the benefit of spring training with the team, Klep went to see Buckeyes owner Ernest P. "Ernie" Wright. Incensed at the injustice, Wright railed, "If Branch Rickey and others of organized baseball can choose material for their liking in order to produce a winning ball club and without question of race or color despite the Southern 'Jim Crow' tradition, then why can't I do the same?"

Observers were divided on Wright's true purpose in signing Klep. Some viewed Wright's statement as an attempt to promote himself as the black Branch Rickey. Others felt that he was only looking for a gate attraction, thinking that crowds would turn out to see Klep, as they did with Robinson. Still another group was convinced that Wright, who characterized Klep as a youngster "with an ambition to be a pitcher on a great ball club," truly believed that he was good enough to make the Buckeyes. Klep *had* made a good showing against the Buckeyes in a post-season exhibition game the previous fall, while pitching for the Glenwood All-Stars of Erie. Whatever his motivations, Wright stood behind his player, and returned with Klep to the Buckeyes' training camp.

A week after returning to camp, Klep was given his first chance to show what he could do with a baseball. On April 7—11 days before Jackie Robinson made his debut with the Montreal Royals against the Jersey City ballclub— the Buckeyes played the Atlanta Black Crackers at Harpers Field in Atlanta.

As the teams went through their pre-game preparations, Klep warmed up on the sidelines. Unlike Birmingham, the Atlanta policemen did not try to prevent the 27-year-old, 5' 7", 170-pounder from playing. The officers simply watched him throw and inquired, "Can he pitch?" They soon found out.

The Black Crackers were a good team for Klep's debut. They were members of the Negro Southern League, which was a class below the Buckeyes' Negro American League. In the first inning Klep retired the side in order without a ball being hit out of the infield. It was to be his best inning.

Cleveland Buckeyes catcher Quincy Trouppe doubled as manager in 1946 when owner Ernie Wright signed Eddie Klep as a reverse Jackie Robinson. Trouppe is pictured two years later with the Chicago American Giants.

Klep yielded his first hit and an unearned run in the next inning, followed by another hit and two more unearned runs in his third and last inning. Leaving the game after his allotted three innings, the husky little left-hander's ledger showed two hits, one walk, and three unearned runs. Most importantly, he was credited with the win in the Buckeyes' 4–3 victory.

During the next four weeks, Klep suffered from inactivity, as the region's Jim Crow laws prohibited his participation as the team toured through Georgia, South Carolina and Florida. The *Cleveland Call & Post* reported, "Braving the taunts, insults, and threats of an outraged southern public, Klep showed true blue and remained with his Negro teammates throughout the spring training season in the deep south."

The Buckeyes completed their spring training and opened their league season May 5 at League Park. The scheduled doubleheader with the Birmingham Black Barons was ushered in with a parade, flag-raising ceremony, and throwing out the first ball. The Buckeyes split the twin bill, but Eddie Klep watched both games from the bench.

Wright maintained a stance on Klep that seemed to echo Branch Rickey's posture with Robinson. "If this lad makes the grade as a top-notch hurler for my team then I will sign him up and use him as any other hurler on the staff." The rhetoric failed to match reality, and Klep had not been utilized as much as the other pitchers on the staff. On May 29, after almost two months of inactivity, Klep pitched four innings in an exhibition game against the Chicago American Giants in Grand Rapids, Michigan. The American Giants were the weakest team in the Negro American League and would finish the first half of the split season in the cellar, but when the game was over Klep was credited with another win.

Klep's opponents were picked much like a boxer being groomed for a title bout. Each was progressively a little better than the previous one.

Klep's first and only appearance in front of the hometown fans was on June 2, when the Buckeyes hosted the Indianapolis Clowns in a doubleheader at League Park. The atmosphere in Cleveland was totally different than in Birmingham. Seating was not segregated and some white fans were counted among the mostly black crowd of 10,000. "There were no incidents from the umpires, players or fans," says Clowns' catcher Buster Haywood. "None of any kind."

The fans received him well. "Everybody clapped their hands and hollered when he came out to pitch that day," remembers Clowns pitcher Jim Colzie. "We did too because Jackie was going up, so we were glad to have him (Klep) there. He wanted to integrate the Negro Leagues."

The circumstances under which he made his entrance were as dramatic as a scripted Hollywood movie production. With the bases loaded in the ninth inning, manager-catcher Quincey Trouppe called on Klep to hang onto a one-run lead, like the cavalry in an old John Wayne movie, arriving at the last minute to save the day. Unfortunately, survival in the Negro Leagues was not like a Hollywood script.

Klep, the fourth Buckeyes pitcher of the game, relieved ace George Jefferson. The first batter that he faced was Goose Tatum, who is best known for his basketball skills and comedy with the Harlem Globetrotters. Tatum lined a single right back through the box, scoring one run to tie the game. After Goose's welcome, Klep tightened down and retired the next two batters, Reynaldo Drake and Buster Haywood.

Just one out away from getting out of the inning, Klep faced the Clowns' playing manager, Hoss Walker, who singled to left field, scoring two more runs and giving the Clowns the lead. Before Klep finally retired the side, four runs had scored, with one of them charged to him. The Buckeyes were unable to mount a comeback in the bottom half of the inning and lost the game, 11–8.

This was Eddie Klep's last appearance with the Buckeyes. Immediately after Jim Colzie pinned a 7–3 loss on the Buckeyes in the second game of the twin bill, General Manager Wilbur Hayes announced Klep's unconditional release. Only a month into the regular season, Ernie Wright's version of the "Noble Experiment" was ended.

Manager Quincey Trouppe told the *Cleveland Call and Post* that Klep "failed to measure up to the fast Negro American League standards." Outfielder Willie Grace agreed with his skipper, "He couldn't have pitched in the league anywhere." Buckeyes pitcher Jim Bolden disagreed. "He was a good enough pitcher. If he had been a black ballplayer he would have stayed with the team."

The *Cleveland Call and Post* had earlier reported that Klep was "one of the most promising prospects of the pitching staff." Although they only played one game against Klep, the Clowns players concurred with Bolden. Catcher

Buster Haywood recalls, "He was a pretty good pitcher. They have good days and bad days. Even Satchel had bad days." Pitcher Jim Colzie remembers, "He was a pretty nice pitcher. He had good stuff. He had a good fastball and a left-hander's ball moves, period, if he throws it hard. And he had a good changeup and a good overhand curveball. He didn't pitch nervous at all. He wasn't scared of anything."

When he was released, Klep's record showed two wins and no losses, but neither decision was in an official league game. The pioneering left-hander pitched only seven innings with the Buckeyes and felt that he had not been given a real opportunity to make the team. According to reporter Cleveland Jackson, Klep "appeared very bitter," yet he made it clear that he "was anxious to continue his baseball career."

Klep said that his "experience with Negro Players had been very cordial and that he was not adverse to playing with another Negro team." The day after he was cut from the Buckeyes, Klep went to the Chesterfield Hotel, where the visiting Clowns were staying, to ask manager Hoss Walker for a chance with the Clowns, but he was turned down.

Jim Colzie recalls the incident, "We were standing outside in front of the hotel, and he came over and wanted to see the manager. Hoss was in the hotel, so Klep went in the hotel and was in there about 20 minutes. He asked could he have a tryout with the team. Hoss told him 'No' and he come out. And we stood and talked around and he said, 'I'll stay until the game is over. I'll see you all at the game.' He walked away and I never saw him again."

In contrast to the hoopla surrounding Jackie Robinson's arrival in white baseball, Klep's entrance and exit from the Negro Leagues were hardly noticed. And his role in the eradication of the color line was virtually an invisible presence.

However, Eddie Klep *did* play baseball again — with the Rockford State Prison team! When he was serving his "hard time," he listed his occupation as "professional ballplayer." It was the one thing in his life that made him proud.

This article was written in December of 1997, at the request of the editor of a proposed baseball publication to be titled The Pennant. *Unfortunately, the funding never came to fruition and the magazine died still on the vine. Thus, this is the first time that it has appeared in print.*

The article deals specifically with Klep's pioneering role in assaulting baseball's color line and touches on his baseball career, but readers will also be interested in the back story, which gives much insight into Eddie Klep as a person.

Eddie's love for baseball was passed down to him from his father. As a youth he found his only success in athletics, primarily playing sandlot and semi-pro baseball. Even after he was married, according to his wife, baseball was "all he ever talked about."

However, his diamond skills did not match his love of the game nor his desire to play professional baseball at the highest level. The unvarnished truth is that if Klep had possessed sufficient talent to play with one of the top teams in the Negro Leagues, he would have been playing in organized baseball's minor leagues at some level. This limitation of his athletic ability was only one delineating factor marking the difference between him and Jackie Robinson.

In contrast to Robinson's admirable character, Klep was not a high-class person and his personal life was a shambles that even Hollywood could not have scripted. It would indeed make a great movie.

Klep's father was killed in 1937, when he was hit by an automated freight car while walking along the Erie Coal Dump ramp and then dragged 150 feet. When the mangled body was brought home, 18-year-old Eddie was there alone to endure the impact of his father's death.

In the aftermath Klep, having already developed a penchant for taking things that did not belong to him, soon expanded his criminal pursuits. Dating from 1937 he had a decade-long string of arrests, totaling more than a dozen, mostly for larceny but also for an array of other crimes, including disorderly conduct, arson, adultery, and assault and battery.

Two of his arrests were sandwiched around his brief career with the Cleveland Buckeyes in 1946. In February, only a month before his confrontation with Bull Connor's police force in the Buckeyes' abortive attempt to integrate the Negro Leagues, Klep was arrested for larceny and jailed for ten days. In May, a scant six weeks after being released by the Buckeyes, he faced trial for burglary, larceny, and receiving stolen goods. This led to his incarceration at Pennsylvania's State Correctional Institution at Rockview, where he played on the baseball team as referenced in this article.

His wife said, "Sometimes you could see the Devil in his eyes. I knew he was a bad seed but I loved him anyway." Klep was a charmer with the ladies and a smooth talker who impregnated his future wife the first time they met when she was only 17. Her mother persistently pressured Eddie to "do the right thing" and get married, but two weeks before the scheduled wedding, Klep attempted suicide and was taken to North Warren State Hospital for mental evaluation. Nearly six months later, after his recovery, he finally succumbed to the parental pressure and was married August 18, 1941, in Erie, Pennsylvania.

Within a month he walked out on his new bride but returned intermittently—when in need of money—to steal something that he could pawn. Eventually, he abandoned his family completely.

His son, Eddie Klep, Jr., who was raised by his wife's parents under a different name, thought that his mother was his sister and didn't learn about his real father until much later. Even then he had little contact with Klep, who failed even to recognize him the last time they met.

After leaving his wife to her own means of support, Klep moved around the country, first to Buffalo, New York, then to Texas and finally to California. Throughout his life Klep had worked intermittently at a variety of menial jobs, and in California he continued this employment pattern and had no steady job. There, although never divorced or remarried, he cohabited with a woman by whom he apparently fathered two children, and lost all contact with his legitimate family. His longtime alcohol abuse contributed to his inability to hold a job and inevitably led to him being institutionalized there. "They say he was a pretty good player as long as he could stay sober through the seventh inning," Klep's son said of his father's alcoholism.

Klep was living in a retirement home in Los Angeles when he died alone November 21, 1981 (or according to the Social Security records, in January 1982) and was cremated in a pauper's ceremony. After his family found out about his death, his ashes were returned to Erie, but there was no burial until almost five years later. In July 1986, at his brother Julius' funeral, Eddie's ashes were tossed inside at the last minute before his brother's casket was closed.

The cemetery marker does not include Eddie Klep's name, so his remains lie at rest in a shared casket in an unmarked grave — a sad end to a forgotten baseball pioneer.

Toni Stone: Lady at the Bat

The second baseman was a target — for baserunners coming in hard to break up a double play, for a pitcher asserting ownership of the inner part of the plate and half of the batter's box, and for the few fans directing their barbed remarks at the keystone player. The understanding was unspoken but everyone knew that it was open season on the new player. And everyone knew the reason. Some of the veteran players resented the rookie's presence on the diamond, while others were merely tolerant. But a few welcomed the "new arrival" despite the obvious difference from the other players.

The second baseman's skin was dark, but it wasn't Jackie Robinson. Racism was the only obstacle that Robinson had to overcome. This player had to overcome sexism as well because the second baseman was a lady. Her name was Toni Stone and she was signed by the Indianapolis Clowns in 1953, making her the first female athlete to play with a team at this level of competition. In 1917 the Havana Red Sox had used a female first baseman, Pearl Barrett, but the Sox' caliber of performance was not regarded on a par with the major leagues.

In contrast, the Clowns were one of the better-known teams in the Negro Leagues and, as the forerunners of the Harlem Globetrotters, always provided the crowds with a blend of baseball and showbiz. Some players voiced the opinion that Toni had been signed simply as a gate attraction. Manager Buster Haywood agreed and indicated that he did not think that she could compete with men. Owner Syd Pollock differed, maintaining that she was signed for her baseball ability. While it cannot be denied that her presence helped fill the ballpark, she was more than just a novelty.

From the earliest years of her childhood, she had wanted to be a baseball player. Born Marcenia Lyle, as a youngster she attended Gabby Street's baseball school in St. Paul, Minnesota, where she began her diamond career as a softball player with the Girls Highlex Softball Club. But by the age of 15, she was playing with a men's team.

After high school graduation, the self-described "tomboy" switched to baseball and later took the name "Toni Stone" because of the phonic similarity.

That was during World War II, when she moved to the San Francisco bay area and began playing American Legion baseball.

A women's professional league, The All-American Girls Professional Baseball League, operated in the midwest from 1943 through 1954 but, like the major leagues of that era, it was rigidly segregated. Toni wrote to the Chicago franchise asking for a tryout, but never received an answer.

Locked out of that league, she joined a black barnstorming team, the San Francisco Sea Lions, before progressing to the Black Pelicans and New Orleans Creoles in the Negro minor leagues. With the Creoles, she earned $300 a month while batting .265 for the 1949 season. The next year, matrimony led to a temporary baseball hiatus. But with the Negro American League suffering from the exodus of black players to organized baseball and struggling to survive financially, Pollock entreated Toni to return to the game she loved. The skilled promoter proved to be a true visionary, and the fans turned out in large numbers to see "the girl" second baseman.

Playing with men was not a problem for the pioneering baseballist. She had played with boys since childhood and could field, throw, run and hit like the male baseball players. And when she made the team, she wore the same kind of uniform as the men. When Pollock asked her to wear shorts, Toni emphatically declined.

She wanted to be accepted on her own, without any special distinction. "I was a ballplayer," Toni says, "and I just wanted to play baseball." League officials agreed that she should not be treated differently from any other ballplayer. When Pollock addressed the issue at a league meeting and asked the other owners to restrict their pitchers to only fastballs when Toni batted, they refused his request.

And Toni *was* treated just like any other player. The ball diamond served as a proving ground where opposing players tested her resolve. She was taken out on double plays, knocked

Toni Stone became the first female player in the Negro Leagues when owner Syd Pollock signed her to a contract with his Indianapolis Clowns in 1953, one year after he had signed a young shortstop named Hank Aaron.

down at the plate and accorded all the other familiarities that come with being a professional baseball player. "When the pitchers knocked me down, I just got back up and went on," Toni says. "Oscar Charleston would tell me, 'Stay loose.'" Those who doubted her determination were quickly convinced, as they learned that she could hold her own on the playing field. She could hold her own in an argument, too, and oftentimes turned the air blue and the umpire's ears red.

In most games Toni would start at second base and play three innings, and then Ray Neil would finish the game. Neil was one of the Clowns' best hitters, and it must have been difficult for him to sit out part of the game so the fans could see Toni play. But the crowds loved her.

Satchel Paige was another gate attraction who only played the first three innings to draw a crowd. On Easter Sunday, 1953, the fans in Omaha, Nebraska, got a double-barreled thrill, when Toni came to bat against Satchel. She was the leadoff hitter and was nervous when she stepped into the batter's box to face the lanky legend. A consummate showman, Paige asked Toni where she wanted the pitch. "It doesn't matter," she responded. Then, with a count of one-and-one after Toni took two pitches, Paige directed the spheroid towards the plate again. "I don't know what kind of pitch it was," she recalls, "but it was right down the middle."

It was a variation of *Casey at the Bat*, but this time, to the great delight of the crowd, "Casey" rapped a base hit. "It went right over second base," Toni remembers vividly. "After I got the hit, Satchel turned his back on me and I guess he had a good chuckle. Then somebody else got a hit and knocked me in. But after I scored, it was zoom ... zoom ... zoom. He didn't give them nothing else." Not the batters, anyway. But he gave the crowd a show and Toni a memory for the rest of her life.

Toni's presence with the Clowns encouraged other female ballplayers across the country, who began writing Pollock requesting a tryout. One player, Doris Jackson, was offered a roster spot as a backup for Toni, but there is no record of her playing in a league game. On the other hand, while Toni had some difficulties hitting the curveball, she still played 50 games and maintained a respectable .243 batting average for the season.

The next year her contract was transferred to Tom Baird's Kansas City Monarchs, and the Clowns signed Connie Morgan as a replacement at second base, while also signing Mamie "Peanut" Johnson as a pitcher and utility player.

Connie Morgan, an all-around athlete who played basketball in the offseason, was younger and smaller than her predecessor at second base. Before signing with the Clowns at the age of 19, she had already played five years with the North Philadelphia Honey Drippers, an all-girl baseball team, and sported a .368 batting average for her tenure with the team.

Mamie Johnson, the smallest of the Clowns' female ballplayers at 120 pounds, earned the nickname "Peanut" because of her size, but the little right hander threw as hard as many male pitchers. Before signing with the Clowns, she played boys sports, including football, while attending Long Branch High School, and had attended New York University, where she studied medicine and engineering.

Toni and the Clowns' new daring duo gave the league three female players in 1954, but none of the trio returned for the ensuing season. Ironically, the All-American Girls Professional Baseball League also ceased operations after the 1954 season, leaving baseball without even a trace of talented female ballplayers.

The year that saw the demise of the ladies of baseball, also saw the rise of another of the Clowns' former middle infielders when Hank Aaron made his debut in the major leagues. Now Aaron is the All-Time Home Run King of baseball and America's national pastime is still waiting for the next female baseball player.

This article was first published in 1994 in the March-April issue of The Diamond: The Official Chronicle of Major League Baseball *under the title "Lady at the Bat: Playing for the Indianapolis Clowns in 1952, Toni Stone Broke the Gender Barrier."*

I conducted a phone interview with Toni and it only took a few minutes to know that she was a ballplayer. I also interviewed Connie by phone and later met her in person at a Negro Leagues reunion in 1995 hosted by the Negro Leagues Baseball Museum in Kansas City. I have met Mamie several times at various venues over the years.

Toni Stone died November 2, 1996, in Alameda, California, at the age of 65, less than three weeks after Connie Morgan, who died October 14, 1996, in Philadelphia, Pennsylvania, at the age of 60 and only three days short of her birthday. Mamie Johnson currently resides in Washington, D.C., and is the subject of a biography.

All three baseball ladies were prominently mentioned in Alan Pollock's poignant memoir Barnstorming to Heaven: Syd Pollock and His Great Black Teams, *which was published by the University of Alabama Press in 2006.*

A final note: In the intervening years since this article was written, Hank Aaron has been supplanted as the All-Time Home run King by Barry Bonds.

Baseball with a Rumba Beat

It is a moment frozen in time: pitcher Rufus Lewis lying unconscious on the ground, batter Adolfo "Tribilin" Cabrera standing over him with his bat raised to deliver another blow after having knocked him unconscious, and Wild Bill Wright charging out of the dugout with his bat poised to hit Cabrera before he could connect with a second blow to the helpless Lewis.

And now for the rest of the story—before and after the photographer's lenses captured the moment for posterity.

The time is 1950 and the scene is a hotly contested Mexican League game between the Mexico City Rojos and the Jalisco Charros of Guadalajara. The Charros would finish first in the second half of the split-season, with the Rojos close behind in a tie for second place. Rufus Lewis, pitching for Mexico, was facing Adolfo Cabrera, the defending batting champion who batted .379 the previous year. Lewis tried to break a curve in on Cabrera's fists but the pitch failed to break and hit the batter.

Still carrying his bat, Cabrera took a few steps down the first base line, as though he were going to first base. When he was about even with the mound, he charged towards Lewis, who took a few steps off the mound but was too surprised to adequately defend himself against the attack. Cabrera's first blow knocked Lewis unconscious and as he lay crumpled on the ground, the enraged Cabrera stood over him and raised the bat to strike the helpless pitcher again.

Players rushed to the scene, trying to verbally dissuade Cabrera from delivering what would have been a fatal blow. Wild Bill Wright, the Rojos' star player who was out of the lineup that day because of a sty on his eye, didn't waste time with words. He grabbed the first bat he saw as he raced from the dugout to intercept Cabrera and protect his teammate. Fortunately, Wright arrived at the scene just in time to save Lewis's life. Wright delivered a resounding blow to Cabrera's head an instant before he again bashed the defenseless Lewis.

Wright was known for his exceptional speed and a slower man might not have arrived in time to save his teammate. The switch-hitting Wright

Bill Wright (foreground) rushed from the dugout to save teammate Rufus Lewis (helpless on the ground) after he had been hit by Adolfo Cabrera (standing over Lewis with bat ready to deliver another blow).

swung left-handed and his was the second and last blow of the brief, almost deadly encounter. Wright had saved his teammate's life.

As both injured players were carried off the field, bloodied and unconscious, the fans cheered and threw cushions and other missiles out onto the playing field. After all, Mexican sports aficionados love bull-fighting, cock-fighting and other blood sports.

I wrote this brief account of the incident in 2000 at the request of Bob Zimmer, who had the accompanying photo displayed in his Cleveland Negro Leagues Museum, and wanted to have an explanatory written description of the altercation to complement the exhibit for visitors.

I first saw this picture in Piper Davis' scrapbook, 25 years ago. It was cut out of a Mexican magazine and a tear in the page had been scotch-taped back together. I interviewed Piper, who was on Cabrera's team, about the incident, as well as two of the principle participants, Rufus Lewis and Bill Wright. I also talked to Jalisco's playing manager, Quincy Trouppe, whose bat was used by Wright.

Wild Bill Wright's swing was right on target—his bat caught Cabrera just below the scalp line, almost scalping him as the blow peeled his scalp part way back from the front of his head. Piper Davis was shaken by the incident and said that he didn't field another ball cleanly the rest of the game. Rufus Lewis adamantly maintained that he had not intentionally hit Cabrera. Wright never regretted his action but expressed some initial concern for his own welfare after the incident. Trouppe did not elaborate about details surrounding the bloody episode.

All of the American players mentioned are now deceased. Quincy Trouppe died August 10, 1993, in Creve Coeur, Missouri. Bill Wright died August 3, 1996, in Aguascalientes, Mexico. Piper Davis died May 21, 1997, in Birmingham, Alabama. Rufus Lewis died December 17, 1999, in Southfield, Michigan.

This photo captured a rare moment in baseball history. Sometimes the most remarkable photographs are not posed, like the famous Iwo Jima shot, which was captured instantaneously by photographer Joe Rosenthal, who never knew what he actually had until the negatives were developed.

As a footnote to the story: Torreon (the first half champs) defeated Jalisco in the play-off between the split season winners, winning in six games to take the championship.

When "The Babe" Came to Mobile

It was April of 1924. The countryside was green with spring and, with a new baseball season just around the corner, hearts were full of hope. Each year when the teams break training camp and head north, dreams are as plentiful as a field's spring seeds.

Mobile, Alabama, always a hotbed of baseball activity and aspirations, was no exception. But this year there was an added excitement — Babe Ruth was coming to town! Nobody else commanded the adulation that surrounded the Babe. He had charisma a generation before the word would find its way into common usage. Everyone loved the Babe. He appealed to men and women alike, and to children he was larger than life. But at the same time, kids recognized him as one of their own and were attracted to him like metal filings to a magnet.

Having spent most of his formative years in St. Mary's Industrial School for Boys in Baltimore, Ruth had an affinity for the "dirty faced kids" that adored him. After arriving in Mobile, he shouldered a tuba and posed for a picture in the middle of the city's Boys Industrial School band. The Babe was always good copy, and the press kept the public well informed of almost everything he did.

Babe's Yankees had won three consecutive American League pennants and, as they took the field for the exhibition game at Monroe Park, they were pre-season favorites in their quest of a fourth title. With the great Bambino in form, few would doubt their chances. He was coming off a season in which he batted .393 and led the league in home runs. Two years before that, Babe had obliterated the single-season home run record with 59 round-trippers.

When the 1924 season was over, the Babe would have another home run crown *and* a batting title, with a .378 average. Three years later he would break his own single-season home run record by slamming 60 baseballs out of American League ballparks. And after playing a dozen more seasons, he would hang up his spikes with a lifetime total of 714 home runs, another major league record. In later years, the Babe would confide to friends that his single-season mark might someday be broken, but he was quite certain that his lifetime record would stand.

The Babe, of course, was wrong in this prediction and could not have even remotely suspected that his lifetime record would be broken by the son of someone watching the game that day in Mobile. Monroe Park was overflowing with baseball fans expecting to see baseball's "Home Run King" hit one of the towering home runs that had become his trademark.

Many who could not gain access to the ballpark watched informally from assorted vantage points. One such observer was a 15-year-old black youngster, who found a makeshift seat on a strong limb after scrambling up a tall pine tree beyond the outfield fence. From this unique perspective, he watched Babe Ruth deliver on the crowd's expectations, and his impression is still vivid:

> I remember when Babe Ruth came to town to play an exhibition game. It was the same time I came to Mobile. I didn't have a family then. I went down to the ballpark, and I went up in a pine tree down there and got a limb way up. And I sat up there and looked at the game. At that time, Babe was wide open, you know. He hit a ball and it hit in a boxcar that was coming along. And the ball went in that boxcar and a fellow found it in Georgia when he was unloading a car.

The youngster's name was Herb Aaron and, as he watched the great Babe Ruth, he never dreamed that nearly a half-century later he would witness another historic home run when his son eclipsed the Babe's lifetime total.

> No, I didn't imagine that someday my son would break his home run record. It never reached to any of us about that. My son Henry never had that in mind. He was just trying to make a payday. You know how some children love something, that's how he was with baseball.

The pride is evident in his voice when he speaks of "My son Henry." Herb had played a little sandlot ball as a young-

Hank Aaron, age 17, leaving Mobile to begin his professional baseball career with the Indianapolis Clowns.

ster, and it was his love for the game that was passed on to his sons. When he later managed a team, he would take them to the ballpark with him and kept a close watch to make sure they didn't get into any trouble.

> I'd tell my wife and she'd know every step they'd make out of the house. My boy was coming up and I managed Henry. He played shortstop, but Tommy was too young. He just followed us around. When Henry was young, he batted crosshanded but when he went up there to the professional leagues, they changed him.

Actually, it was between the time he left Mobile and when he signed with the Boston Braves organization that he was converted from his crosshanded batting grip. Before he got to the major leagues, his trail took a few unusual turns.

The first professional team to sign him was Syd Pollock's Indianapolis Clowns of the old Negro Leagues, and that was when Hank was changed to a conventional batting grip. After his three months as an infielder with the Clowns, Aaron's baseball career is well chronicled. As he followed the path that led to breaking Ruth's lifetime home run record and to the Hall of Fame, Hank's most faithful fan was the youngster who had scrambled up the pine tree on that day so long ago. As a father he watched proudly as his son received the accolades of mankind, but he also remembers different times that the cheering crowds never saw. "I've seen him come home and sit down and cry because he couldn't hit Koufax," he says, before adding proudly, "Then the next day he knocked a double off him and a single and home run."

Herb Aaron was always there to help his son in any way he could, but there is no hesitation when giving the credit for Hank's success. "Henry was a natural ballplayer. The man that made him a ballplayer is the same one who made me and who made you. That's the Good Lord up above."

In 1991 I went to Mobile, Alabama, to research Satchel Paige's years in his hometown. My first quest was to locate the place where Satchel was born. So I located the street (now bearing a different name) and the vacant lot where his parents' house had been located when he was born there. I also located the school in which he was enrolled and the playground where he learned to play baseball. I located his best friend from his childhood—the one who gave him his nickname "Satchel" and was in Mt. Meigs reformatory with him. I located and talked with Satchel's sister, Palestine, who was about as colorful as her famous brother.

I also talked to the fathers of two major league baseball players who remembered Satchel. One was Amos Otis' father, who still carried a scar on his face from his childhood where he had been hit by a metal washer that a young Satchel had thrown from across the street for no apparent reason. The other was Hank Aaron's father. He talked a while about his recollections of Satchel but it didn't take him long to begin talking about "my son Henry." And the best story I got from Herb Aaron is the one that is written here and published for the first time.

I met Herb Aaron again at Atlanta's Fox Theatre at the premier of the TBS original documentary movie made about Hank's life, Hank Aaron: Chasing the Dream. *Herb Aaron was obviously still proud of his son Henry.*

Barry Bonds broke Hank Aaron's career home run record on August 7, 2007, when he hit his 756th homer to become the new Home Run King, but Hank Aaron will not be forgotten — just as Babe Ruth was not forgotten when Hank broke his record.

President Bush Hits a Homer: Negro League Players Honored at the White House

In his collegiate days George Bush was noted as a smooth-fielding first baseman with a light stick. But on February 19, 1992, he seemed more like Babe Ruth to four fortunate former Negro League players who were honored at the White House.

As representatives of the Negro League Ballplayers Association, Monte Irvin, Leon Day, Jimmie Crutchfield and Josh Gibson, Jr., were invited guests at the Presidential program in the East Room of the White House, recognizing February as Black History Month. With General Colin Powell, Chairman of the Joint Chiefs of Staff, and Judge Clarence Thomas, newest Supreme Court Justice, among the distinguished dignitaries present for the ceremonies, President Bush welcomed the quartet of ballplayers in his opening remarks and afterward, at a reception in the Abraham Lincoln Room, personally greeted each of them.

"We were sitting on the front row and to see him call our names and get up and take a bow was simply outstanding," said Monte Irvin. "To just honor those fellows who never got a chance to play in the major leagues and let them finally experience the feeling of being wanted and of being honored made me feel very good. And the fact that we talked to him (President Bush) and got a chance to take a picture with him was very, very gratifying."

But this was not Irvin's first time to meet George Bush. Having starred in the major leagues as well as in the Negro Leagues, Irvin was well known to the President. They had met previously, when Bush was Vice President, at an old-timers game in which the current Chief Executive had donned a first baseman's mitt to demonstrate that he still retained a recognizable residue of the fancy footwork he had demonstrated around the initial sack in his college days. The Prez also took his turn at bat in the exhibition game and rapped out a base hit, one that he will probably remember longer than any other that he ever collected.

Nor was this Irvin's first trip to the White House. "I got a chance to go to the White House in 1969, when it was the Centennial of Baseball, to meet

President George H. W. Bush recognized four former Negro Leagues players at the White House in 1992. Pictured is Jimmie Crutchfield meeting the President. Only in America!

with President Nixon," he explained, "And then President Reagan invited all the Hall of Famers to the White House for a special luncheon."

But for the other players, the occasion provided a first opportunity to meet the leader of their country and proved a most rewarding experience. "It was a big thrill," acknowledged Leon Day afterwards. "I had met a Cuban president and I had met a Mexican president, but that was the first time I had ever met an American president."

The former Newark Eagles ace is a living legend from the Negro Leagues and a strong candidate for the Hall of Fame, but he continues to be overlooked by some members of the Veterans Committee. It is ironic that Day had met the Latin American dignitaries during his baseball prime while he had to wait until he was 75 years of age to meet the president of his own country and be recognized for his accomplishments. The hard-throwing right-hander had blown his fastball by batters throughout the hemisphere, from Canada to Venezuela, and the fastball artist holds the single-game strikeout record for both the Negro National League (18) and in Puerto Rico (19), as well as the career strikeout record for the Negro Leagues All-Star Game. Belatedly, his achievements are being acclaimed in his own country.

Earlier in the day, the players had met with three congressmen (including former NBA star Bill Bradley) for photos and recognitions. When introduced to the New Jersey Senator, Josh Gibson, Jr. quipped, "I used to watch you with the Knicks." Bradley was gracious and genuinely interested in learning more about the Negro Leagues.

Gibson, whose baseball career was just beginning as the Negro Leagues were ending, tried to follow in the footsteps of his famous father, whose name he bears. The elder Gibson, who was called the black Babe Ruth, died in 1946, two years before his son made his professional debut with Youngstown, Ohio, at the age of 17, straight out of high school. The following season Josh, Jr. signed with the Homestead Grays and played third base under the tutelage of his mentor, Sam Bankhead, during the Grays' last two seasons of existence. With the demise of the Negro Leagues as a viable entity, he followed Bankhead to Canada for a season, but an injury contributed to an aborted career.

Gibson was the youngest of the quartet of former players, while the honor of being the eldest went to a man often called the black Lloyd Waner, Jimmie Crutchfield. "Crutch" was a small, gutsy hustler whose all-around ability and team contributions were recognized by teammates, opponents and fans alike, and during his 16-year career, he played in five East-West All-Star Games. The fielding genius used to practice catching fly balls behind his back to entertain the fans, and on occasions he would make a behind-the-back catch in a game.

But while black fans cheered these remarkable catches, white Americans were never privileged to see the fielding stylist in action. Now, 60 years later, Crutchfield, whose wife is a descendent of former President William Henry Harrison, was a guest at the White House and shaking hands with the President of the United States.

"To meet the President and to talk to him was quite an honor," Crutchfield said later. "Everybody doesn't get a chance." And Crutchfield almost missed *his* chance. In Chicago, a heavy fog had grounded all flights and it was feared that the 82-year-old outfielder might not be able to get to Washington in time for the ceremonies. But Providence intervened and after a seven-hour delay, he was able to get a flight out in time to meet the President. Eschewing domestic politics and foreign affairs, Crutchfield found a more comfortable topic of conversation with the Chief Executive. "I told him I knew he liked baseball and that he played first base in college," the octogenarian related. "He said, 'That's true, but I couldn't hit the curveball.' " Gesturing typically, President Bush added, "I couldn't hit anything."

It was a busy day for the previously forgotten stars of a bygone era and truly one for them to cherish. Following their full day, the players returned to their hotel to share a fine dinner and even better memories, some recent and some remote.

Crutchfield pulled a newspaper clipping out of his wallet and unfolded it to show a box score of the first game that he had ever played. The year was 1930 and he was in center field for the Birmingham Black Barons, playing behind a young stringbean pitcher with a disappearing fastball, who was to become a baseball legend. His name, of course, was Satchel Paige.

At the end of the season, the two players went their separate ways but, less than a year later, Crutchfield and Paige were reunited on the Pittsburgh Crawfords. With the Crawfords, Crutchfield joined Cool Papa Bell and Sam Bankhead to form an outfield triad that takes a back seat to no other in baseball history. Satchel loved to pitch with this trio of gazelles in the outer gardens. If there were two outs and a ball was hit to the outfield, Satchel didn't even look back, he just started towards the dugout.

"Satchel was always giving credit to his outfield," says Crutchfield, who loves to relate his favorite "Satchel story" which illustrates Paige's high regard for the Crawfords' outfield. "I have to laugh every time I think about this," he chuckled as he warmed up to the story. "One day in Pittsburgh I was in center field and a rainstorm was brewing out beyond the center field fence and the wind was blowing the rain in towards the playing field," he said, setting the scene. "Satchel said he looked back and saw that rain coming across the center field fence and while he stood there and watched it, we caught every raindrop before it got to the infield."

Satchel was prone to exaggeration, but Crutchfield can back up all of his own stories. That's why the former fielding whiz carries his clippings — to dispel the possibility of an argument. "I can prove everything that I say," the former outfielder laughs.

It had been a full day in every way — full of honors, full of fun and full of camaraderie. And each player left with a belly full of good food, a heart full of memories and a pocket full of dreams come true.

Only in America.

This article was first published in 1992, in the Vol. 4 No. 2 edition of Old-tyme Baseball News. *The President Bush mentioned in this article is George H. W. Bush. Monte Irvin called me and asked, "How would you like to go to the White House with all expenses paid?" Of course, I accepted the invitation in a heartbeat.*

The next time I saw Jimmie Crutchfield after this event was at the Meadowlands, and he sought me out to let me know how much he appreciated the article. "Crutch" smiled and, with a twinkle in his eye, said "Only in America," the words with which I had ended the story.

Of the four players who were honored, only Monte Irvin is still living.

A Bit of Americana — 1986 Ballpark Dedication Renews Memories

It's a way of life that's gone ... and almost forgotten. The lifestyle of baseball in the Negro Leagues. It was an arduous existence which consisted of—as one former player descriptively rhymes the experience—"long rides, low pay, and a game every day." Throughout, the players endured the hardships and maintained an indomitable spirit. Negro League veteran Judy Johnson, who now can look back over eight and a half decades, expresses his own colorful optimism which characterizes that spirit. "The sun was always shining somewhere," the Hall of Fame third baseman says, "and wherever it was shining there was a game being played."

These games were played in major league parks, in cornfields, and sometimes in their own ballparks. Today's kind of "progress," which knocks down trees and then names streets after them, has also effectively destroyed most of the structural links with baseball's history by tearing down the old stadiums and replacing them with concrete. Only two of black baseball's "green cathedrals" still stand as sentinels of the past to remind us of "days that used to be."

Both of these surviving locations are in the state of New Jersey. One is Hinchliffe Stadium in Paterson, and the other is Grove Street Oval in East Orange. The Oval was also known as the Grove Street Senior Ball Diamond and is still used as a community ball diamond. The site is in a residential area and is bounded on the north by Grove Place, on the west by Grove Street North, on the south by Eaton Place, and on the east by Greenwood Avenue.

On June 6, 1986, in a cultural and historical event, the East Orange Oval Park was recognized as an historic site and renamed Monte Irvin Field in honor of the city's own baseball great.

Although he was born on a sugar plantation near Columbia, Alabama, on Feb. 25, 1919, at six years of age Monte moved with his family to Orange, where he spent his childhood and formative years. They lived in an integrated, but rough and tough, neighborhood. "There was good feeling between white and black boys in Orange," Monte says. "We played together, fought together, and had good times together." Monte's father, like many others of the Depression era, worked long hours to bring home wages of $18–$20 a week to support his family. These men, according to Monte, are the real heroes.

In an environment where he could easily have gone the wrong way, Monte turned to sports to point him in a positive direction. As the youngest of 11

Cultural & Historical Event

Commemorating
The Naming of the
East Orange Park's Baseball, Diamond
to Monte Irvin Field

The Celebration of the
East Orange Oval Park As An Historic Site

The Official Opening of the East Orange Parks

Friday, June 6th, 1986
1:30 P.M.

East Orange Oval
Eaton Place, East Orange, New Jersey

Pictured is the program from the ceremony when East Orange, New Jersey, named the former Grove Street Oval in honor of Monte Irvin.

children, Monte had learned to play baseball from his older brother Bob, who had bought his six-year-old brother his first ball glove.

In elementary school, Monte played soccer, and at Orange High School, he excelled at football, basketball, baseball, and track, earning 16 varsity letters. Always a gifted natural athlete, among his schoolboy accomplishments was to set a state record of 192' 8" the first time that he threw a javelin competitively.

Ultimately, sports were the vehicle that provided him with an education, and a baseball career that carried him to the Hall of Fame. This honor represented a pinnacle of success that he could not have even envisioned as a youngster. Now, contrary to Thomas Wolfe's assertion, Monte Irvin had come home again.

Arriving at the site prior to the official ceremonies, the Hall of Famer stepped on the field and, taking a visual stroll, shared rekindled memories.

As a youngster Monte had walked the five miles from his home to the field to watch the old-time great black baseball teams play. "At that time there was no television and everybody used to flock to the park," Monte explains. "Because the park was close by and it was during part of the Depression and nobody had any money. So they would go to the park and enjoy themselves."

Pointing over to a low wall paralleling the third base line, he recalled how the fans would bring their own chairs and sit in that area while watching the game. Other fans would ring the outfield and sometimes sit on the roofs of surrounding structures. General admission was 25 cents while grandstand seats were 50 cents. The grandstands are gone now and, gesturing behind home plate to where they had once stood, Monte recalled how the grandstand prices were later raised to 75 cents.

Looking out toward the playing field, Monte nostalgically commented on how big the field had looked when he was a youngster. Pointing toward left field, he recalled the ground rule double for balls hit over the fence between the foul line, which was just 240 feet away, and a pole located in left-center field.

The fence consisted of garage walls that were about 25 feet high and stood in place of the present chain link fence. A school playground serves as a buffer between the fence and the elementary school now located just beyond where a string of poplar trees once stood. The scoreboard had been in left field too, while the clubhouse had been down the right field line in foul territory.

In right field, just as it was long ago, there is still no fence. But 280 feet from home plate trees remain interspersed, delineating the far reaches of the playing field from the tennis courts and street beyond, just as it had been when Monte had played there.

In deepest center field there was a four-foot-high water fountain, and balls that hit it were still in play. A white house still stands beyond the fountain in back of center field. Monte recalled once hitting a grand slam that cleared the house. Deepest center field was listed as 360 feet but to clear the house a ball would have traveled well over 400 feet.

These distances which once had looked so far to Monte — both as a kid watching the great black teams and later as a young player with the Newark Eagles — now seemed almost like they were nothing at all. As a major leaguer Monte had hit balls a lot further many times, but today he was again looking through the eyes of a ten-year-old.

Carloads of former players had arrived from Baltimore, Philadelphia, and the surrounding New Jersey area. Returning to demonstrate their support and to share in the memories evoked by the ceremonies, they were also looking at the field through the eyes of their younger selves and conjuring up their own personal memories of the field.

Charlie Biot, a former center fielder with the Newark Eagles, recalled a game in which Josh Gibson, in each of three consecutive trips to the plate, hit a home run over that little white house. Monte puts the legendary black slugger's accomplishments in perspective. "Gibson, without a doubt, was the greatest hitter I ever saw, black or white. He would have broken Ruth's record. The fans saw the Babe from the left side; they would have seen Josh from the right side."

Ray Dandridge, the Eagles' hot corner wizard, recalled playing on the field in 1934. "We played some helluva games on this field," the infield great said. Although not able to recall any specific games because "it was so long ago," he did remember having pitched in the Oval against some white semi-pro teams.

Speaking to former Eagles teammate and pitching ace Leon Day, he jested, "I pitched as good as you did!" Day replied, "Sure you did," and winked at the other Negro League veterans listening. One of them jocularly reminded Dandridge, "They let you pitch because they didn't want to waste a pitcher."

Among those laughing at the jibe was Pat Scantlebury, who also had pitched on the field. During the forties, whenever the Polo Grounds was unavailable, owner Alex Pompez' New York Cubans sometimes played their home games at the Grove Street Oval and the dapper Panamanian played with Pompez' team for several years prior to making it in the majors with the Cincinnati Reds.

As the guests, dignitaries and media assembled, the fond remembrances were temporarily interrupted for the formal ceremonies. After the welcome, the audience stood to salute the flag and remained standing as the high school bands played the National Anthem. Among the crowd standing at attention were 16 Negro League veterans demonstrating their allegiance to the country that had too late accorded them full rights of citizenship.

Despite the slights and injustices that they encountered both on and off the playing field, there is a marked lack of bitterness on their part. "It was a sign of the times," explains Monte. "But you see the main difference was the whole thing was different then. Segregation was a known thing. And they just didn't believe in any kind of experiment. You know, it's easy to sit back and criticize but that's the way it was back then. I can't understand it but at that time they didn't want blacks to play in the big leagues."

Since that time a lot of water has passed under the bridge, and with this passage our country has matured socially and produced many changes during the interim which permitted Monte's transformation from a four-year-old boy skipping rocks across a pond in rural Alabama to the dignified elder statesman being honored on this occasion.

Following the invocation and introductory remarks, a proclamation was read stating that the Grove Street Oval would henceforth be known as Monte Irvin Field. In accepting the honor, Monte received a standing ovation. Amidst the appreciative applause, he stepped to the podium and addressed the audience.

"This is a very special day for me today," said the Hall of Famer, who had started his professional baseball career in 1937 playing weekends on the very same field.

He had joined the East Orange Triangles, a mixed team in a mixed league, as an oversized schoolboy in 1932, and the Newark Eagles of the Negro National League picked him up from the Triangles. At that time it was fashionable for talented high school athletes to pick up some extra money by playing baseball summers and weekends. In addition to playing in East Orange, Monte recalls, "We used to go up to Paterson East Side Park and there may be three or four thousand people sitting around watching a ball game. So we would stage the games. We might have two black teams or a black team and a white team and it was a big attraction.

"Baseball was king at that time. So in order to earn a few dollars, my buddy used to come by to pick me up around ten o'clock in the morning and by the time we got to Paterson it would be about 11:30 and by the time we got dressed and practiced and warmed up the game would start at one o'clock. We'd play the game and around the second or third inning they would pass the hat to pay for uniforms and expenses, and a few players would get paid. Not all of them did. If they did real well, then just about everybody would get a few dollars."

To preserve his amateur standing, Monte had "borrowed" the name of a friend and played under the alias of "Jimmy Nelson," a practice that he continued after joining the Newark Eagles following his high school graduation in 1938.

"I go off to college and the same situation exists," Monte relates. "So I played again under an assumed name. Jimmy Nelson was a catcher, a fine-looking fellow with a good physique and looked good in his uniform. I was Jimmy Nelson when we would go out west to play the Grays, or go to Kansas City or up in Rochester, Syracuse, or Buffalo. And when we came home all I would do would be to work out with the team before the game started and get dressed and sit in the stands or sometimes on the bench if the umpire would permit it."

Not many people know that Monte almost didn't graduate high school at all. During his senior year he contracted hemolytic streptococcus, an infection which resulted from scratches received in a basketball game. For seven weeks he was near death, and only necessary blood transfusions from caring donors saved his life. He recovered just in time to play with the Triangles that summer and earn a scholarship to Lincoln University.

Having almost lost his life, the youngster savored the joys of life all the more. Monte reflected on his personal memories, capturing the past significance of the park. "Some of the happiest moments of my life were spent right here on this field," Monte asserted while quickly adding, "I would like to just reminisce for a moment."

The man whose greatest thrill in baseball was stealing home at Yankee Stadium during the first inning of the first game of the 1951 World Series, stood looking out over the ball field of his youth, only a short distance but a long way in time and circumstances from Yankee Stadium. The path between the two had not been an easy one. Who would have ever dreamed that what had begun at The Grove Street Oval would one day lead to a World Series at Yankee Stadium and, eventually, to the Hall of Fame?

"My first visit to this park was way back in 1928. We used to come in here to see the truly great, great players. This is the first place that I ever saw the Pittsburgh Crawfords." That was a few years later, around 1932 or 1933. "The Crawfords that year had Satchel Paige, Josh Gibson, Judy Johnson, Oscar Charleston, Bill Perkins..."

One could almost visualize spectres from the past once again taking their positions on the field as Monte ticked off their names. In those days of the color line the players from the Negro Leagues served as idols and role models for the black youth.

"We came in here and watched baseball played the way it should be played. It inspired me later on to try to learn how to become a ballplayer, too. It motivated me and it certainly made me very happy and helped me achieve whatever success I have achieved."

The success that the modest Irvin has achieved includes a professional baseball career that spanned 18 years, a World War, and World Series triumphs in both the Negro Leagues and the Major Leagues. Although most of his prime years were spent in the relative obscurity of the Negro Leagues, he still played in the Major Leagues until just a few months short of his 38th birthday. In his eight major league seasons, he registered a .293 lifetime batting average.

"I remember after I became a player with the Newark Eagles and we were playing a key game down here against the East Orange B.B.C. The bases were loaded and we were ahead 3–2 and the last out was hit to our center fielder, Jimmie Crutchfield, and to show you what a great talent he was, he caught the last out behind his back.

"When he came off the field our owner, Mrs. Manley, said 'Jimmie, if you ever do that again it'll cost you $200.' He said 'Aw, I just wanted to give the fans a thrill. Besides, you've already advanced me next month's salary, go ahead and fine me.' That's how good he was."

Monte paused for a moment to take another deep breath of memories. "It was just so many thrills."

The East Orange B.B.C. was an aggregation of marginal major league talent on the way up or on the way down. The rivalry between Newark and East Orange back in the late thirties was big and sometimes attracted crowds as large as 5,000 to witness a game between the two teams.

Sometimes the East Orange contingent wanted to win so badly that they would engage in nefarious means. One time they put the baseballs in the refrigerator the night before the game. When the Eagles batted they used the frozen balls and when East Orange batted they used the regular balls. Other times they would enlist the aid of the umpires to give the Eagles a dose of "home cooking" with a key call at a crucial time in the game.

"I remember Willie Wells, who was our manager and our captain and our shortstop, who said, 'Guys you know when we go up to East Orange, sometimes when we get in a tight situation they'll squeeze us.' He said, 'I'm going to use some psychology today.' He goes up to the two umpires and he says to them, 'Fellows, are we going to have a good game today?' They said, 'Yes.' He said, 'Remember I don't want you to give us anything but at the same time I don't want you to take anything away from us.' He did that to — in a key situation — get a called strike when it was right down the middle. And fortunately that did happen and it worked out all right."

Wells, who is still living in Austin, Texas, is but one of Irvin's former teammates from the Negro Leagues whose baseball ability clearly warrants a place in the marbled halls of Cooperstown. "Wells had great hands and was a clutch hitter," says Monte. "He hurt his arm pitching and to compensate, he developed a knack for getting rid of the ball quick. Before the injury he had a very, very strong arm. Afterward, since his arm wasn't as strong, he consequently played in real shallow. But he was great going back on pop flies. And what he lacked in arm strength, he made up for in wisdom. He was very, very smart about playing hitters. Because very rarely would anyone hit a ball that he couldn't get to. When he had to go backhand the ball and get the ball to first base, he'd get you out.

"He was a clutch player. He always came up with the big play or he would come up with the big hit. He was just as good a fielder and a much better hitter than Pee Wee Reese. He was one of the best curveball hitters I ever saw, and a very smart hitter. He was our leadoff hitter but he had good power and was a good hitter in the clutch.

"Pee Wee is in the Hall of Fame and I think that there's a chance that Wells will get into the Hall of Fame too. I hope so because he deserves it. I just hope he hangs on a little longer. His name has been mentioned for several years."

Two other living players, Ray Dandridge and Leon Day, whose credentials merit inclusion in the Hall of Fame, were present for the ceremonies. Dandridge was the Brooks Robinson of the Negro Leagues while Day was their ace moundsman who delighted in hooking up with Satchel Paige in pitching duels.

"One day we were playing against Satchel Paige and Leon said, 'Get me a run.' But Satchel had us shut out," Monte says, recalling a game when the two great pitchers were locked in a scoreless battle. "And Leon hit a home run that won the game. That's the kind of player he was."

"If you could have seen this man when he was in his prime," Monte marvels, shaking his head. "Leon Day was probably the finest all-around player I've ever seen. He was a good pitcher, had the heart of a lion, and a real good fastball. He threw as hard as Bob Gibson. And he had a small but good curve, and had control of it. He could field his position. He was a good hitter. He could outrun me. He played second base and played a great outfield."

"When the going got tough you wanted Leon Day on your side." Monte alludes to Mets superstar Dwight Gooden in describing Day. "If Dwight Gooden continues to pitch the way he has, he may become the kind of pitcher that Leon Day was. We always said that if we had one game to win, we wanted Leon to pitch."

"I'm proud of having known Leon Day. And Danny..." again he shakes his head in awe. "Dandridge and Wells were two of the finest infielders I've ever seen," he states without reservation. "I'm talking about bar none. I've seen Red Rolfe. I've seen Brooks Robinson. I've seen Graig Nettles. I've seen all the great third basemen. But I've never seen anybody that could make the plays any better than Dandridge."

"And once you saw him you'd never forget him because he was short and bowlegged. But he was quick as a cat and he had an adequate arm. If the ball got to him real quick, he would always time it so that his throw would just beat you. When he had to hurry it was the same way, the throw would just beat you.

"He was the best I've ever seen on a swinging bunt. Because he was already short and he'd come in full speed, take that ball and toss it underhand and just get you. It was a thing of beauty just to see him come in and flip that ball underhand without even slowing down on it. It was the damnedest thing I've ever seen."

The Brooklyn Dodgers' Billy Cox was the premier defensive third baseman in the National League when Monte was with the New York Giants. "Cox was a super fielder with a good arm," Monte agrees. "But Dandridge was a better hitter and just as good or better fielder."

"You know, it's hard to describe his style of fielding. You had to see him play. People would have paid just to see him play third base. He was something! The way that he went after a ball ... the way that he would backhand a ball with that big glove of his and the way he would come up with a hard-hit ball and he'd take it and shake it before he'd throw it to first base.

"I saw him and I have so much respect for him. He was the darnedest third baseman I ever saw. He was very spectacular but not showy, understand. Certainly not a showman in the way he fielded, like Willie Mays with the basket catch. But something about the way he moved made him separate and apart from all the rest of the third basemen.

"They loved him in Mexico. They thought he was the best third baseman in the world. They still talk about him." Monte pauses to reflect momentarily on the bottom line concerning the man with the velvet hands. "Dandridge was one of the best ever," he summarizes, giving his unequivocal appraisal.

Like Willie Wells, Ray Dandridge has also been mentioned as an outstanding candidate for the Hall of Fame, missing election only by a very narrow margin. Baseball authorities who have seen him play agree that he should already be enshrined.

One of these is Dodgers manager Tommy Lasorda, who played with Ray in Cuba. "Ray was about 40 years old when Tommy Lasorda first saw him," Monte recalls. "He said he had never seen a better fielding third baseman than Ray Dandridge."

Although he was a magician at the hot corner, Ray could also perform magnificently at other infield positions. Monte remembers, "One year they put Dandridge at second and Wells at shortstop and you should have seen them. What a combination that was. Unbelievable! And you had to shoot a ball through the infield in order to get the ball through the middle.

"That's the first time that I ever saw where on a ball hit to the shortstop's left and he's going over and he takes the ball and gives it to the second baseman, who's right there, and the second baseman would throw the ball to first to get the man. No double play, just get the batter at first. When they worked that play, that was the first time I had ever seen it.

"There was so much great talent in those days. It's just too bad that some of those great fellows didn't get a chance to play in the major leagues."

Monte, only recently retired from his position in the Commissioner's office, continues to champion the cause of those players who were denied a rightful place in the major leagues. The task of generating long overdue recognition for these unrecognized baseball greats is difficult and ofttimes frustrating. "It's a crime that no one important on the white side saw them in action or recorded their feats," Monte emphasizes. "The test of a man's merit should be his ability."

At the dedication of the Negro League Hall of History at Ashland, Kentucky, in 1982 Monte had voiced the same feelings. Discussing players such as Roy Campanella, Ernie Banks, Willie Mays, Hank Aaron and himself, who started in the Negro Leagues and, once given the opportunity to play in organized ball, made it to the Hall of Fame, Monte said, "You can see where we are."

And lamenting the generations of black players who came before Jackie Robinson "kicked the door ajar," he added, "Most of them never got a chance. You ask yourself, 'What would they have done?'" The question is rhetorical. No one will ever know. We can only speculate by extrapolating the past from the present. Just as great black players exist today, they also existed then. They can be measured only in terms of what they accomplished on the baseball diamonds to which they were restricted.

Regardless of the obvious injustice of this exclusion, there is little residual resentment on behalf of the players. "The most amazing thing is a lack of bitterness" Monte points out. "You can't miss what you never had." However, Monte adds, "They do want some recognition."

Thus on a day that was designed to be his alone, he shared the spotlight with those players who were not fortunate enough to have been afforded an equal opportunity to play in the major leagues. Had it not been for them, there would have been no Jackie Robinson, and had there been no Jackie Robinson there would have been no Hank Aaron or Willie Mays and certainly not any black baseball players with multi-million-dollar contracts today.

Monte's first salary was a far cry from those contracts. When he joined the Newark Eagles in 1938 he made $125 a month plus one dollar per day meal money. "Looking at the contrast in salaries between today and my day, I wish my momma had better timing," he sometimes laughs. The other players who came along too early for either the big salaries or the major leagues know what he means.

"We really didn't make any money," he reminded those players present at the ceremonies, "but you stuck with it. Remember we used to say, although we were only making $200 a month, it was better than working. It was better than having a job because the average salary was $15–$20 a week for other jobs and if we made $50 we were still ahead of the game. And all this comes back to me now."

Monte inhaled another deep breath of memories, but the memories were too many to be expressed in such a short time. The meager pay was only one small part of the camaraderie shared by the players in the Negro Leagues. "I made more money when I was in the majors and the caliber of baseball was better and the playing conditions were better, but we had fun in the Negro Leagues." Monte emphasizes, "We *did* have fun!" *And* memories that couldn't be bought for money. The overflow from that flood of memories would be shared later at the reception at Upsala College.

Replenished, Monte again looked over the field of his youth and continued his address, expressing the obstacles that men who played there had to overcome, and challenging future generations to take advantage of the opportunities afforded them by the sacrifices made by those who had begun in places like the Grove Street Oval.

"A couple of years ago Satchel Paige had a park in Kansas City named after him. Last year Ray Dandridge had the West Side Park named after him. And the fact that I'm the man honored today makes me very happy tonight. To be so honored makes me very happy, and very grateful, and very appreciative.

"I hope that by naming this park after me, it will be an inspiration to some of the youngsters coming along today." Speaking of the hardships that he and the other veteran players had encountered, Monte addressed the young people present. "We didn't have an easy time. We knew it was tough but it made better men of ourselves. When things get tough that's okay. The tough get going in a situation like this. Stick to it," he advised. "Stay with it."

Don Newcombe, the only man to win the Rookie of the Year Award, the Cy Young Award, and the Most Valuable Player Award in his career, understands the reference. Newcombe was one of the first blacks signed after Jackie Robinson, and was a teammate of Jackie's during part of the time when he was subjected to the pressures of breaking baseball's color line. The big, right-handed fireballer knows the strength of character that is required to "stick with it."

When Branch Rickey was scouting the Negro Leagues for the right man to become the first black player in the Major Leagues in modern times, Monte Irvin was one of the leading candidates.

In discussing Robinson's ordeal, Newcombe acknowledges, "Irvin and Campanella are the only two others that could have done it." Monte doesn't think that there was a better candidate than Robinson but concurs with Newcombe's assessment of Campanella.

"The only other candidate was Roy. His father was Italian, he was popular, and he was a catcher so he's back there by himself where he's not as conspicuous. Jackie was out there in the middle of the field, he's black, and he stood out like a sore thumb. And he was so aggressive, so proud, and not going to back down. You know the problems he had. He said, 'To hell with it.' He just had that type of attitude. So he had the problems that he had. And Campy had the problems, but he had sort of an easy manner about him." This allowed Campy to cope with the problems successfully.

Monte believes that, had he been a little older, Willie Mays' name should be added to the list. However, his feelings about himself in that role are ambivalent. "I think that I could have been the first one," Monte assents. "In fact I had been selected by Mrs. Manley and the rest of the owners. I was supposed to be the guy. It was supposed to have been me." But timing is everything. And Monte still has reservations about whether, under the existing circumstances, he could have or would have taken all of the pressure and harassment that Robinson endured.

At the time of Branch Rickey's "great experiment," Monte had only recently returned from the service with buck sergeant's stripes on his sleeve, three years of "athletic rust," and a bad case of "war nerves." Under those circumstances, he does not feel that he was ready physically or psychologically for undertaking a task with such far-reaching ramifications.

At that time Monte was unaware of the owners' meeting where it was unanimously agreed that he should be the first, and it wasn't until almost 35 years later that former Newark Eagles owner Effa Manley told him about the meeting. "She told me in Ashland, Kentucky," Monte declares.

It was in 1979, at the first reunion for Negro League veterans, when Mrs. Manley confirmed that Monte had initially been the first choice for the pioneering role that Robinson played.

"Monte was the choice of all of the Negro National League and American League owners to serve as the number one player to join a white major league team. We all agreed in a meeting that he was best qualified by temperament, character, ability, sense of loyalty, morals, age, experience, and physique to represent us as the first black player in the white majors since the Walker brothers back in the 1880s.

"But Branch Rickey lifted Jackie Robinson out of Negro ball and made him the first. It turned out all right but we all felt Monte Irvin would do best representing us. Robinson later resented the 'treatment' he got in the Negro Leagues but Monte has had nothing but praise for what we tried to do for the players under most difficult circumstances for all of us."

Had it not been for World War II, Rickey may have selected Irvin instead of Robinson. But fate intervened. While Robinson was being discharged from the army as a result of his protests against segregation in the service, Monte was in Europe in the middle of a war.

While Robinson was playing his only season of black professional baseball with the war-time weakened Kansas City Monarchs, Monte was walking guard duty at a prisoner-of-war camp in Germany. And while Robinson signed a contract with the Dodgers organization and was playing at Montreal, Monte felt a need to work back into his pre-war playing condition before committing to Rickey's persuasion.

But again timing was everything. Had Branch Rickey contacted Monte before the war, or waited a sufficient time afterwards while he progressed in his efforts to regain his pre-war playing form, Monte would have been ready.

"In 1941 and 1942 I was playing my best baseball," Monte explains. "I had a good arm, I was doing great fielding, but more than anything else I could hit and I had an easy time." Monte led the Negro National League in batting in 1941 with an average of .394 and opened the 1942 season as an established superstar. Early that spring the Eagles had what Monte considers the most talented team in the history of the franchise.

But because the penurious Effa Manley would not give him a $25 a month increase so that he could get married, Monte signed with Mexican millionaire owner Jorge Pasquel. In Mexico Monte almost won the Triple Crown, recording league highs with a .397 batting average and smashing 30 HR in only 68 games, while narrowly missing the RBI title. "I went home sometime in October and Jorge would send me money every month and say, 'I want you to come back down.'

"So, in February I went to the draft board to get permission to come on down to spring training and they said, 'Well, if you don't pass the physical you can go.' I was married and had a job so I didn't have any idea that I was going to go into the Army. I took the exam and they passed me, and off to the Army I went.

"I had started out really turning around in 1941 and in '42 I was even more improved but then I had to go in the Army and that destroyed it. I was assigned to an all-black engineering outfit and served in England, France, and Germany. I went to France in 1943 and I didn't get a chance to play any ball in the service or anything else. I was always having to worry about everything else in the world. I was in France and Belgium during the Battle of the Bulge. But I never got a chance to play. I came out of service and I was never the same guy coming out as when I went in. I lost my timing and I was three years older."

After Germany surrendered in early May, Monte was one of the many soldiers who were returned stateside. He got back just in time to play in the last five games for the Newark Eagles. It was around this time that Rickey contacted him and, at that time, Monte didn't feel that he was in proper playing condition. "This was before I was ready," he states.

"Because I could have gone" Monte reiterates. "Rickey contacted me in 1945. I told him that I would talk to him later. At that time they said they were going to start another league. We learned later what they intended to do."

Had Rickey made clear his intentions or made his move a few years earlier or later, then baseball history may have been written differently. "In fact, I did sign with them," Monte says, recalling the circumstances extant at the time, "but I told them I wasn't ready for this year and when I got ready I'd let them know and I could play. So in order to kinda regain my old form, I played ball in the winter of 1945 in San Juan, Puerto Rico."

While Monte was working himself back towards the pre-war personal level of play to which he had become accustomed, Branch Rickey made the decision to go on with his plan. Jackie Robinson was his selection to be the player to re-integrate baseball. No black player had performed in the major leagues since 1884. Other owners, like the Washington Senators' Clark Griffith and the Pittsburgh Pirates' Benny Benswanger, had talked about it but nobody wanted to be the first owner to make the break with tradition. "No one said, 'Damn it, if you can play baseball you can play anywhere,'" explains Monte.

Like most Negro League veterans, Monte agrees that Jackie was not the best player as far as ability alone was concerned. "We didn't think that much of him. At the time we thought there were better players in our league. We knew once Jackie signed that was the end of the Negro leagues.

"The younger guys like Sam Jethroe, Don Newcombe, Dan Bankhead, and Larry Doby were happy because it meant they had a chance to play in the big leagues. But the older guys figured they wouldn't get the chance because of their age and soon they wouldn't have a league of their own any more."

That is just the way that it did happen. The major league owners established a policy of not signing the older players. The veterans reacted in a variety of ways. Josh Gibson's drinking became worse and he died in 1947 at the age of 35, a heartbroken, disappointed and embittered man. Buck Leonard turned down an offer to play with the Browns and finished his career in Mexico. Monte himself just barely qualified under the owners' cut-off age of 30 when he was finally signed.

While Jackie was pioneering a revolutionary concept at Montreal, Monte had returned to the Eagles, leading them to a pennant with a .401 batting average while leading the league in RBI. His sterling performance continued into post-season play where he hit .462 and slugged three homers to spearhead the Eagles' Negro World Series victory over the Kansas City Monarchs. The following season, although Monte continued to lead the league in home runs and RBI, his teammate on the Eagles, Larry Doby, was the one selected in July of that year to become the first black player in the American League.

The purchase package for Doby's contract totaled $10,500 and was the first time that the major leagues had acknowledged the legitimacy of Negro League contracts. As usual Mrs. Manley was her outspoken self, and while agreeing that Doby was a fine prospect, openly deplored the major league owners' oversight in not signing Monte. "The best all-around player that we have had for years is our superman, Monte Irvin," she declared to all who would listen. What she said was true and, while Monte never fully regained his pre-war playing level, he still demonstrated sufficient skills to indicate that he could be a major league star.

Disappointed in being overlooked, Monte played in the Cuban winter league to keep his renewed skills honed and returned to the Eagles the following season. By then some observers considered him to be a "war casualty" because he was still unsigned by the major leagues.

Branch Rickey, unlike Bill Veeck with Doby, refused to give the Eagles any monetary compensation for Monte's contract. The Mahatma considered the Negro Leagues to be "in the zone of a racket" and adamantly insisted on continuing his policy of not paying for the rights to black ballplayers.

"The Dodgers released me because Mrs. Manley wanted some money and Rickey said he wasn't going to give her any money," Monte says. "I found out later that he said why should he spend five or ten thousand dollars when he could get me for free. So Mrs. Manley says, 'Well, you took Don Newcombe and you're not going to take Monte because I'm not going to let you. Furthermore I'll fight you in court.' So he didn't want any kind of bad publicity or any unnecessary lawsuits and he released me. So the New York Giants picked my contract up. That's the best thing that ever happened to me."

Monte had returned to Cuba again for the 1948–1949 winter baseball season, and that's where the Giants signed him. He had to take a pay cut of $5,000 to make the jump. To compensate for his loss in salary he asked Mrs. Manley to give him a part of the $2,500 that the Giants had paid for his contract. Instead the hard-nosed business woman paid her lawyer and bought herself a fur stole.

Monte relates how a few years ago at the Negro League reunion in Ashland, Kentucky, she was still wearing the stole. Monte told her, "You made a good buy, Mrs. Manley." The still feisty former owner replied, "Not as good as the Giants did." And she was right!

The Giants sent Monte to Jersey City, their AAA farm club, in the spring of '49. He remained there until July when, with a .373 batting average, he was brought up to the parent club. The following year he returned to Jersey City for a brief interval during which he hit .510 with ten home runs and 33 RBI in only 18 games.

The level of play there was less than what he had faced in the Negro Leagues. But while the black players had the talent to play in the majors, Monte feels that they needed a little time in the minor leagues to get adjusted to playing with white players. "The gap was just too wide," Monte explains. "See, we had some good ballplayers but they played individual baseball. Learn the organized way of playing and then it would be easy. You know play down there and start to feel comfortable. After awhile it's a brand new game. There was a transition period and it was a good time to do it in the minor leagues. Jackie would never have made it if he hadn't had the year at Montreal. The best thing that could have happened to Willie Mays was to start in the minors."

He attributes the failure of Willard Brown and Hank Thompson initially with the St. Louis Browns in 1947 to this lack of acclimation. "They didn't know what to expect," he says. "They had always been told the major leagues were so tough. They were bound to wonder, 'Can I make it?' The first thing that they had to teach them was discipline. Show up every day on time. Play team ball rather than individual baseball. Take them to spring training and keep them in the minor leagues. Pay them and now bring them up. Bring them up slowly. Then they would have been all right. But they didn't do that, and both of them got disgusted and wanted to leave." Thompson later got another chance, in 1949 with Monte on the Giants, and proved to be a good major league ballplayer. "Once you see what its like," Monte explains, "it's a piece of cake."

By that time Jackie Robinson had already run interference for other black players coming into the major leagues, and the initial resentment had been debilitated somewhat. Many barriers had been broken down and the pressures, while still present, were not as great. Monte credits Whitey Lockman and Bobby Thomson for helping in his adjustment to the major leagues.

Later on Monte helped a young Willie Mays "all I could" in making the adjustment when he joined the Giants. "He needed instruction off the field in little things," says Monte, adding, "Durocher handled Mays just right." Monte credits Leo with being a great manager while leaving something to be desired as a person.

Ray Dandridge had helped Willie during his brief intermission at Minneapolis prior to joining the Giants. Monte believes that one of the reasons that Ray himself wasn't brought up a year earlier was due to an unofficial quota system that the major league owners followed. Another reason was because "Ray Dandridge was bringing people out to the ballpark." Another excuse used by the Giants organization is discounted by Monte. "They said that he was too old, but all we knew was if we could have brought him up in 1950 we could have won the pennant that year. Durocher would have played anybody."

Chub Feeney, currently the National League President but then an official in the Giants organization, claimed that the Giants' position was that "We were merely looking for the best possible talent." While this was true for Irvin and Mays, it was not true in Ray's case.

"Those fellows in the minor leagues who saw him at Minneapolis say it's a crime that he never got to play in the major leagues," Monte continues. "They said that even though he's 40 years old, they ought to give the man a chance. But he never did get a chance. He told me one day, 'All I want to do is play — just get dressed and go out on a major league field and play one game. And I would be the happiest man in the world.'" But Dandridge languished at Minneapolis where he won MVP honors, and the Giants had to wait until 1951 to win a pennant.

The Giants could not have won that flag without Monte's contributions which consisted of a .312 average, 24 HRs, and a league-leading 121 RBI. His outstanding play on the diamond also helped the Giants to another pennant in 1954. But his baseball exploits were not as great as his contributions in helping to break down the color barrier outside of baseball as well.

"You don't have these barriers now," he told the young people at the ceremonies. "All you have to do now is learn your trade well. There is equal opportunity and if you work hard and do the things that you're supposed to do, you can certainly succeed."

One person who played in the Oval as a youngster and to whom the players served as an inspiration was John C. Hatcher, now the Mayor of East Orange, who read the City Council's proclamation re-designating the park as Monte Irvin Field. When Monte was a youngster some business establishments in East Orange did not welcome Negroes. Now the mayor of the city is black. In the 1960s folk songwriter Bob Dylan had penned the lines, "The times they are a-changin'." The times have changed, thanks to a helping hand from the game of baseball and men like Monte Irvin.

"Again my eternal thanks to all of you. I'm very, very appreciative and very happy today," Monte said in conclusion. "Thank you so much."

During the ceremonies, the Society for American Baseball Research (SABR) presented a plaque which will be placed on one of the columns at the

Eaton Place entrance to preserve the field's identity with the Negro Leagues. The presentation was a culmination of the efforts of SABR ballparks authority Phil Lowry, who first envisioned permanent markers for historic baseball sites.

When the on-field ceremonies, pictures, and interviews were finally ended, Monte was the last one to leave the field, pausing for one last look — one last memory from the days of his youth.

As he left the park he observed, "It's sad in a way to see how the neighborhood has gone down. It used to be a nice neighborhood." When Monte left the field he left behind a slice of Americana, too easily forgotten by too many people. Appropriately, SABR's plaque at the entrance to the site will serve as a reminder of a way of life from "days that used to be."

This article was written in 1986 after attending the ballpark dedication described, but it was considered too long for inclusion in publications of the Society for American Baseball Research (SABR). A copy of the manuscript has been housed in the SABR Research Library since that time.

Monte Irvin now lives in Houston, Texas, where he moved after many years of retirement in the Sunshine State. Many of the players with whom he shared his day have passed away in the intervening 25 years. Ray Dandridge, Leon Day, Judy Johnson, Jimmie Crutchfield, Pat Scantlebury, and Charlie Biot—just to name a few—have all passed on.

On the positive side, six former Newark Eagles (Ray Dandridge, Leon Day, Willie Wells, Larry Doby, Biz Mackey, Effa Manley) have been inducted into the Hall of Fame in the interim.

As a final note, in addition to the two New Jersey sites mentioned, there are two other ballpark locations with Negro League connections that merit mention. Rickwood Field in Birmingham, Alabama, built in 1910, is the oldest surviving professional ballpark in the country and, although not a black ballpark, served as the home field for the Birmingham Black Barons for many years when the white Barons were on the road. Among the Black Barons to play there was a young center fielder named Willie Mays.

Also, during the early 1930s, Hamtramck Stadium served as the home field for the Negro National League's Detroit Stars and the Detroit Wolves of the East-West League. In the stadium's inaugural game, Ty Cobb threw out the ceremonial first pitch. The ballpark's grandstand is still standing, and efforts are under way to preserve the field once tread upon by the spiked shoes of superstars Satchel Paige, Josh Gibson, Turkey Stearnes and numerous other black members of baseball's Hall of Fame.

Buck O'Neil: A Remembrance

When John Jordan "Buck" O'Neil, Jr. died October 6, 2006, at the age of 94, baseball lost its greatest ambassador, the Negro Leagues lost their greatest spokesman, and I lost a friend.

My sense of loss is shared by countless others across the country, for Buck was beloved by all who met him. More than 10,000 people of all ages and backgrounds gathered to pay their respects as he lay in state at the Negro Leagues Baseball Museum in Kansas City. Buck had been an all-star first baseman with the Kansas City Monarchs in the old Negro Leagues, but the multitudes were not there to simply pay homage to a ballplayer, they were there to honor the *man* who had touched their lives.

America discovered Buck O'Neil in 1994 when his dignified grace and charisma beguiled the camera and thrust him into a focal role in Ken Burns' highly acclaimed documentary on baseball in America. Buck was a natural story teller and, as he shared stories about life in the Negro Leagues, his genuine warmth, wit and sincerity came through to the viewers. This, more than anything else, elevated him into the spotlight as an American icon. Buck later joked about how he became an overnight star at the age of 82.

I had discovered Buck and his vast reservoir of baseball lore many years earlier through my research on the Negro Leagues. His career in the Negro American League spanned 19 seasons, during which he won two batting titles, played on five championship teams, appeared in three All-Star Games and managed a championship team. Two prime years were lost to military service in the U. S. Navy during World War II but Buck was always proud to be an American and never regretted serving his country.

After the elimination of baseball's color line, Buck became a pioneer in the integration of the major leagues. He was the first black scout with the Chicago Cubs and later also scouted for the Kansas City Royals. While with the Cubs, he became the first black coach in major league baseball.

When a reporter suggested to him that he had been born too soon, Buck responded, "Waste no tears for me. I didn't come along too early. I was right on time." Buck never wavered from this position. He had no regrets about his time in baseball and felt that he had played with and against some of the greatest players of all time. He understood fully that had it not been for men like himself, there would have been no proving ground for Jackie Robinson to develop the necessary baseball skills to eradicate the color line when the opportunity came.

The grandson of slaves, Buck was born November 13, 1911, in Carabelle, Florida, and he never forgot his roots. This is underscored by a poignant story that Buck related about a trip that he and Satchel Paige took to South Carolina's Drum Island, where Africans were once brought to America and sold into slavery. The two friends stood silently for several minutes, each alone with his own thoughts. Finally Satchel spoke, "Seems like I've been here before," and Buck answered, "Me, too." In telling the story Buck explained, "Because my great-grandfather might have been there. My great-grandmother might have been there."

Buck also remembered his roots in the Negro Leagues. As a member of the Veterans Committee, he championed the stars from that era for the Hall of Fame. This year he made what was to be his final appearance in Cooperstown when, after being passed over himself by a special committee, he graciously spoke on behalf of the 17 who were elected.

Buck was instrumental in founding the Negro Leagues Baseball Museum

Buck O'Neil is pictured in his role as manager, observing the field of play from his trademark position on the dugout steps. This photograph served as a model for his bronze statue at the Negro Leagues Baseball Museum in Kansas City.

and served as Chairman of the Board for 16 years. Recently, the museum has undertaken a $15 million project to create The Buck O'Neil Education and Research Center, which will be his enduring legacy.

When I think back over the quarter century that I knew Buck, I remember the twinkle in his eye, his infectious smile, and his impeccable integrity. Throughout his life Buck exuded love. He loved baseball, he loved jazz music, he loved people and he loved life. Buck had only one rule for living that he espoused: "Love what you do in life. It's as simple as that. Take pride in it, take joy in it, and you'll live longer." He lived by his own axiom and never stopped loving baseball.

Even more than baseball, he loved the special lady that he has rejoined in heaven. In his autobiography, *I Was Right on Time*, the dedication reads: "To my beloved wife of 50 years, Ora Lee Owen O'Neil."

Above all else, Buck loved the Lord and to the very end believed that he had been blessed in life.

So were those of us who had the privilege of knowing him.

This article was written shortly after Buck O'Neil passed into eternity on October 6, 2006. It was first published in the November-December 2006 issue of The Crisis.

Remembering Ray: The Hot Corner Hall of Famer Will Not Be Forgotten

"Why did you take so long?"

I remember Ray Dandridge directing this question to the Veterans Committee at his induction into the Hall of Fame in the summer of 1987. And I remember him saying poignantly in the same speech, "I have loved the game of baseball. And today, it looks like maybe baseball loves me, too." Years before, Ray had told me that if he were ever elected to the Hall of Fame, "It would be a beautiful thing!" I can't forget him telling me that tears ran down his cheeks when Hall of Fame president Ed Stack telephoned to inform him that his long wait was over.

These memory "bites" provide a rare glimpse of the softer side of the man I knew as Ray Dandridge. Ray was unpretentious. With him, "What you saw was what you got." He generally eschewed diplomacy for directness and was a practitioner of "telling it like it is" long before Howard Cosell helped the phrase to become fashionable.

In the 13 years that I knew Ray we became friends. Coming from different generations and disparate backgrounds, to some we may have appeared to be baseball's "odd couple." In the beginning our common ground was a love of baseball, but as the miles and time that we shared together increased, our friendship outgrew that tenuous constraint.

I first knew him when he was one of the forgotten "sundown stars" from the shadowy world of the Negro Leagues, and I observed that his "hat size" was not changed by the belated honors bestowed upon him at Cooperstown. In retrospect, my remembrance of Ray is in vignettes from those years that passed all too quickly.

I remember Ray reminding me, "I guess you know you're in the ghetto," when I first met him in the summer of 1981 at his home on Littleton Avenue in Newark's central ward. I can see him now, "popping the top" of a beer and telling me the first of his many stories from the 22 years he spent playing baseball, summer and winter. I remember him nodding off to sleep later that same day, while I pored over a boxful of clippings spread out over the pool table in his basement. And I remember him sitting on the stoop of his house as darkness approached, watching to make sure I made the right turn when I left the "hood."

I'll always have the image of him at the Negro League reunions in Ashland, Kentucky, wearing his Stetson and looking like he had just stepped out of a Marlboro commercial. And who can forget the little toreador dance that he did when he was celebrating.

Ray was never impressed with the rich and famous. I remember how he would turn down invitations to the White House or to prestigious black tie dinners hosted by Hollywood celebrities, yet look forward to "rappin' with the guys" at the Cozy Corner in his old neighborhood. I remember him always having time for children, and the way he made them feel special. I especially remember a young girl at a card show in Orlando, Florida, who told him, "You know why I like you? Because you're good to little people."

A happy Ray Dandridge answers questions in front of the camera at the announcement ceremonies when he was elected to the Hall of Fame in 1987.

The characteristic that she recognized was also evident when Ray threw out the ceremonial first pitch at a "Little Lassie" softball game in his adopted hometown of Palm Bay, Florida. To Ray, it made no difference whether it was an inconsequential girl's softball game at an obscure local field or a World Series game at the Hubert H. Humphrey Metrodome in Minneapolis, he took the mound and performed his duties with the same aplomb. And I remember how the Dodgers "rolled out the red carpet" at Dodgertown when Ray threw out the first pitch for a spring game in Vero Beach.

Through the years, we made several treks to the Dodgers' training camp and everyone, from the brass to the fans, adored him. Ray could never remember anyone else's name, but everyone always remembered him. Tommy Lasorda was one of that legion, and I remember how the Dodgers' skipper's face lit up when seeing Ray for the first time since they played against each other in Cuba almost 35 years earlier.

It was the same way with Roy Campanella when the two met unexpectedly at Dodgertown for the first time in almost 40 years. Campy recognized Ray instantly and greeted him with his nickname from the Negro Leagues, "Hello, Squatty." And I won't forget Hoyt Wilhelm, who played with Ray at Minneapolis in 1950, wanting to be recognized and giving Ray a "hint" by doubling up his knuckles like he was going to deliver his famous "butterfly" pitch.

I remember Willie Mays, another teammate at Minneapolis, coming to Cooperstown for the first time since his own induction to be with Ray when he went into the Hall of Fame. Willie showed the same respect during Ray's last few days, by calling the hospital to speak to him after learning of his condition.

Another of the almost endless cadre who remembered Ray's hot corner heroics was Frank Robinson. As a teenager, he had watched Ray play with Oakland in the Pacific Coast League. When he informed Ray of this, Robinson also disclaimed any possibility that he would ever manage again. A few days later, when Frank Robinson was named manager of the Orioles, Ray phoned me to confirm what Robinson had told him about never managing again.

Similar phone calls were commonplace, and I know I'll miss our telephone "rap sessions" and the many times when I came home and found his standard message on my answering machine: "Hey, Riley! This is Ray Dandridge calling. Give me a call when you come in."

And I'll miss the days when we would sit around his kitchen table "cussing and discussing" anything and everything. I remember Ray laughing about how his father had been bribed for $50 to let him leave home to play professional baseball in Detroit, and Ray asked him, "Where is Detroit?" A few years later a similar scenario presented itself, but with a little different twist, when Ray was given a generous advance to go to Venezuela. He took the cash home, spread it out on the bed and told his wife, "I don't know where Venezuela is, but that's where I'm going."

Among his stories of life after baseball, Ray used to tell about tending bar in Newark and listening to customers argue about who was the greatest third baseman, without realizing that the answer to that question was standing across the bar from them.

I remember Ray telling about the "punks" who had burglarized his home in Newark and stolen most of his trophies and keepsakes from baseball. And I remember what he said he would do to them if he ever found out who they were.

These stories came from conversations that we shared all across the country in our travels, by plane and by car. I remember how at ease Ray was on the big jets but yet couldn't wait to get off the commuter planes, and couldn't understand why I thought it would be fun to pilot one.

And I remember, during one of our automobile trips, stopping in his hometown of Richmond in the wee hours of the morning and going by the street where he lived as a child and the field where he played sandlot baseball. And I listened as Ray talked about those early years, when a trip to the bathroom required leaving the house. And when he was a scufflin' sandlotter playing against Buck Leonard and Dave Barnhill, with none of them ever dreaming what lay ahead. And I also remember Ray talking about the childhood years that were spent in Buffalo, when the times were hard and the winters were cold, and he would walk along the railroad tracks picking up lumps of coal from the cinders, where they had fallen from the train.

On our long trips together, we listened to the radio and when we were between stations, I would pop in a tape. And I remember Ray, who liked the big band sound, listening to my country music tapes while we were traveling together, tapping his fingers in time with the beat and nodding his head when he heard some lyrics that he could relate to his own experiences.

And on his 80th birthday, I introduced him to another kind of music when I gave him a tape of the rap album that included a song that I had written about him and other players from the Negro Leagues. And I remember how he smiled when he listened to the words, "Black baseball, they paved the way ... with players like Dandy, the Devil and Day..."

Ray liked good music, and he also liked games of chance. I remember his penchant for pinochle, dog tracks and jai-alai. On the one occasion that I accompanied him to the fronton, he won the first two matches but never again for the rest of the day. And I remember the pinochle games, when Ray, Leon Day, Monte Irvin and his other friends would banter back and forth good-naturedly.

After being ignored to the point of invisibility, Ray genuinely appreciated being "rediscovered" and enjoyed the attention and autograph sessions during his last years. And I remember in business ventures, how he didn't like to owe anybody anything or to be beholden to anyone for any reason.

I can still picture Ray playing catch in his front yard with his German Shepherd "Pepper" by tossing a pine cone and having her leap up and catch it like a Frisbee. And I remember that Ray's last "roommate" at the hospital was an avid baseball fan and as the two lay in bed, each suffering with cancer, their common wish was "just to be able to play catch in the sun one more time."

I remember his special sense of humor, and how he liked to be jolly and to keep people laughing. And he maintained his ability to do that, even in his last days at the hospital where the nurses all talked about how "witty" he was. I remember when his days were growing short, how he smiled when I related one of his favorite stories about him barreling towards home plate and yelling to Campy, who was taking the throw, "I got you now!" And I remember another weaker smile, the last time he recognized me before he passed away.

During our years together, Ray often talked about his wife, children and grandchildren, adding affectionately, "And I'm the Godfather." I have a mental picture of a church full of family and friends at the funeral, and I know that Ray Dandridge will live as long as any of them has a memory.

Throughout his baseball career, Ray always liked to wheel and deal, often wrangling about contract terms with team owners. He always thought everything was negotiable, even in his post-baseball years. I can just see Ray now, negotiating with St. Peter about the terms under which he will enter the Pearly Gates. And when he is finished, he'll have the fluffiest cloud, the biggest harp and the shiniest halo.

There's no doubt in my mind that I'll see him again some day. And when I get up there, he'll probably turn around, look at me with a twinkle in his eye and say...

"Why did you take so long?"

During my 35 years of researching the Negro Leagues, I made many friends, but I was probably closer to Ray than to any other player, especially after he moved to Florida, only a short 30-minute drive down I-95 from my home.

Ray passed away February 12, 1994, in Palm Beach, Florida at the age of 80. This was written very shortly afterwards.

Buck Leonard: A Tribute

I first met Buck Leonard in the summer of 1981 at his home in Rocky Mount, North Carolina. Through the years we spent countless hours together and forged a friendship that lasted until November 27, 1997, when he passed away at the age of 90 after a full and exemplary life. I was asked to speak at his memorial service, and this is the eulogy that I delivered at that time.

Eulogy Delivered at Buck's Funeral Services
St. James Baptist Church
Rocky Mount, North Carolina
December 2, 1997

In *Ecclesiastes 3:1*, it is written: "To everything there is a season, and a time to every purpose under the heaven."

The writer of *Ecclesiastes* identified several things that had their own season and a special time. Some of those are especially meaningful to us today.

"There is a time to mourn" — as we are all mourning now, each in our own way.

"There is a time to speak" — as I am speaking now and as others will speak, both formally and informally, talking about the kindness and goodness that epitomized the life of Buck Leonard. Whether it was helping a young baseball player and providing guidance and counseling; or encouraging a youngster to learn the importance of an education; or helping provide a small child with sufficient clothes for the winter; or sharing his memories with a writer to help preserve a segment of baseball history that he was a part of for so many years.

Ecclesiastes says: "A good name is better than precious ointment." Buck Leonard had a good name all the days that he walked the earth.

"There is a time to love" — and Buck Leonard was loved, by his family and by his friends. And in his time Buck Leonard also loved. He loved baseball. He loved fishing and his hunting dogs. He loved trains and crossword puzzles. He loved quartet singing. And he loved his church.

On a different level he loved people — and he looked for the good in them. He loved his family, without exception. He loved his mother and father. He loved his brothers and sisters. And he loved his nieces, nephews and his step-children — and all the other members of his extended family. And most especially he loved Sarah, and he loved Jean.

Buck Leonard's den in his home at Rocky Mount, North Carolina, was a virtual museum of Negro Leagues baseball history.

And on another level, he loved the Lord.

"There is a time to lose"—as we have all lost a friend, a loved one. And the world has also lost. For the world, it was a loss of greatness. Not because Buck was a great baseball player—although we all know he was that—but rather because of the greatness of his spirit.

"There is a time to keep"—as we will keep the special memories that Buck Leonard created for each of us. And as long as we keep these memories in our hearts and in our minds, he will always be a part of us.

Over the 23 years that I knew Buck, we spent a lot of time together, especially in the years before his stroke. During that time, we talked a lot about baseball. But there were other times when there was no tape recorder and no pencil taking notes, when we talked about other things.

He shared some of his thoughts—about his aspirations and his disappointments, and about life itself. Many of our conversations were personal and shall remain private. But there is one memory that I have that I would like to share with you today.

One summer on the way back from Cooperstown, he stopped to visit his sister in Washington, D.C., and I also made a stop on the way down. But we had arranged to meet at his house at a specified time and we arrived almost simultaneously. As we went into his house, he stood in the doorway to his den, looked at all the trophies, photographs and memorabilia from his baseball career, and said, "I don't know what's going to happen to all of it after I'm gone. I told everybody that I didn't care what they did with all this stuff. I'm not going to worry about it—I'm going to Heaven."

That statement stayed with me over the years and when we worked together on his autobiography, that's the way we closed the book.

Ecclesiastes says, "There is a time to be born and a time to die."

Ecclesiastes also says that the day of death is better than the day of one's birth. In his passing, Buck has merely gone from a place to a place—from a place called life to a place called Heaven.

And I know that I'll see him there someday.

In order to attend Buck Leonard's funeral and memorial services, I drove from my home on Florida's Space Coast to Orlando, Florida, where I boarded a train and rode all night to arrive at the railroad station in Rocky Mount, where Buck had worked prior to beginning his professional baseball career. I then took a taxi to his home at 605 Atlantic Avenue. From there I rode to the St. James Baptist Church with Wilmer Fields, one of Buck's former teammates with the Homestead Grays.

At the church I followed Don Marr (president of the Baseball Hall of Fame at Cooperstown, New York) and Buck O'Neil (Chairman of the Board at the Negro Leagues Baseball Museum at Kansas City, Missouri) in eulogizing Buck.

Afterward, I rode with Don Marr to the cemetery for the graveside services and then back to St. James' fellowship hall, where the ladies from the church had provided a meal for everyone.

From there, it was back to the train station for the return trip to Orlando, where my wife was waiting for our drive back home.

Index

Aaron, Hank 12, 133, 138, 181, 225, 227, 234, 248
Aaron, Herb 232–34
Abraham Lincoln Room 235
Acipco Cast Iron and Pipe Company 194
Acme Giants 159
Adair, Benjamin 73
Adams, Bert 51–2
Aguascalientes, Mexico 186–87, 230
Alabama Sports Hall of Fame 199
Alabama State College 192
Alameda, California 227
Albany, New York 178
Alexander, Grover Cleveland 7, 49–50
Alexandria, Virginia 157
All-American Girls Professional Baseball League 225, 227
All-Star Dream Team 157
All-Star Game Yearbook 26, 99, 128
All-Time All-American team 100
The All-Time All-Stars of Black Baseball 56
Allen, Newt 59, 80, 84–5, 172
Allen, Touissant 78
American Association 14, 20–22, 125
American League 25–6, 34, 50, 70, 97, 117, 165–66, 215, 231, 253
American Legion baseball 225
American Negro League 14, 45, 65, 96, 107, 109
Americana 256
Ammon Field 128
Amoros, Sandy 4
Anson, Cap 22
Archer, Jimmy 30, 32
Army Quartermaster's Depot 45
Ashland, Kentucky 248, 250, 253, 261
Atlanta, Georgia 195, 203, 206, 209–11, 218
Atlanta Black Crackers 3, 209, 21
Atlanta Sports Hall of Fame 211
Atlantic Avenue 267
Atlantic City, New Jersey 46–7, 62–3
Atlantic City Bacharach Giants 45–6, 60, 62–65, 71, 74–5, 82–3, 86
Atlantic City Little League Commissioner 46
Austin, Texas 152, 245

Bacharach, Harry 63
Bacharach Giants *see* Atlantic City Bacharach Giants
Bacharachs *see* Atlantic City Bacharach Giants

Baird, Tom 226
Ball, George 28
Ball, Walter 32
Baltimore, Maryland 21, 25, 26, 77, 80–1, 94, 96–9, 103–04, 107, 156, 165, 167–68, 183–85, 231, 242
The Baltimore Afro-American 93, 135
Baltimore Black Sox 40, 62, 64–6, 68–9, 76, 95, 97, 99, 105, 107–09, 157
Baltimore Elite Giants 3, 9, 111–12, 114, 130, 157, 165–66, 168, 183, 185, 210
Baltimore Orioles 25, 94
Bancroft, Dave 52
Banks, Ernie 248
Barkley, Sam 22
Barnhill, Dave 3, 9, 116, 129, 135, 170–74, 263
Barnstorming to Heaven 205, 227
Barrett, Pearl 224
The Baseball Encyclopedia 43, 139
Battey, Earl 113–15
Battle of the Bulge 252
Beckwith, John 66, 68, 95–6, 107
Belanger, Mark 147
Belgium 210, 252
Bell, Cool Papa 12, 15–6, 25, 60, 68, 87, 89–93, 121–22, 125–28, 131, 172, 238
Bell, William 208
Bender, Chief 39, 42, 50, 55
Benson, Gene 3, 9, 173, 179–82, 190
Benswanger, William 172, 252
Berardino, Johnny 190
Bertha, Minnesota 73
Bill Wright's Dugout 186
The Biographical Encyclopedia of the Negro Baseball Leagues 4, 110
Biot, Charlie 242, 256
Birmingham, Alabama 121–22, 192, 194–96, 198–200, 217–18, 220, 230, 256
Birmingham All-Stars 195
Birmingham Black Barons 3, 9, 11, 121–22, 127, 192–94, 217, 238, 256
Bismarck, North Dakota 126
Black, Joe 4, 98, 216
Black History Month 4, 235
Black Pelicans 225
Black Sox Park 94
Blackman, Henry 95
Blackwell, Ewell 153, 186
Blount, Tenny 58

269

Index

Bob Feller's All-Stars 181, 190
Bolden, Ed 63, 65–6, 76, 114
Bolden, Jim 220
Bonds, Barry 11, 17, 136, 227, 234
Booker, Pete 31–2, 34, 36
Boston Braves 176, 233
Boston Red Sox 51, 118, 198
Bradley, Bill 237
Bragana, Ramon 186
Bragg, Jesse 52
Brett, George 56
Brevard Hotel 198
Brewer, Chet 66–7, 122
Bridgeforth, William 99
Britt, George (Chippy) 90–2, 108
Brock, Lou 12
Brooklyn Dodgers 98, 111, 130, 140, 161, 177, 198, 210, 216–17, 247
Brooklyn Royal Giants 45, 61–2, 64, 72
Brown, Butts 155
Brown, Dave 59, 62, 71–5, 116
Brown, Jim 85
Brown, Larry 89–92
Brown, Mordecai (Three Finger) 28, 31
Brown, Ray 17, 127–28, 176–77
Brown, Willard 16–7, 153, 160, 163, 172, 198, 254
Brown University 24
Buck Leonard: The Black Lou Gehrig 110, 132, 216
The Buck O'Neil Education and Research Center 259
Buffalo, New York 40, 176, 223, 244, 263
Bugle Coat and Apron Supply Company 94
Bugle Field 77, 80–1, 94, 97
Burk, Bill 129, 131–32
Burnett, Tex 148
Burns, Ken 9, 257
Bush, George H. W. 4, 156, 235–38
Bush, Joe 55
Bush Mountain 206
Bushwicks 105
Butler, Pennsylvania 105
Butts, Pee Wee 98, 173
Byrd, Bill 3, 9, 97–8, 111, 165–69, 184
Byrd, Hazel 168

Cabrera, Adolfo (Tribilin) 228–29
Cadiz, Ohio 23
California 169, 186–87, 195, 223, 227
California Winter League 186
Cambria, Joe 97
Camden Yards 156
Campanella, Roy 4, 9, 14, 94, 98, 111–15, 130, 157, 165–69, 184–87, 210–11, 215, 248, 250, 262
Canada 21, 214, 236–37
Canadian Provincial League 151
Carabelle, Florida 258
Caracas, Venezuela 157, 191, 212, 214
Caribbean 148, 190

Carr, George (Tank) 63
Carter, Joe 12
Catholic Protectory Oval 73
Catskill Mountains 175
Centennial of Baseball 235
Cepeda, Orlando 56
Chalmers, Dut 51–2
Champions of the South 94, 107
Chance, Frank 32
Chandler, Spud 190
Chapman, Sam 190
Charleston, Oscar 95, 108, 122–23, 125–26, 128, 145, 155, 178, 226, 244
Chase, Hal 48
Chattanooga, Tennessee 195
Chesterfield Hotel 221
Chicago, Illinois 22, 25–6, 28, 34–6, 45, 60, 78, 81–2, 85, 91, 93, 103, 124, 163, 201, 203, 225, 237
Chicago American Giants 14–5, 36, 39, 45, 53, 58–9, 61–2, 64, 69, 71, 74, 76, 82–3, 85, 87, 92, 98, 114, 118, 151, 172, 219
Chicago Cubs 28–9, 31–2, 35–6, 127, 163, 257
The Chicago Defender 30, 57–8, 80, 84, 87, 93
Chicago Giants 58
Chicago League 35
Chicago Leland Giants 38, 44
The Chicago Tribune 29
Chicago Unions 35
Chicago White Sox 34, 36, 38, 41, 114, 191
Chicago White Stockings 22
Cienfuegos, Cuba 151
Cincinnati, Ohio 27
Cincinnati Reds 242
Citizens Republican Club 65
City Island Park 217
Civil War 21
Cleveland, Ohio 19, 23, 68, 98, 184, 220
Cleveland Buckeyes 9, 173, 217, 219, 222
The Cleveland Call & Post 219–20
Cleveland Negro Leagues Museum 229
Cleveland Stars 68
Cobb, Lorenzo S. 58
Cobb, Ty 12, 14, 34, 37–8, 41–3, 151, 256
Cockrell, Phil 64, 77, 104
Cocoa, Florida 198
Cole, Robert A. 69, 92
Cole's American Giants 69
Colonial Warehouse 211
Columbia, Alabama 239
Columbia Giants 26
Columbus, Ohio 97
Columbus Blue Birds 165
Columbus Buckeyes 45
Colzie, Jim 220–21
Comiskey, Charles 25–6, 33
Comiskey Park 15–6, 87, 91, 93, 112, 130, 172, 201, 203
Congress Avenue 152

Connor, Theophilus Eugene (Bull) 217, 222
Connors, John 61–2
Coombs, Jack 39
Cooper, Andy 17
Cooper, James Fenimore 111, 165
Cooperstown, New York 4–5, 9, 12, 13, 17, 38, 43, 56, 109, 111, 115, 132, 157–58, 164–65, 168, 208, 210, 245, 258, 260, 262, 267–68
Cosell, Howard 260
Cox, Billy 247
Cozy Corner 261
Cravath, Gavy 49, 51
Crawford, Sam 41–2
Crawfords *see* Pittsburgh Crawfords
Creve Coeur, Missouri 230
The Crisis 259
Crutchfield, Jimmie 3, 4, 9, 120–21, 123–24, 126, 146, 148, 172, 235–36
Cuba 36, 39–41, 72–3, 96, 139, 150–51, 168, 173, 190, 247, 253, 262
Cuban Giants 14
Cuban Stars 61–2, 64–5
Cuban Winter League 36, 102, 157, 253
Cuban X-Giants 38, 44
Currie, Rube 64, 79, 82
Cy Young Award 118, 249

Dallas, Texas 71
Dallas Black Giants 71
Dandridge, Ray 3, 8, 12, 102, 108–09, 131, 134, 142–49, 168, 173, 184–88, 208, 211, 242, 246–47, 249, 254–56, 260–62, 264
Dandy, Day and the Devil 110, 144, 149, 151
Davids, Bob 174
Davis, Harry 42
Davis, Johnny 3, 9, 148, 162, 172, 188–89, 191
Davis, Piper 3, 9, 192–93, 195, 197–200, 229–30
Davis, Roosevelt 165
Davis, Steel Arm 87, 89–92
Day, Leon 94, 97–9, 103–04, 106, 110, 129, 135, 146, 148, 153–58, 161–63, 167, 169–70, 188, 208, 211, 235–36, 246, 256, 263
Dayton Marcos 58
Daytona Beach, Florida 217
Dean, Dizzy 118, 186
DeMoss, Bingo 59
Detroit Stars 40, 58, 61, 63, 102, 256
Detroit Tigers 34, 38–43, 118
Detroit Wolves 68–9, 256
Devlin, Art 53–4
Dexter Park 61
The Diamond 23, 141, 157, 199, 227
Dickey, Bill 133
Dickey, Steel Arm 74–5
Dihigo, Martin 12, 16, 66, 88, 107, 186
Dismukes, Dizzy 68
Dixon, Rap 66, 87, 89–92, 96–7, 99
Doby, Larry 115, 161–62, 165, 188–89, 202, 215, 252–53, 256

Dodgertown 168, 261–62
Donaldson, John 48, 58
Dougherty, Pat 28, 30, 33–4
Drake, Reynaldo 220
Dropo, Walt 198
Druid Hill 94
Drum Island 258
Duncan, Frank 79, 85, 170, 190
Duncan, Frank (Pete) 35–6, 50
Duncan, Vern 49
Durham, North Carolina 104
Durocher, Leo 173, 254–55
Dylan, Bob 255

Earle, Frank 52–4
Earle Mack's All-Stars 50
East Orange, New Jersey 2, 239–40, 243, 245, 255
East Orange B.B.C. 245
East Orange Oval Park 4, 239
East Orange Triangles 243
The East Room 123, 235
East-West All-Star Game 9, 15, 46, 87, 89, 91, 93, 97, 103, 112, 130, 139, 151, 171, 175–76, 178, 194, 201–02
East-West League 15, 68–9, 97, 256
Eastern League 198
Eastland Hotel 25
Eaton Place 239, 256
Ebbets, Charlie 55
Ebbets Field 55, 188
Ecclesiastes 265, 267
Edwards, Ralph 186
Ehmke, Howard 97
Eibel, Hack 51–2
Elite Giants *see* Baltimore Elite Giants
Elmira, New York 198
England 210, 251
The Equator 23
Erie, Pennsylvania 218, 222–23
Erie Coal Dump 222
The ESPN Baseball Encyclopedia 40
ETO Championship 153
Europe 3, 45, 71, 251
Evans, Felix (Chin) 3, 9, 201–05
Evers, Johnny 32

Farley Stars 46
Farrell, Jack 97
Farrell, Luther 65
Federal League Stars 52
Feeney, Chub 255
Feller, Bob 155, 163, 181, 186, 190
Fenway Park 117
Fields, Wilmer 267
Florida 35, 44, 148, 159, 173–74, 191, 198, 201, 204, 217, 219, 258, 261, 264, 267
Florida Hotel Winter League 35
Florida International League 191
Florida Sports Hall of Fame 46
Florida Winter League 35

Foggy Bottom 94, 107, 109
Fondy, Dee 173
Forbes, Frank 52
Forbes Field 127, 136, 139
Fort Benning 122
Fort Dix 153
Fort Lauderdale, Florida 173, 191
Foster, Rube 1, 7, 12, 14, 26, 28–36, 38–9, 44–5, 48, 57–60, 62–3, 66–8, 71, 77, 80, 82
Foster, Willie 8, 14–5, 17, 64–5, 67, 82–7, 89–93, 116, 122, 128
Fowler, Bud 14
Fox Theatre 234
Foxx, Jimmie 97, 136
France 153, 210, 251–52
French, Larry 186

Gaines, Jonas 97–8
Gardner, Jelly 84–5
Gaston, Robert (Rab Roy) 106–07
Gatewood, Bill 54, 120–22
Gehrig, Lou 1, 12, 110, 127, 129, 131–32, 135–36, 138–39, 141, 145, 159, 216
Georgia 44, 122, 211, 219, 232
Georgia House of Representatives 211
Germany 153, 251–52
G.I. World Series 153
Gibson, Bob 244, 246
Gibson, Josh 1, 3, 4, 8, 9, 15–6, 67, 90–1, 93, 100, 108, 112–13, 122, 125–141, 145, 147, 159, 161, 163, 176–77, 184, 188–89, 201–03, 207–08, 216, 237, 242, 244, 256
Gibson, Josh, Jr. 235, 237
Gilkerson's Union Giants 73
Gilliam, Junior 4, 98, 191
Girls Highlex Softball Club 224
Glimmerglass 111, 165
Gomez, Rueben 4, 191
Gooden, Dwight 246
Grace, Willie 220
Grand Rapids, Michigan 219
Grant, Charlie (Tokohama) 25–7
Grant, Frank 17
Graves, Lem 129, 131
Grays *see* Homestead Grays
Great Depression 60, 68, 117, 125, 209
Green, Joe 28, 58
Greene, Joe 160
Greenlee, Gus 15, 69–70, 92–3, 122, 125–27, 145
Greenlee Field 125–27
Grier, Red 65
Griffith, Clark 8, 130, 136–38, 140–41, 216, 252
Griffith Stadium 104, 130, 136–40, 188
Grimes, Burleigh 168
Grove, Lefty 9, 97, 116–17
Grove Street Oval 239–40, 242–44, 249
Grove Street Senior Ball Diamond 239
Guadalajara, Mexico 228
Gunthers 35

Haas, Mule 97
Hamtramck Stadium 256
Hank Aaron: Chasing the Dream 234
The Hank Aaron Room 207, 211
Harlem Globetrotters 194, 220, 224
Harney, George 82
Harper 35
Harpers Field 218
Harris, Vic 89–92, 108, 127, 176
Harrisburg Giants 62, 64, 96
Harrison, William Henry 237
Hartnett, Gabby 127
Hatcher, John C. 255
Havana Red Sox 66, 224
Hawkins, Lem 77, 84–5
Hayes, Johnny 146, 148
Hayes, Wilbur 220
Haywood, Buster 220–1, 224
Heard, Jehosie 25
Heath, Jeff 190
Hegan, Jim 190
Heintzelman, Ken 153
hemolytic streptococcus 244
Hemsley, Rollie 190
Henderson, Rats 63
Henderson, Rickey 37
Higgins, Bob 22
Hill, Pete 7, 14, 17, 26, 31–42, 95, 99
Hilldale 14, 45, 61–6, 68, 72, 74, 76–81, 113–14
Hilldale Daisies *see* Hilldale
Hinchliffe Stadium 239
Hofman, Solly 32
Holland, Bill 67
Holloway, Crush 95, 104
Hollywood, California 29–30, 79, 220, 222, 261
Homestead, Pennsylvania 126
Homestead Grays 1, 3, 8, 9, 12, 15–7, 38, 65, 67–9, 95, 97, 100, 103, 105–09, 112, 116, 125–26, 129, 131, 133, 136–38, 145–46, 155, 157, 159, 163, 170, 175–76, 180, 183, 188, 202, 210, 212, 216, 237, 267
Hooker, Len 161
Hooper, Harry 51
Hot Springs, Arkansas 25
Houston, Texas 189, 256
Howard, Del 28
Hubbell, Carl 16
Hubert H. Humphrey Metrodome 61
Hughes, Sammy T. 98, 184
Hunter, Bert 90, 92
Hutchinson, Fred 35
Hyde, Bubba 203

I Was Right on Time 259
Indianapolis ABCs 36, 58, 62–3, 95, 114
Indianapolis Clowns 159, 205, 219, 224–25, 227, 232–33
The Indianapolis Freeman 58
The Indianapolis Ledger 58

Insider's Baseball 174
International League 22, 214
Irvin, Bob 241
Irvin, Monte 1–6, 8, 12, 100, 104, 110–13, 115, 129, 134, 142 148, 155, 161–62, 166–67, 173, 188–92, 201–03, 208, 211, 235, 238–41, 243, 245, 250–51, 253, 255–56, 263
Italy 253
Iwo Jima 230

Jacob Ruppert Memorial Trophy 97–8
Jackson, Bo 194
Jackson, Cleveland 221
Jackson, Doris 226
Jackson, Rufus (Sonnyman) 127
Jackson, Shoeless Joe 14
Jackson, Stanford 83–5
Jackson, Tom 62
Jacksonville, Florida 44, 148, 216
Jalisco Charros 228, 230
James, Bill 174
James, Nux 52–4
Jamesville 106
Japan 99
Jefferson, George 220
Jenkins, Fats 91–2, 97
Jersey City, New Jersey 218, 254
Jethroe, Sam 173, 190, 252
Jim Crow 218–19
Johnson, Connie 161
Johnson, Grant (Home Run) 31, 33–4, 36, 39, 41–2, 49–51
Johnson, Jack 36
Johnson, Judy 12, 15, 45, 63–4, 66, 68, 78–80, 91–3, 122, 125, 128, 239, 244, 256
Johnson, Mamie (Peanut) 226–27
Johnson, Walter 7, 34, 38, 50, 54, 133
Johnson Stars 46
Johnston, Wade 34–5
Jones, Slim 3, 9, 16, 114, 116–19, 170
Joseph, Newt 83–5
Judge, Joe 51–2

Kankakee, Illinois 66, 68
Kansas City, Missouri 35, 46, 58
The Kansas City Call 93, 163
Kansas City Monarchs 1, 3, 14, 16–7, 58–9, 61, 63–4, 67, 69, 73, 76–7, 80, 82–3, 108, 114–15, 132, 155, 159–60, 162, 170–1, 189, 204, 212, 226, 251, 253, 257
Kansas City Royals 257
Keenan, James J. 61–2, 65
Keller, Charlie 190
Keltner, Ken 190
Killefer, Bill 49, 51
Kimbro, Henry 98
Kincannon, Harry 116
Klem, Bill 146–47
Klep, Eddie, Jr. 222
Klep, Edward Joseph (Eddie) 9, 217–223
Klep, Julius 223

Knox, Elwood C. 58
Koufax, Sandy 116, 168, 233
Kuhn, Bowie 5, 130

Labine, Clem 191
Lake Glimmerglass 111
LaMarque, Lefty 161
Lanier, Max 186
Lardner, Ring 30
Larry King Show 156
LaSorda, Tommy 168, 247, 262
The League of Colored Baseball Clubs 127
League Park 219–20
Lee, Scrip 80
Leland, Frank C. 31, 33, 38
Leland Giants 28, 32–36, 39, 44
Lemon, Bob 190
Leonard, Buck 1, 3, 8, 9, 12, 55, 100, 105–07, 109–10, 112–13, 115–17, 119, 127, 129, 131–32, 135–41, 145, 159, 163, 170, 173, 176, 189–90, 201–03, 212–13, 215–16, 252, 263, 265, 267
Leonard, Dutch 190
Leonard, Lugenia (Jean) 132, 266
Leonard, Sarah 266
Lewis, Cary B. 58
Lewis, Rufus 161, 189, 228–30
Lincoln Giants *see* New York Lincoln Giants
Lincoln Stars 45, 51, 54
Lincoln University 44
Lindsay, Bill 35–6
Lindstrom, Fred 79
Little Falls, Minnesota 73
Little Lassie 261
Littleton Avenue 260
Lloyd, John Henry (Pop) 2, 7, 12, 14, 26, 31, 33, 36, 38–9, 41–7, 49–51, 53–4, 63, 66, 90, 93, 120, 147, 237
Lockman, Whitey 254
Long Branch High School 227
Lopez, Al 114
Lord Baltimores 94
Los Angeles, California 113, 115, 186, 223
Louisville, Kentucky 19–21, 147
Louisville Eclipse 21
Lowry, Phil 256
Luderus, Fred 516
Lundy, Dick 14, 17–8, 63–4, 66, 68, 89–93, 96–7, 99, 147–48, 188
Lyle, Marcenia 224
Lyons, Jimmie 53–4, 58–9

Mack, Connie 26, 96
Mackey, Biz 113–15, 148, 167, 184, 188, 201, 256
Macmillan *Baseball Encyclopedia* 139
Macon (Georgia) Acmes 44
Maglie, Sal 186
Maisel, Fritz 96
Malarcher, David 59–60, 64, 69, 82, 85
Manley, Abe 145
Manley, Effa 135, 245, 250–51, 253–54, 256

274 Index

Mann, Earl 209–10
Manning, Max 161
Marcelle, Oliver 63, 66, 73, 96
Marianao, Cuba 173
Maris, Roger 133, 136, 138
Marquard, Rube 7, 52–56
Marquard's All Leaguers 55
Marr, Don 267–68
Marrero, Connie 173
Marshall, Bobby 28
Marshall, Rube 54
Martin, Fred 186
Martin, Pepper 173, 191
Maryland Park 94
Mathewson, Christy 38–9, 53
Matlock, Leroy 126
Matthews, John 58
Mayaguez, Puerto Rico 190
Maynard, Johnny 105
Mays, Willie 2, 4, 9, 11–12, 127, 143, 162, 173, 179–81, 192–93, 195–99, 247–48, 250, 254–56, 262
McCreary, Fred 104
McDougald, Gil 116
McDuffie, Terris 148
McGill, Nathan K. 87
McGraw, John 25–27, 40, 54
McGwire, Mark 17, 133, 136
The Meadowlands 238
Memphis Red Sox 3, 159, 201–2, 209
Mendez, Jose 17, 36, 39, 48, 58, 64, 80
Mexican Hall of Fame 9, 185
Mexican League 5, 98, 100, 135, 139, 151, 157, 183–86, 228
Mexico 73–4, 98, 134, 139, 143, 147–48, 150–51, 168, 183–84
Mexico City 4
Mexico City Rojos 228
Meyer 30, 32
Meyers, Chief 54–6
Miami Beach Flamingos 173
Miami Department of Recreation and Parks 174
Miami Giants 159
Mike Glenn Foundation 211
Mike Donlin's All-Stars 36, 50
Milan, Tennessee 183
Mills, Charlie 58
Minneapolis, Minnesota 173, 198, 255, 261–62
Minneapolis Millers 173
Mitchell Report 136
Mobile, Alabama 231–33
Mohawk Giants 50, 188
Monroe, Louisiana 123
Monroe Park 231–32
Monte Irvin Field 4, 239, 243, 255
Monte Irvin: Nice Guys Finish First 4, 110
Montgomery, Alabama 192
Montgomery Grey Sox 74
Montgomery Rebels 191
Montreal, Canada 181, 214, 216, 251, 253–54
Montreal Royals 217–18

Moore, Dobie 59, 79–80
Moore, James Benjamin, Jr. 206
Moore, James (Red) 3, 9, 98, 146–47, 206–07, 209–11
Moore, Mary 211
Moore, Mike 32
Moore, Sadie Robinson 206
Moran, Pat 28–9, 32
Morgan, Connie 226–27
Morney, Leroy 87, 89–92
Morris, Barney 186
Morton, Charles 21
Most Valuable Player Award 249
Mothel, Dink 84–5
Mount Pleasant, Ohio 20
Mount Winen, Maryland 157
MTO Champions 153
Muehlenbach Park 78, 81
Mullane, Tony 21–2
Mullin, George 39, 41–2
Murray, Patrick 23
Mutual Association of Eastern Colored Baseball Clubs 61
Mutual Broadcasting System 156

Nashville, Tennessee 97, 99, 183
National Anthem 242
National Association of Colored Professional Baseball Clubs 57
National Baseball Hall of Fame 5, 8, 12, 43, 56, 80, 93, 109, 152, 164–65, 212
National League 11, 59, 70, 94, 97–8, 109, 111, 118, 137, 146, 156, 175–76, 198, 243, 247, 255
The National Pastime 211
Negro American League 3, 16–7, 70, 98, 127, 159, 172–73, 194, 196, 218–20, 225, 257
Negro League Hall of History 248
Negro League Players Association 4
Negro Leagues Baseball Museum 46, 227, 257–58, 268
Negro Leagues Baseball Museum Yearbook 36
Negro National League 1, 3, 8, 14–7, 45, 58–62, 64, 68, 70–1, 74, 76, 82–3, 86, 97–8, 109, 111, 114, 117, 125, 127–8, 132, 135, 137, 145, 155–56, 158–59, 165, 173, 175, 183, 188, 202, 210, 236, 243, 250–51
Negro Southern League 15, 69–70, 74, 218
Negro World Series 1, 8, 14, 17, 59–60, 63–5, 76–7, 80, 82–3, 85, 114–5, 127, 132, 155, 159, 161, 163, 173, 178, 198, 217, 253
Neil, Ray 226
Nelson, Jimmy 243–44
Nettles, Graig 142, 246
New Jersey 142, 237, 239–40, 242, 256
New Orleans Creoles 225
The New York Age 21, 50–1, 53, 55
New York Bacharach Giants 61
New York Black Yankees 46, 69, 184
New York Catholic Protectory 188
New York City 61, 71–2, 162, 212
New York City Championship 72

New York Cubans 3, 116, 129, 135, 171, 173, 242
New York Giants 1, 2, 5, 12, 25, 39, 48, 52–54, 75, 79, 111, 155, 161, 173, 177, 247, 253
New York Lincoln Giants 44–5, 49, 51, 53, 61–2, 64–7, 71, 73
New York Lincoln Stars *see* Lincoln Stars
New York Tigers 159
The New York Times 214
New York University 227
New York Yankees 1, 5, 48, 98, 125, 133, 138, 145
Newark, New Jersey 22, 115, 140, 142, 153, 162, 163, 177, 208, 245, 262–63
Newark Browns 68
Newark Dodgers 148
Newark Eagles 1–3, 6, 8, 13, 61, 98, 115, 123, 129, 135, 143, 145–47, 149–50, 153, 155, 161, 166, 170, 172, 176, 188–89, 202, 207, 210, 236, 242–45, 248, 250, 252, 256
The Newark Herald 115
Newark Stars 64
Newcombe, Don 4, 115, 249–50, 252–53
Newsom, Bobo 186
Newton Street 152
Nice, France 153
Nielsen, Billy 31
Nixon, Richard 236
Noble Experiment 217, 220
North Carolina Central University 104
North Philadelphia Honey Drippers 226
North Warren State Hospital 222
Northwest League 21
Nunn, Bill 92
Nuremberg, Germany 153
Nutter, Isaac H. 63

Oakland, California 173, 262
Oberlin College 21
Oh, Sadaharu 135
OISE (Overseas Invasion Service Expedition) 153
Oldtyme Baseball News 31, 40, 56, 119, 123, 158, 163, 168, 178, 182, 187, 204, 238
Olympic Field 52–3, 55
O'Neil, Buck 3, 9, 159–64, 209, 257–59, 268
O'Neil, Ora Lee Owen 259
Orange, New Jersey 4, 239–41, 255
Orange High School 241
Orlando, Florida 261, 267–68
Otesaga Hotel 111, 165
Overall, Orval 28–9, 31–2
Owen, Mickey 186

Pacific Coast League 173, 191, 198–99, 262
Page Fence Giants 26
Paige, Satchel 1, 8–9, 12–3, 15–6, 49, 56, 60, 66, 94, 97, 100–01, 117–18, 121–22, 125–28, 145, 154, 156–57, 159, 161–63, 170–71, 188, 190, 207, 226, 238, 244, 249, 256, 258
Palatka, Florida 44

Palm Bay, Florida 261
Partlow, Roy 216
Pasquel, Jorge 251
Paterson, New Jersey 239, 243
Paterson East Side Park 243
Patton's Third Army 153, 210
Payne, Jap 31–2, 35
Pearson, Lennie 98, 148, 189, 207
Penn State University 126
Pennsylvania's State Correctional Institution 222
Perkins, Bill 244
Perry, Gaylord 168–69
Petway, Bruce 31, 33–4, 38–9, 41–2
Philadelphia, Pennsylvania 44, 51, 61–2, 65, 80, 83, 85, 102, 134, 165, 169, 182, 227, 242
Philadelphia Athletics 39, 50
Philadelphia Giants 26, 33, 38, 44
Philadelphia Nationals *see* Philadelphia Phillies
Philadelphia Phillies 48, 51, 54
Philadelphia Stars 3, 103, 106, 108–09, 114, 117–18, 155, 178–81
Philadelphia Tigers 64
The Philadelphia Tribune 93
Pittsburgh Alleghenys 125
The Pittsburgh Courier 49, 56, 93, 127, 135, 146, 157
Pittsburgh Crawfords 2, 15, 17, 69, 92, 103, 108–09, 121–22, 125–26, 128, 133, 145, 238, 244
Pittsburgh Keystones 38, 128
Pittsburgh Pirates 28, 44, 252
Plank, Eddie 39
Poles, Spot 49–51
Pollock, Alan 205
Pollock, Syd 66, 205, 224–227
Polo Grounds 139, 155, 177, 198, 242
Pompano Beach, Florida 201, 204
Pompez, Alejandro (Alex) 62, 242
Pop Lloyd Field 46–7
Posey, Cum 15, 38, 65–6, 68–9, 100, 108, 126–27, 129, 146, 157, 161
Powell, Colin 235
Powell, Dick 97, 99
Powell, Willie 82
Providence Grays 24
Pryor, Wes 35
Puckett, Kirby 179
Puerto Rican League 135, 190
Puerto Rican Winter League 156
Puerto Rico 139, 148, 150, 162, 188–91, 236, 252

Quartermaster's Depot *see* Army Quartermaster's Depot

Radcliffe, Alex 89–92, 172
Radcliffe, Ted (Double Duty) 68, 108–09, 127, 130, 209, 211

Reagan, Ronald 236
Rector, Connie 67
Redding, Dick (Cannonball) 14, 17, 48, 72
Reese, Pee Wee 246
Renfroe, Othello 190
Reynolds, Bill 49
Richmond, Virginia 263
Rickey, Branch 8, 25, 37, 130, 140, 179, 213–14, 218, 250–53
Rickwood Field 196, 217–18, 256
Riley, Jim 168
Rizzuto, Phil 190
Roberts, Ric 136, 139, 206
Robinson, Brooks 12, 142, 212, 246
Robinson, Eddie 191
Robinson, Frank 262
Robinson, George W. 62
Robinson, Jackie 3, 7–9, 11–2, 17, 20–3, 25, 37, 46, 55, 127, 130, 140, 142, 162, 172, 179–81, 195, 198, 201, 212–19, 222, 224, 248–52, 254, 258
Robinson, Neil 172
Robinson, Norman 196
Robinson, Wilbert 54, 62
Rochester, New York 244
Rockford State Prison 221
Rocky Mount, North Carolina 107, 132, 140, 212, 216, 265–67
Roe, Preacher 168
Rogan, Bullet 8, 14, 17, 59, 64, 77–80, 82–5
Rolfe, Red 142, 246
Rommel, Eddie 97
Rookie of the Year Award 249
Rosenthal, Joe 230
Rosner, Max 61
Rossiter, George 62, 65, 94, 96
Ruffin, Leon 148, 208
Ruppert Stadium 153
Russell, John Henry 89–92
Ruth, Babe 1, 12, 17, 38, 47, 94, 127, 132–33, 135–36, 138, 141, 145, 159, 208 231–32, 234–35, 237
Ryan, Nolan 56

SABR 174, 211, 255–56
SABR Research Journal 174, 191
SABR Research Library 256
Sain, Johnny 176, 190
St. James Baptist Church 265, 267
St. Louis Browns 140, 198, 254
St. Louis Cardinals 117–18
St. Louis Stars 16, 60–1, 67–9, 98, 150–51
St. Mary's Industrial School for Boys 231
St. Paul, Minnesota 224
St. Paul Gophers 28, 34
Salazar, Lazaro 186
Sally League 191
San Antonio Black Aces 114
San Diego Padres 191
San Francisco, California 225
San Francisco Sea Lions 225

San Juan, Puerto Rico 190, 252
Sanders, Deion 194
Santa Clara Leopards 72–3
Santo Domingo 126
Santop, Louis 14, 17, 49–51, 56, 63, 79
Santurce, Puerto Rico 191
Satchel Paige's All-Stars 181
Scales, George 69, 115
Scantlebury, Pat 242, 256
Schaefer, William Donald 156
Schenectady, New York 50, 188
Schorling, John M. 33, 60
Schorling's Park 82
Schulte, Frank 29–30, 32
Score, Herb 91, 116
Scott, Elisha 58
Scottsboro Trial 99
Scranton, Pennsylvania 198
Seay, Dick 146–48, 188, 207–08
Sheckard, James 29, 32
Shibe Park 77, 80, 85
Simmons, Al 97
Sioux City, Iowa 73
Sisler, George 131
Smith, Chino 66
Smith, Ford 161
Smith, Hilton 17, 160–61, 190
Smith, Ozzie 150, 152
Snow, Felton 97, 111, 179
Society for American Baseball Research *see* SABR
Sosa, Sammy 17, 133, 136
South America 214
South Carolina 219
Southern Express Company 44
Southfield, Michigan 230
Spahn, Warren 116, 176
Sparrow, Roy 92
Speaker, Tris 14, 34, 37–8, 122
Spearman, Henry 101
Spedden, Charles P. 62, 94–5
Springfield Missionary Baptist Church 211
Stack, Ed 144, 260
Stallings, George 53
Stanley, Joe 32
Stearnes, Turkey 14, 17, 89–93, 256
Steel and Industrial League 194
Steinfield, Harry 32
Stephens, Jake 103, 109
Stetson 142, 261
Steubenville, Ohio 21, 23
Stone, Ed 148
Stone, Toni 9, 224–25, 227
Stovey, George 22
Street, Gabby 224
Streeter, Sam 89–90, 92
Strong, Nat C. 58, 61–2
Strong, Ted 160–163, 172
Strothers, C. W. 62
Strothers, Tim (Sam) 31–2, 35
Sullivan 51–2

Summers, Ed 39, 41
Suttles, Mule 15–7, 60–1, 68, 87–93, 97, 99, 146–47, 188, 203–04, 208
Sweatt, George 78, 85
Sykes, Doc 94, 99
Syracuse, New York 22, 244

Tampa, Florida 153
Tatum, Goose 220
Taylor, Ben 17, 36, 40, 62, 72, 96, 99
Taylor, C. I. 36, 58, 127
Taylor, Candy Jim 93
Ted Williams' Hitters Hall of Fame 132
Ted Williams Museum Yearbook 132
Texas 152, 223, 245, 256
Texas State Cemetery 152
Third Army 153, 210
This Is Your Life 186
Thomas, Clarence 235
Thomas, Clint 63
Thomas, Valmy 191
Thompson, Hank 4, 190, 198, 254
Thompson, Sandy 84–5
Thomson, Bobby 254
Thunder Twins 8, 127, 130–132, 135, 137–39, 141
Thurman, Bob 191
Tiant, Luis Sr. 173
Tinker, Joe 29, 31–2
Tokohama, Charlie (Chief) 25–7
Toledo Blue Stockings 20–1
Toledo Mudhens 170
Topeka, Kansas 58
Toronto Blue Jays 12
Torreon, Mexico 230
Torriente, Cristobal 14, 17, 59, 75, 84–5
Traynor, Pie 127
Trent, Ted 122
Trimble, William E. 60
Tri-State League 36
Trouppe, Quincey 219–20, 229–30
Tucker, Henry 62
Turner, Pop 104
Turner Field 207, 211

UCLA 215
Union Hotel 23
United States Army 5
United States League 213
United States Navy 160–61, 257
U.S. Steel Mill 126
U.S. Supreme Court 217
University of Alabama Press 205
University of Florida 159
University of Michigan 21
University of Minnesota 28
Upsala College 249
Utah Beach 153

V-E Day 153
Veeck, Bill 140, 253

Venezuela 157, 179, 181, 190–91, 212–13, 236, 262
Veracruz 151, 157
Vernon, Mickey 190
Vero Beach, Florida 168, 261
Veterans Committee 13, 144, 156, 168–69, 236, 258, 260
Vietnam War 21

Wagner, Honus 7, 12, 28, 33, 38, 43–4, 63, 150
Walker, Dixie 215
Walker, Edsall 3, 9, 175–78
Walker, Fleetwood 7, 14, 18–24, 250
Walker, Hoss 220–21
Walker, Welday 7, 250
Wallace, Dick 29, 31–2, 53–5
Walsh, Ed 34, 38, 41
Waner, Lloyd 120, 237
Warfield, Frank 63, 66, 68, 79, 96
Washington, Chester 127
Washington, D.C. 94, 97, 104, 109, 177, 183, 186, 227, 237, 267
Washington Pilots 68
Washington Potomacs 62, 64
Washington Senators 8, 51, 79, 130, 133, 136–37, 140, 173, 216, 252
Wayne, John 220
Welch, Winfield 194
Wells, Willie 3, 8, 14, 16–8, 60–1, 68, 73–4, 87, 89–93, 142, 145–48, 150–52, 176–77, 184, 188, 207–08, 211–12, 245–47, 256
Wertz, Vic 12, 162
West, Max 191
West Baden Sprudels 36
West Side Park 249
Westfield High School 194
Westport Park 94
White, Chaney 63
White, Sol 26, 44
White, William Edward 7, 18, 23–4
White House 4, 123, 156, 235–38, 261
White Sox Park 33, 36
Whitehurst Freeway 109
Whitted, George 51
Whitworth, Richard 58
Wickware, Frank 33–4, 36, 48, 50, 73
Wilhelm, Hoyt 262
Wilkinson, J. L. 58–9, 76, 163
Willett, Ed 39
Williams, Smokey Joe 7, 13, 17, 48–56, 62, 67, 85, 100, 108, 126
Willie Wells Boulevard 152
Wills, Maury 12
Wilson, Artie 190, 194, 203
Wilson, Dan 16
Wilson, Hack 97
Wilson, Jud (Boojum) 3, 9, 14, 17, 66, 68, 89–97, 99–102, 104–05, 107–09, 127–28, 178
Wilson, Lefty 73
Wilson, Rollo 65–6

Wilson, Tom 70, 183
Winters, Nip 63–4, 72, 77–80
Wolfe, Thomas 183, 241
Woodland Hills, California 169, 187
Woods, Parnell 172
World Series 1, 5, 6, 12, 14–5, 26, 28, 32, 51, 55, 64–5, 76, 79–80, 85, 96–7, 106, 117–18, 127, 153, 162, 178, 244–45, 261
World War I 39, 45
World War II 3, 5, 8, 12, 16, 98, 153, 159–61, 184, 210, 225, 251, 257
Wright, Bill 3, 9, 98, 183–87, 228–30
Wright, Ernest P. (Ernie) 9, 218–20
Wright, George 31–2
Wright, Johnny 216
Wyatt, Dave 58

X-Giants *see* Cuban X-Giants

Yankee Stadium 45, 67, 98, 117, 130, 134, 139, 190, 210, 244
Yokely, Laymon 66, 96
Young, Fay 30–1
Young, Pimp 68
Young Receivers 44
Youngs, Ross 48
Youngstown, Ohio 237
Yount, Robin 56

Zimmer, Bob 229
Zimmerman, Heinie 29, 32
Zulu Giants 159

www.ingramcontent.com/pod-product-compliance
Ingram Content Group UK Ltd.
Pitfield, Milton Keynes, MK11 3LW, UK
UKHW041929140426
5217IPUK00014B/385